PREPARING

FOR WAR

Praise for *Preparing for War: The Extremist History of White Christian Nationalism—and What Comes Next*

"A clear-eyed, compelling study of the road to January 6 and the possible future of the politics-versus-religion battle in the US."

—*Kirkus Reviews,* starred review

"This persuasive account documents the rise of White Christian nationalism and warns of the very real threat it poses to American democracy."

—*Booklist*

"A rigorous and earnest grappling with the intersection between religion and politics."

—*Publishers Weekly*

"Bradley Onishi is an expert on what's fueling extremism from the religious right, which is acting increasingly as though it's ready for combat."

—*Rolling Stone*

"Makes the case for a nuanced conversation about how contemporary strains of White Christian nationalism relate to earlier iterations of conservative Christian politics."

—*Politico*

"In his excellent book, Onishi blends his expertise in religion with his personal experiences in evangelical communities to make sense of the January 6 attack and rising Christian nationalism. If you care about maintaining a separation between church and state, and if you want insights into those who do not, make sure to check out Onishi's critically important and wonderfully written book."

—*The Revealer*

"Part memoir, part history of Southern California's formative role in the rise of the religious right, Onishi's book traces his growing estrangement from the faith he once zealously championed."

—*Religion News Service*

"What comes alive in Onishi's absorbing and often disturbing work is the simple ordinariness and ubiquity of what he explores. How so much of what often passes as regular—and unremarkable—features of American life and culture have also helped cultivate the context in which a radical White Christian nationalism could take hold."

—*Religion & Politics*

"If you were alarmed by the January 6 attack on the US Capitol and the wave of racially motivated mass murders that have taken place over the last few years, you should read Bradley Onishi's *Preparing for War*."

—*The New York Journal of Books*

"This disturbing look at the rise of White Christian nationalism proves that the January 6 insurrection was the (far from natural) result of a subculture of racist violence that has been growing in the United States for years."

—*Alta*

"A deep dive into how the new White Christian nationalist movement has gone from origins of worshipping Jesus to maintaining a racial status quo through the religious platform."

—*Rawstory*

"Onishi's thorough research, close observation, and clear writing are invaluable in helping to understand the insurrection as well as some of the many puzzling aspects of the Trump presidency."

—*The Christian Science Monitor*

"In this compelling and scholarly mix of memoir and cultural and political history, Onishi brings to bear his experience as a former Christian nationalist movement insider to expose the radicalism behind the January 6th insurrection. Gripping and essential reading for anyone who wants to understand the threat that this movement poses to American democracy."

—Katherine Stewart, author of *The Power Worshippers: Inside the Dangerous Rise of Religious Nationalism*

"In *Preparing for War*, Bradley Onishi traces the history of White Christian nationalism from the John Birch Society to the Big Lie and the January 6 terrorist assault on the US Capitol—a narrative enlivened by the author's own intersections with the movement. This is an excellent and important book, both chilling and prophetic."

> —Randall Balmer, historian and author of *Bad Faith: Race and the Rise of the Religious Right*

"Hinging on the Capitol insurrection on January 6, 2021, *Preparing for War* presents the New Religious Right in light of their aggressive political ambitions. Bradley Onishi is ringing the alarm bells. He believes we are not at the end but rather a beginning of a religiously sanctioned extremism that threatens our American democratic future. Following the best scholarship on the nature of Christian nationalism and the further developments of the Religious Right, Onishi roots his story of historical changes in his life experiences in Southern California. The challenge is for all of us to examine how these momentous shifts have affected our own lives, and then seek ways to counteract the destructive paths being forged in our communities and our nation. This is a book to read with care."

> —Dr. Gerardo Marti, William R. Kenan Jr. Professor of Sociology at Davidson College, and author of *American Blindspot: Race, Class, Religion, and the Trump Presidency*

"Bradley Onishi takes us on a sweeping yet personal journey through modern American religious and political history to understand the violent, extremist strains of White Christian America that led to the January 6 insurrection. With insight from countless interviews, deep scholarship, and his own escape from White Christian nationalism, Onishi's *Preparing for War* is a clear account of what happened and a clarion warning about what is coming. Compelling and timely."

> —Andrew Seidel, attorney and author of *The Founding Myth: Why Christian Nationalism Is Un-American*

"*Preparing for War* is Bradley Onishi's exposition of White Christian nationalism from its roots in the antebellum South, to the 'family values' discourses that took control of the Republican Party in the 1980s, all the way to the reactionary movement that still puts Donald Trump at the helm of a culture war. That movement wants to turn back time to a point when everyone other than White Christian men knew their place, and White Christian men had a social order to keep everyone else in their places through violent displays of both public and private force. At this moment, when those reactionary forces threaten to regain control of the American state and impose their theocratic vision on the rest of us, Onishi's thorough and meticulous history is crucial. If you've ever found yourself confused and questioning how a nation supposedly founded for 'religious freedom' could evolve to become a 'Christian nation' bordering on theocracy, *Preparing for War* is necessary reading."

—Tori Williams Douglass, writer, speaker, educator, and creator of White Homework

PREPARING FOR WAR

THE EXTREMIST HISTORY OF WHITE CHRISTIAN NATIONALISM— AND WHAT COMES NEXT

BRADLEY ONISHI

Broadleaf Books

Minneapolis

PREPARING FOR WAR
The Extremist History of White Christian Nationalism—and What Comes Next

30 29 28 27 26 25 24   1 2 3 4 5 6 7 8 9

All Scripture quotations are from the New Revised Standard Version Bible, copyright © 1989 National Council of the Churches of Christ in the United States of America. Used by permission. All rights reserved worldwide.

The Library of Congress has cataloged the first edition as follows:
LCCN: 2022951212
LC Classification: BR526 .O64 2023

Cover design: Faceout Studio

Hardcover ISBN: 978-1-5064-8216-3
eBook ISBN: 978-1-5064-8217-0
Paperback ISBN: 979-8-8898-3349-9

To Kendra and Kaia,
the strangers who are my home

CONTENTS

PREFACE TO THE PAPERBACK EDITION

"I hate to say it, but this country needs a dictator."

The clip made the rounds in the days after the Iowa caucuses in late January 2024. The caucuses serve as a visual reminder of how our elections are supposed to work. Each year, news programs film Iowans, whom Americans from Anaheim to Boston to Atlanta assume are all corn farmers, gathering to cast their votes in a ritual that emblematizes the sharing of power and cooperation demanded of those who want to live in a democracy. It's like the first day of Advent for the American voting season.

This year was different. A correspondent for The Young Turks interviewed the man at a Team Trump Iowa Commit to Caucus event in Coralville, Iowa. He's middle-aged and wearing a red Trump hat. His face is weather-worn, leathery as the jacket he wears.

"I hate to say it, but this country needs a dictator": It's easy to write off a man-on-the-street interview as an expression of the fringe. A fanatic who made his way onto television. Someone made for the age of social media, where the thirty-second clip would get millions of views and reactions and play endlessly for weeks.

But a month later, another man said this: "Welcome to the end of democracy. We are here to overthrow it completely. We didn't get all the way there on January 6, but we will endeavor to get rid of it and replace it with this, right here."

There's no writing off this one as a blowhard on the street, some extremist of no consequence. Make no mistake, the man who said this *is an extremist*. According to the Southern Law Poverty Center, he has "worked with a global network of extreme far-right and pro-authoritarian figures in his activism. He printed his second book through a publishing house where white supremacist Theodore Beale, known by the pen name Vox Day, serves as lead editor" and "collaborated on content for the online publication Rebel News at least twice with Jeffrey and Edward Clark, brothers who were active in online Neo-Nazi circles." He is also a conspiracy theorist who popularized the Pizza Gate hoax.

The man who said this is Jack Posobiec, a right-wing provocateur affiliated with Turning Point USA and has over two million followers on X (formerly known as Twitter). Posobiec proclaimed his desire for the end of democracy not from a high school gymnasium in Iowa but from the main stage at CPAC in February 2024. CPAC, the Conservative Political Action Conference, showcases the vanguard of American conservatives at its gatherings here and abroad.

CPAC may host extremists like Posobiec, but it is not fringe. Extremists can, and often do, take political power. Expressing a desire to overthrow democracy is an extremist position. But it is also now a mainstream one in the United States.

When I began researching this book in 2019, making such a statement would have likely ended your political career. Even that short time ago, if the candidates and elected officials and public personalities at CPAC had not decried someone like Posobiec and his antidemocratic ideas, they would have been swarmed by the press. They would have been forced to answer why they shared a stage with someone trying to undo the sacred values of our nation.

That is no longer the case.

Other speakers at CPAC 2024 included Rep. Elise Stefanik, Rep. Jim Jordan, Senator J. D. Vance, then presidential candidate Vivek Ramaswamy, and, of course, Donald J. Trump. None of them disavowed Posobiec or his statement.

We can point to many factors that created this situation. But one is now so ordinary—like the family picture on the wall or the decorative plant at the far corner of the kitchen—that most of us don't see it. The January 6 insurrection was, simply put, an attempt to end democracy. Those rioting might have done so in the name of justice for a stolen election or a rigged process or a deep state conspiracy. But if we ask about what it was meant to *do*—not what its proponents *believed*—we arrive at a straightforward conclusion: January 6 was engineered to stop the democratic election of the president of the United States of America. It was an attempt to overthrow democracy.

GOP officials, right-wing commentators, and members of the conservative influencer class have had many opportunities to decry January 6 as not only extremist but also fringe. They've now had years to do so. They could designate the insurrection out of bounds. Not allowed. Something that can't be memorialized or celebrated by anyone who claims to be a patriotic American.

That hasn't happened. Since the time I wrote *Preparing for War* in 2021, January 6 has become an Alamo moment for MAGA Nation and Trumpists from sea to shining sea. We've witnessed "border convoys," led by some of those present at J6, caravanning to the southern border in order to prevent the country from being "overrun" by "globalists" who they claim are conspiring to keep US borders open and destroy the country." Ashli Babbitt, the woman shot and killed by Capitol Police at the insurrection, has become a martyr whose face appears on flags and patches across the country. Politicians such as Rep. Marjorie Taylor Greene and Rep. Elise Stefanik label those jailed for participating in the insurrection as "hostages" and "political prisoners." In October 2023, Mike Johnson—a man who did everything possible to overturn the 2020 election in the courts and is close to those who mobilized supporters to be at the Capitol on January 6—was elected speaker of the House, third in line for the presidency.

State courthouses have been evacuated due to bomb threats. Federal judges in Trump cases have been doxed. A state representative in Arizona proposed a bill that would have declared Donald Trump the winner of the presidential election in that state before the election even took place. Theologians, historians, thinktank pundits, and philosophers have published books and papers, arguing that perhaps a post-constitutional America with a "red Caesar" or "Christian prince" would be a better way forward for the country. Pastors and provocateurs have expressed a desire for blasphemy laws and other measures that would punish Americans for not obeying what they take to be biblical law. These are the small fires everywhere that the unextinguished embers from January 6 left to burn. They are reducing our democracy to ashes, and they are doing it in order to build something else.

We didn't get here by accident.

Preparing for War is about the six-decade movement to overthrow American democracy as we know it. While Trump's ascendancy to the presidency and the events following January 6 may have been shocking, they were the outcome of sixty years of Christian nationalist organizing to "retake" the country from those who want to "destroy" it. If the idea that "this country needs a dictator" or the desire to "overthrow" democracy is now mainstream, it is because of the white Christian nationalist organizers, pastors, fundraisers, politicians, and shadow network operatives who have been preparing for war on their own country since the 1960s.

For them, power, rather than democracy, is the sacred value because they believe God has chosen them to order the country according to his vision. If God has dominion over all the earth, they see themselves as the dominators of human society—the enforcers of God's plans.

I know this because I was once one of them.

—Bradley Onishi

BEFORE AND AFTER

PROCESSING THE CAPITOL INSURRECTION is akin to coming to terms with a national home invasion. That violent mob's breach of a secure and sacred space on January 6, 2021, resulted in nothing less than a collective trauma. Decades of threats, calls for civil war, and White grievance politics burst forth into a vulgar display of vengeance. It was a day that divides time into Before and After. It was dismantling.

But as time has passed, it has become clear that January 6 was not an aberration or even some historically bewildering event. It was the logical outcome not only of the Trump presidency and election defeat but also of the long history of White Christian nationalist rhetoric, organizing, and influence across the United States. This book is partly a religious history of the events at the Capitol on January 6, 2021. But it is mainly a history of the events, movements, religious leaders, and religious communities that made that event possible.

It is also a history of my own involvement in those communities and movements. As a former White Christian nationalist who is now a scholar of religion, I have both an insider's view and a scholarly perspective on the long road to J6. This book recounts the historical narrative by using my own history with the movement as a prism for understanding its principles, doctrines, emotions, and extremisms. I use my personal experience and training as a scholar to analyze the past and present and to forecast what comes next for MAGA Nation and the White Christian nationalists at its core.

As I processed the events from that horrific day, I began to ask the three questions that would become the foundations for this book. How did the rise of the New Religious Right between 1960 and 2015 give birth to violent White Christian nationalism during the Trump presidency and beyond? What aspects of the White Christian nationalist worldview—the worldview I once held—propelled some of the most conservative religious communities in the country to ignite a cold civil war? And how can understanding the history of White Christian nationalism help us anticipate how it will take shape in and influence the public square in years to come?

In chapters 1–5, we will answer the first question. Chapter 1 is a primer on White Christian nationalism—and my participation in it—and its development over the last half century. In chapters 2 and 3, I trace the history of extreme right-wing politics and White Christian nationalism in Southern California and the American South in the 1960s and 1970s. These chapters show how the development of the New Religious Right set the stage for the White Christian nationalist takeover of the Republican Party. In chapters 4 and 5, I examine the results of this takeover in the ouster of Jimmy Carter at the hand of his fellow White Christians and the White Christian nationalist support for Ronald Reagan.

In chapters 6–8, I answer the second question through studies of various components of the White Christian nationalist worldview—from sex, gender, and the national body (chapter 6) to authoritarian leadership and strongman masculinity (chapter 7), to the use of conspiracy theories to transform what is considered real, true, and actual (chapter 8).

If the first eight chapters tell a historical narrative of modern White Christian nationalism, chapters 9–11 analyze its present and future. Chapter 9 is a detailed analysis of the religious elements of the January 6 insurrection that reveals how White Christian nationalism was an integrating force for Trump's coup attempt. Chapter 10 explores the myths and relics that have developed in MAGA Nation since the insurrection. I argue that January 6 was the first battle in MAGA Nation's war on American democracy. Chapter 11 forecasts what MAGA Nation and White Christian nationalism may look like long after Trump has left the scene. Here I focus on the large-scale migration of Christian supremacists to the "American Redoubt," and their dreams of a theocratic state separate from the American republic.

No definitive answers as to how we arrived at this political moment exist. There are many ways to tell this story and to investigate the historical events leading up to the insurrection. There are also too many figures and historical markers to cover in depth. Some scholars have centered on figures such as Billy Graham and Richard Nixon; others have taken a longer view by going back to the nineteenth century to illuminate the present; and others have zeroed in on gender, sex, and immigration in order to understand the history of White conservative Christianity in the United States. I am indebted to the scholars and journalists who have followed these routes, and this book draws on their insight at many points.

I am also indebted to the many Black authors who have articulated why it is time to capitalize White, as I have done throughout this book. While Black has been capitalized for some time, White has not been. Many style guides recommend capitalizing the former but not the latter. In my view, it is important to capitalize White to draw attention to it as a racial category that demands observation and investigation. For too long, whiteness has been invisible, especially to White people. As Nell Irvin Painter says, "We should capitalize 'White' to situate 'Whiteness' within the American ideology of race, within which 'Black,' but not 'White,' has been hypervisible as a group identity." By capitalizing White, we call attention to the specific racial category that has a particular history in the United States and beyond.

In order to focus this work, I decided to tell the story of the rise of White Christian nationalism since the 1960s, when various cultural and political movements transformed the United States and led to the extension of various civil rights and forms of cultural representation to religious, racial, sex, gender, and ethnic minorities. This set off a counterrevolution that resulted in, among other things, religious support for the Trump presidency and the central role of Christian nationalism at the January 6 insurrection. Tracing this path makes it possible to see how the myth of the White Christian nation provided the basis for our polarized public square—what amounts to an American cold civil war—and the worst attack on the Capitol in two centuries.

Chapter 1

WOULD I HAVE BEEN THERE?

I SPENT THE FIRST sunlit hours of January 6, 2021, bobbing in the Pacific Ocean. Having awakened at dawn and gone surfing, I was surprised that no other surfers were in sight that morning; it was a rare but welcome phenomenon. With all that room to think, my thoughts expanded into the endless blue of the ocean around me. Two surprising Democratic victories in Georgia's Senate runoff elections the day before had made me jubilant. As the sun rose above Northern California, I thought of Raphael Warnock, a Black minister, and Jon Ossoff, a Jewish man in his early thirties, representing the Peach State in the Senate. The Democrats would now have control, by the slimmest of margins, of the White House and both houses of Congress.

My face was numb from the forty-degree air and fifty-degree water, but my body was glowing with anticipation. Maybe we are headed for better days, I thought, sitting on my board, looking at the horizon and tracing the long continuous arc of the Monterey Bay from Santa Cruz to Seaside. After four years of living under a contracted and sinister vision of America, I was ready for the country to unfurl itself from the myopia of the previous administration and move forward once again.

As a scholar who teaches courses on the racism, misogyny, xenophobia, and homophobia that mark American history, I should have known better. I *did* know better. I have told my students a million times: Even if the arc of the universe bends toward justice, it's not a straight line. It's a zigzag, or a curve that doubles back on itself, one full of loops and hairpin turns.

Nonetheless, it was hard not to feel relieved or even buoyant. Before going home, I took a selfie with the ocean in the background. In the frame, the sun is soft and golden; my hair is still wet, and I'm smiling calmly. When I look at that photograph now, I am amazed at the hope that glimmers in my eyes, the sense of anticipation in my smile.

By the time I got to my office later that morning, everything had changed. When I sat down in front of my computer, images of rioters breaching the US Capitol began to stream across my screen. In a matter of minutes, ebullience transformed into dread as I watched a mob overtake the Capitol in an attempt to overturn the 2020 presidential election. The initial video footage showed throngs of people, many flying Trump flags and wearing MAGA hats, descending on the Capitol in droves. They pushed through barriers, overran Capitol Police, and seized the building. It looked for all the world like footage of an invading force toppling an enemy government.

The first picture I posted to social media was a still shot from the base of the Capitol, looking upward to the rotunda. A large blue Trump flag takes up the bottom third of the frame. Two men in black are holding it on either side, one of them triumphantly waving his free hand in the air. Smoke hovers throughout the image. Contrasted with the illuminated rotunda in the top third of the picture, the gray haze creates an eerie aura. The Capitol looks like a haunted house. It is a startling depiction of the most important and iconic building in American democracy.

I used to live on Capitol Hill in Washington, DC, less than a mile from the Capitol. Though I passed it almost daily, while walking to the gym or heading to the grocery store, the gravitas of the building struck me each time it came into sight. The image of its desecration now unnerved me. Like millions of other Americans, I felt like democracy was crumbling before my eyes.

As video of the mob kept streaming across my screen, I began to notice something else. Religious symbols started to come into view. In one frame, I saw an enraged man waving a "Jesus Is My Savior—Trump Is My President" flag, with the besieged Capitol in the background. Rage and resentment saturate the photograph. In another frame, I saw banners with Bible verses and, in yet another, a statue of Jesus being carried as an icon of insurrection. The image that plagues me still is a panorama shot in which the Trump, Christian, Gadsen ("Don't Tread on Me"), and Confederate flags all fly in a row. The flags are so close to one another that they touch. That line of flags, with the mob of rioters dotting the Capitol steps—well, it seems like footage from a country that has been overtaken by intruders. If you didn't know better, you'd think that the rioters had replaced Old Glory with a new set of flags representing their new nation and its political leader–religious figurehead.

Watching the insurrection play out on my screen, I remembered that the night before, the second Jericho March had taken place not far from the Capitol. Billed as a prayer rally by the organizers, that march was a who's who of MAGA Nation's most ardent religious and conspiratorial leaders—from Michael Flynn to Alex Jones to Eric Metaxas, the writer and radio host turned Trumpian celebrity. I thought of the first Jericho March, held about a month prior, on December 12, 2020. Friends from home in Southern California had told me that people from the evangelical megachurch I used to belong to had attended that event.

I squinted at the screen, peering more closely. Were people I knew from church at the second Jericho March on January 5? Were people I used to sit next to in church storming the Capitol now, as the world watched and waited to see if they would succeed?

Later that night, as people across the globe began digesting the horrific reports and graphic videos from an armed insurrection, one thought kept looping through my mind: *I could have been there.*

MAYBE I'M A JESUS FREAK

In eighth grade, it can be hard to find ways to see your girlfriend outside of school, especially on a weeknight. So when Kelly invited me to Wednesday night Bible study at Rose Drive Friends Church, I said yes immediately. Listening to a Bible lesson was well worth it if we could sneak away for ten minutes to make out in the field behind the church. Plus, I knew a bunch of kids from school who went to this place. Maybe it would be fun.

Rose Drive Friends Church is in Yorba Linda, a small enclave in the northern region of Orange County, California. Other than being the birthplace of former president Richard Nixon, it's commonly known as one of the towns that borders Anaheim, the home of Disneyland and the Anaheim Angels of Major League Baseball. Only thirty miles from Los Angeles, Yorba Linda feels like it's a world away from both the glamour of Hollywood and the city streets where riots erupted after the 1992 acquittal of police officers who brutalized Rodney King.

Kelly dumped me soon after that first Wednesday, but the youth group quickly became my second home. When I went that first night, I expected to encounter corny adults like Ned Flanders from the *Simpsons*. Instead, I met cool youth leaders who had tattoos and played in Christian punk bands. They taught me how Jesus would forgive my sins and grant me eternal salvation. They taught me that the answers to my existential crises about meaning and purpose lay in God's plan for my life. They explained that the Bible wasn't a boring ancient text but a "personal love letter from my creator."

My conversion was extreme. Until April 1995, I was an eighth grader living in the grunge era, blasting Nirvana, Pearl Jam, and the Smashing Pumpkins through his portable CD player—one who was experimenting with drugs, sex, and vandalism; who had been suspended from school; and who had worried his parents by dyeing his hair every color possible. But soon after visiting Rose Drive, I became a bona fide Jesus freak. Landing in the youth group at Rose Drive Friends, I felt like I had discovered a hidden world, one that had existed right in front of me but that I had somehow missed or willfully ignored.

Soon my identity became wrapped in purity pledges, dedications and rededications of my life to my savior, and evangelism to the lost. I traded childhood friends for a new flock at church. Instead of sneaking behind the movie theater to light up a smoke, I stood in front of the theater with my new comrades, hoping to talk to anyone who passed by about their eternal destiny and God's plan for their life. We fashioned ourselves as a chosen minority living amid a Southern California culture given over to rebellion, licentiousness, fornication, and obscenity. We lamented that our neighbors and our country had abandoned the faith of our forefathers for secular humanism and Darwin's theory of evolution. At school, we handed out pamphlets decrying the atrocities of abortion. And we awaited the rapture with bated breath, knowing that Jesus would return at any moment to take us home.

At fourteen, I went from a smart-mouthed kid to a zealous convert. I was the guy who leads a Bible study at school lunchtime, proselytizes to strangers on the boardwalk at the beach, and refuses to leave the house without a Bible in hand. In 2001, I married my high school sweetheart and became a full-time youth minister at Rose Drive Friends Church. In that role, I would oversee a flock of two hundred kids as their spiritual leader. I was twenty years old.

WHAT IS EVANGELICALISM?

The histories and belief systems of the different strands of American evangelicalisms are complex; they look quite different depending on what time period you examine as well as the dimensions of class, politics, and geography. Race is especially decisive when sorting

American evangelicalisms. Yet the basic teachings across a broad swath of evangelicalisms are pretty simple: The Bible is the errorless Word of God. It should be read and followed as literally as possible. Unlike in Catholicism, hierarchy and tradition aren't sources of authority. Instead, dynamic preachers invite worshippers into services more akin to contemporary tent revivals than solemn ceremonies. Evangelicals don't care about celebrating dead saints or (except for a very few) maintaining liturgical traditions of the church. They locate authority in the Bible and those who, in their minds, teach it faithfully. Spreading the gospel is a top priority for evangelicals, because they believe that all those who die without accepting Christ as their personal savior will spend eternity in hell.

Many evangelicals expect Jesus will return soon, and evangelical kids who come home to an empty house sometimes wonder if their family has been raptured to heaven and they have been left behind for some unacknowledged sin. Other religions are seen as false teachings with little to no value. Interreligious dialogue is something of an oxymoron for most evangelicals, because they don't see other religions as legitimate. Moreover, evangelicals see themselves as "not of this world" because their true home is in eternal paradise with Jesus and God the Father. The "world" is an evil enemy, given over to sin and licentiousness. There is no cohering of faith with culture. Instead, there is a battle between them that goes back to the serpent's temptation of Adam and Eve in Genesis 3. This is why most evangelicals are allergic to discussions of social justice. They see social or political solutions to inequality, racism, and other issues of injustice as soft approaches to fixing worldly problems, and they prefer what they see as a biblical approach, which they consider to be individual salvation, to fixing social ills. Real Christians don't focus on feeding the hungry. They feed hungry souls.

LOSING MY RELIGION

In 2005, after eleven years in the movement and seven years in ministry, I left evangelicalism. My elders in the church had always told me that if I read too many books, my brain would railroad my heart and lead me away from the church. Turns out they were right.

When I began to read widely in theology, philosophy, and church history during and after college, my perspective started to expand and change. It became clear to me that the timeless truths we had attributed to the Bible in my church were modern inventions. I learned that our staunch commitment to voting Republican in order to oppose abortion of any kind was fueled by GOP operatives who preyed on our care for the unborn in order to garner millions of votes. From there, I digested the histories of evangelical theologies of sex, gender, race, and immigration. As I read and studied and reflected on my own experience, the picture grew ever more complex and yet much more vivid: White evangelicalism is a movement thoroughly entrenched in American nationalism, White supremacy, patriarchy, and xenophobia.

It wasn't easy to come to these revelations while I was still in ministry. Some Sundays I would lead prayers in front of two hundred teenagers while wondering if I still believed in God. In March 2005, I received notice that I had been accepted into a master's program in theology at Oxford University in the United Kingdom. This was my way out. When I arrived in Oxford in September of that year—a city of transcendent spires, cobblestone streets, ornate libraries, and medieval traditions—it was the first time in my adult life I was free to be myself without worrying that I was setting a bad example for the kids in my youth group or the church as a whole. Studying in the same places as John Locke and Duns Scotus, and drinking my first beers in the same pub where J. R. R. Tolkien and C. S. Lewis used to meet weekly, was as exhilarating as it was terrifying. My only job was to read theology and, in essence, figure out my approach to faith, politics, and the human condition. No one was policing my thoughts or my writing. I didn't worry about who would see the stack of books on my desk and wonder if I was sliding into "liberal" Christianity or, worse, secular humanism. In a city grounded by a thousand years of history, there was no longer an anchor to my life. No church barriers keeping me inside a set area. It was my responsibility to figure out how to re-create my sense of self and the moral contours of my world. That period in Oxford set me on an intellectual and personal journey that I am still on today.

What I realized then, and have been processing ever since, is that the Christianity I converted to was as much about a particular myth of the United States as it was about the gospel of Christ. Scholars now call this "Christian nationalism." I didn't have the term to label it back then. In the decade after I departed the church in 2005, I identified how the American myth had twisted American evangelicalism into a tradition that prioritizes patriotism over compassion, national defense over loving one's neighbor, and protecting the unborn more than loving anyone on earth.

Since leaving evangelicalism, I have pursued a scholarly life in Oxford, Paris, and across the United States. While I no longer identify as a Christian, I have spent the last decade and a half as a scholar of religion consumed by questions surrounding faith, the divine, and the ways humans make meaning. My time and energy have been devoted to understanding the histories of Christianity, from early church fathers and medieval mystics to modern reformers and American preachers and revivals. But it wasn't until 2018 that I was ready to merge my scholarly projects with my personal history. The ravages of the Trump administration led me to want to help both insiders and outsiders understand why more than 80 percent of White evangelicals and 60 percent of White Catholics voted for Donald Trump. It seemed like my insider scholarly lens might provide a decoder ring to help explain why some of the most conservative religious Americans supported the forty-fifth president's sexual misconduct, acts of cruelty, crass rhetoric, lack of religious literacy, and overtures to White supremacy and xenophobia.

In 2016, I took a job at Skidmore College in upstate New York. This put me only two hours away from my good friend Dan Miller, who teaches at a college nearby. Dan is also a former evangelical minister who is now a scholar of religion. We met at Oxford and have been friends ever since. In July 2018, I drove the short distance to his town in western Massachusetts. We had a beer at a bar near his house and threw around ideas about how to use our personal experiences and academic training to help a larger public understand the religious elements of MAGA Nation—that coalition of Americans, mostly White ones, who supported Trump and his America first ambitions. We eventually landed on the idea of starting a podcast.

When Dan and I started recording the *Straight White American Jesus* podcast a few months later, we wanted to explore issues related to race, gender, sex, and politics in order to unpack a puzzle that, to the casual observer, seemed not to make sense. How could those who touted the Bible at every turn support a man who clearly had never read it? How could the pastors who called on Bill Clinton to resign after his sexual misconduct support a thrice-married president who had paid hush money to a sex worker and gleefully described sexually assaulting women? Why would they not abandon a man who neither spoke of Jesus nor attended church as he pursued a border wall, a Muslim ban, and tax cuts for the rich? Our wager was that we could provide a helpful perspective on the religious-political trappings of the Trump era by addressing these questions and more.

Our goals were humble. We thought a podcast would help some of our colleagues and friends get a handle on important issues. If nothing else, it would be cathartic to relate the religious support for the Trump administration to our evangelical pasts. We had no idea how relevant our research and conversations would become. As we launched our show and invited guests to come talk with us about what we were all seeing, we knew our conversations were important. We knew it was crucial for our nation to figure out what mix of nationalism, racism, and religion had gotten Trump elected.

What we didn't know was that within two years' time, an armed mob would storm the Capitol intending to hang the vice president and assassinate the Speaker of the House after being convinced that the election—and "their" country—had been stolen from them.

WOULD I HAVE BEEN THERE?

As I saw the rioters enter the Capitol on January 6, many of them carrying "Jesus 2020" flags and wearing "Faith, Family, Freedom" shirts, I began to worry and wonder. Over the next few days and weeks, it would become clear that busloads of White evangelicals were indeed among the rioters, having traveled to Washington, DC, with neighbors and friends from church. Would I have been there if I had not left the movement? Or if I hadn't gone myself, would I have been watching the images in tacit support, perhaps praying for the "patriots" willing to do God's will even when it's not easy?

A few days after the J6 insurrection, friends from my old church informed me that dozens of people from churches in our home region had been there and that there were even more back home who approved of the rioters' actions. What seemed like a fringe movement of violent Trump supporters was populated by the small business owners, accountants, and lawyers from the affluent suburbs surrounding my old church. With a wave of nausea, I admitted to myself that had history unfolded in a different pattern, I could have been one of them.

On one hand, I told myself, you would have known better. After all, over time you have transformed from a youthful zealot to a heady professor. Your brain would have never let your body get on a plane to DC. You would have seen the folly in such a move, right? *Right?*

On the other hand, my headiness is exactly what had made me so extreme. After working through the logical components of evangelical teachings—like the idea that Jesus could return at any moment—as a teenager I had committed myself to living them out in the most stringent and pure ways, even if it meant social awkwardness and disapproval from my family. I had clearly been a zealot, and I couldn't know now how far that zealotry would have taken me.

I felt like I was occupying two perspectives on the whole spectacle. As a former insider, my body came alive with the memories of the righteous indignation that fueled my anger about issues like abortion and the "attacks" on Christianity by the US government. I remembered trusting pastors and elders whose faith inspired me to forgo critical thought for radical obedience. If that meant saving my country from ruin by "stopping the steal," I imagine that saying a prayer and jumping into the fray like the patriots of 1776 would have made sense to me. In ways that startled me, it wasn't hard to think myself into the rioters' shoes.

Yet as a scholar who has been analyzing White Christian nationalism for years, I realized that the Capitol insurrection was the logical outcome of a half century of patriotic Christians preparing for combat. It was set in motion by the New Right—a conservative political movement, birthed in the 1960s, ready to use any means necessary to stop the cultural revolutions and return the country to the hands of White, landowning men. In the 1970s, the Religious Right—an explicitly political coalition of evangelicals and Catholics set on restoring old-time religion and family values—joined forces with the New Right. Together they form the *New Religious Right*. In the half century since they linked up, their Christian nationalist mission has been to take America back for God and the people they deem worthy of holding power in his name.

In many ways, it was the White Christian nationalism of the New Religious Right to which I converted back in eighth grade. Thus, for me, January 6 was the physical manifestation of the culture war in which I had been a soldier for eleven years—one that pitted God's patriots on one side against godless traitors on the other. For more than a decade, I had learned the war's topography. Front and center was the fight to take the country back for God. Christians needed to rise up, enter positions of leadership and influence, and ensure the nation didn't fall into the hands of godless socialists and radical leftists—even if ascending the political hierarchy and maintaining power required antidemocratic strategies.

On one flank was a separate but related battle against "government schools," waged through unregulated homeschool curricula and private academies. On the other was the struggle to maintain the "traditional family" against the "gay agenda" and the women's rights movement. This clash merged with the militant proborn movement, standing up to the "holocaust" of abortion. Soldiers in this war were trained in a particular model of masculinity. As a teenager, I was taught by the male elders in my life that the best examples of Christian manhood came from Mel Gibson movies like *Braveheart* and *The Patriot*, in which a courageous hero refuses to allow the government to take his people's way of life and successfully ignites a revolution.

What I knew instinctively on January 6 was that Christian nationalists' war on our democracy didn't start after the November 2020 election. It didn't even start with Trump. It has been raging for over half a century. Trump's Big Lie simply provided the impetus to take it from the political and cultural levels to an actual attempted coup.

As I began to catalog artifacts from that day, scrolling for hours through #capitalsiegereligion (started by Smithsonian curator Peter Manseau), two things became evident. First, religious symbols were everywhere—rioters carrying crosses and icons of Mary, tough guys wearing Bible verses stitched onto chest patches declaring war on God's enemies, people breaking out in impromptu worship songs, the Proud Boys kneeling and praying together in a circle before violently overtaking law enforcement to enter the Capitol. Second, White Christian nationalism was a major unifying phenomenon among the insurrectionists.

It became clear that, if we were ever going to understand what seemed like an unthinkable set of events, we were going to need to reckon with how White Christian nationalism helped birth MAGA Nation.

WHAT IS CHRISTIAN NATIONALISM?

White evangelicalism and White Christian nationalism are not the same thing. White Christian nationalism far exceeds the bounds of

White evangelicalism. There are White Catholic Christian nationalists. And strangely enough, according to recent scholarly work, even some adherents of other faiths qualify as White Christian nationalists. One way to think of White Christian nationalism is as a stream that runs throughout evangelical, Catholic, and other religious traditions and communities. Some White Catholics, for example, are White Christian nationalists. Others are not. It's possible to be a White evangelical or White Catholic without being a White Christian nationalist. However, during the Trump era, White Christian nationalism became so prevalent among these communities—especially in White evangelicalism—that it became hard to separate the two categories.

Recent data shows that over 80 percent of White evangelicals are Christian nationalists, to some degree. This is why the two categories are often conflated. As we will see in chapters 2 and 3, White evangelicals have been formative in the development of White Christian nationalist culture and politics since the 1960s. Thus, while it is a mistake to think of White evangelicalism and White Christian nationalism as synonymous, they are indeed intimately linked.

According to the sociologists Samuel Perry and Andrew White-head in their groundbreaking book *Taking America Back for God*, Christian nationalism exists on a spectrum. Some Christian nationalists are extremist and prone to violence. Others are less hard-core but willing to affirm Christian nationalist tenets about the supposedly Christian founding of America or God's plan for the country. Christian nationalism is a spectrum because, according to Perry and Whitehead, it is less about Christian beliefs and doctrines and more about "historical identity, cultural preeminence, and political influence." Rather than a stable ideology, it is a cultural identity. It's more a matter of how one thinks of oneself and the stories one draws on than a coherent theological belief system.

For Perry and Whitehead, Christian nationalism has three foundational components: the myth of the Christian nation, nostalgia for past glory, and an apocalyptic view of the nation's future.

Understanding each of these three dimensions of Christian national-ism is essential to figuring out what happened on January 6 and what is likely to happen in the future.

The easiest way to envision the first facet of Christian nationalism is as the marriage of cross and flag. In ideological terms, Christian nationalists believe that this country was built for and by Christians. They follow a particular vision of the Puritan preacher John Winthrop's idea that America was founded as a nation to be a "city on a hill," a light to the world. They see themselves as central to the narrative of the United States not only as a nation under God but one elected by God to play an exceptional role in world history. The Christian elements— belief in God's rule and election—are fused with a White nationalist ideology: that the United States is superior to all other nations, that we should take an "America first" approach to policy and trade, and that White people deserve to remain at the top of social, political, and eco-nomic hierarchies. Christian nationalists believe that the United States is a "Christian nation," even if—and this may be surprising—some of them do not regularly attend church, read the Bible, or pray. For not all Christian nationalists are traditionally religious. If you believe that the nation was chosen by God, was founded on religious principles, and has strayed from its divine founding to a sinful state of being, then you might be a Christian nationalist—even if you are only loosely (or not at all) a practicing Christian.

By using the Christian nation myth, Christian nationalist propaganda isn't limited to a certain subset of White evangelicals. It doesn't matter what your denominational affiliation is; you can unite with other believers in a Christian nationalist movement centered on "saving" the nation from "godless ruin." While the data shows that more than 80 percent of White evangelicals register as Christian nationalist to some degree, the myth is expansive enough to include non-Protestants. Perry and Whitehead show that nearly half of American Catholics also chart as Christian nationalists to some level. There are also members of the Latter-day Saints (Mormons) and even some Jews who fit the category.

This explains one of the confusing aspects of Christian nationalism: it often doesn't correlate to denominational identity or personal
religious practice. Many Christian nationalists haven't been to church
in decades, swear like sailors, and couldn't find the book "Two Cor-
inthians" (as Trump once called it) in the Bible. The "Jesus 2020" and
"Trump Is My President—Jesus Is My Savior" flags are a signal of
group identity—indicators of what group they belong to and what
story they are living out—rather than an indicator of their personal
religious practices.

In addition to believing that the United States was founded as a
Christian nation, Christian nationalists share the conviction that the
country has declined over time due to the growing prominence of
outside invaders and ungodly forces. As Perry and Whitehead argue,
Christian nationalists view the United States as similar to Israel in
the Hebrew Bible (what Christians call the Old Testament): if the
nation disobeys God's commandments, it should expect divine ret-
ribution and ruin. And Christian nationalists hold the keys, in their
own minds at least, to what God wants, what he commands, and who
is to blame when the nation gets "punished."

For example, days after 9/11, Jerry Falwell—one of the figure-
heads of modern White evangelicalism and a formational figure in
the Religious Right—said that the terrorist attack was God's punishment for our nation's sins:

> Throwing God out successfully with the help of the federal
> court system, throwing God out of the public square, out of the
> schools. . . . The abortionists have got to bear some burden for
> this because God will not be mocked. And when we destroy
> 40 million little innocent babies, we make God mad. [T]he
> pagans and the abortionists and the feminists and the gays and
> the lesbians who are actively trying to make that an alterna-
> tive lifestyle, the ACLU, People for the American Way—all of
> them who have tried to secularize America. I point the finger
> in their face and say "you helped this happen."

For Falwell, feminists, members of the LGBTQ community, and the ACLU are invaders similar to enemies of the nation of Israel. Not only is the punishment a direct result of what he takes to be disobedience, but it also reflects how the nation has allowed those with no right to leadership and authority—women, racial minorities, sexual-identity minorities, and others—to shape the country's ethos.

This perspective is shared among Falwell's evangelical cohorts. In the wake of Hurricane Katrina, prominent evangelical megachurch pastor John Hagee said, "I believe that New Orleans had a level of sin that was offensive to God, and they were recipients of the judgment of God for that." Franklin Graham, son of Billy Graham, had this to say: "This is one wicked city, OK? It's known for Mardi Gras, for Satan worship. It's known for sex perversion. It's known for every type of drugs and alcohol and the orgies and all of these things that go on down there in New Orleans. There's been a black spiritual cloud over New Orleans for years." The prevailing idea among Christian nationalists such as Falwell, Hagee, and Graham is that as a Christian nation, the United States has a covenant with God that trades obedience and loyalty for protection and blessing. The nation's perceived decline is, in their view, a result of the United States breaking its covenant with God.

Thus, any difficulty the nation faces can be chalked up to collective disobedience and need for a return to the good old days of loyalty to God. This is why nostalgia politics, hinging on the promise to "make America great again," tap into the lifeblood of Christian nationalism. Politicians working this angle promise to return the country to what they take to be the ideal state: an American garden of Eden, founded by American patron saints such as Thomas Jefferson and George Washington and destined to be the greatest nation on earth.

Lurking beneath the patriotic rhetoric of restoring the nation to its former glory is a desire to reinstate a retrograde social and political order. The goal is to return to a state wherein straight, White, native-born Christian men take their rightful places of authority and leadership. Everyone else—including women, racial minorities, religious minorities, and certainly the LGBTQ community—must accept their place as either lower on the American register or outside of it altogether. "The 'Christianity' of Christian nationalism represents something more than religion. . . . It includes assumptions of nativism, white supremacy, patriarchy, and heteronormativity," Perry and Whitehead write. "It is as ethnic and political as it is religious."

This is the sinister underbelly of Christian nationalism's nostalgia politics. The calls for a nation's renewed loyalty and obedience to God are also calls for a return to a time when straight, White Christian men had exclusive control of the nation's political and cultural spheres. It is a movement, in essence, to right-size America by taking it back from people of color, women, immigrants, and LGBTQ people as well as Muslims, secularists, and other religious or nonreligious groups. In essence, "make America great again" is code for "make America White and Christian again."

The final defining trait of Christian nationalism is its apocalyptic tone. The evangelical emphasis on the end of the world is transposed into a crisis narrative that envisions the country as on the precipice of a catastrophic decline. If real Americans don't take decisive action, the story goes, they will not simply lose their majority in the houses of Congress or see a political opponent in the White House; the country as they know it will be gone forever.

As a teenager I learned firsthand how motivating crisis narratives can be. Soon after I converted, my youth leaders introduced me to films like *Thief in the Night*, which claims Jesus could return at any moment to take all Christians to heaven, leaving unbelievers to endure a great tribulation and then an eternity of punishment. As a convert prone to letting logic govern his life in extreme ways, I decided that the best use of my time would be to convert as many people as possible before the end of the world. So I stood outside movie theaters with pamphlets about the gospel, walked up to strangers at lunch at my high school with my Bible in hand, and interjected Jesus into otherwise pleasant conversations with second cousins at family functions. Even though I was captain of the basketball team my senior year, I was the only guy on the squad without a letterman's jacket. How could I spend money on such a frivolous item when we could direct those funds to people who needed to hear the good news of Jesus Christ?

Christian nationalism applies this crisis logic on a national political scale. Politicians and pastors warn that unless patriots and good people of faith take action, the country will be destroyed by "godless, communist" movements, which now include feminism, Black Lives Matter, and secularism. "The hard truth is you won't be safe in Joe Biden's America," then vice president Mike Pence said before the 2020 election. Donald Trump did him one better by claiming the election is "a choice between a socialist nightmare and the American dream." This sentiment was echoed by Christian nationalist pastors such as Brian Gibson, who said that if Biden won, it would be "the death of America," because electing Joe Biden is a "win for Marxism." For Christian nationalists, the choice is not between two viable political candidates; it's between saving the nation and witnessing its demise.

It's a short step from apocalyptic thinking about elections to the demonization of your political opponents. In this system, it's logical to believe that they are capable of—and perhaps already committing—the worst atrocities imaginable. This is how conspiracy theories such as QAnon are so readily adapted to a Christian nationalist worldview, as we will see. If you believe the country is in a cosmic war between good and evil, it's not hard to take the jump to thinking that there is a grand conspiracy, wherein a cabal of global elites are trying to take down the United States in service to Satan. This worldview also makes it possible to demonize your political enemies—literally. "She is an abject, psychopathic, demon from Hell," popular conspiracy theorist Alex Jones said about Hillary Clinton in 2016. "I'm telling you, she's a demon."

Christian nationalism primes people to conspiratorial extremism by expanding the apocalyptic cosmology I adopted as a teenager into a national political register. The script reads like this: we have a short time to save the country; if we don't treat this as a red-alert situation and devote all our time and energy to this campaign, the country will be destroyed forever by Marxists and socialists.

Political opponents become demons. Elections become end-times events. And the nation's history is viewed as a cosmic war, with enemies of the republic on one side and God-fearing patriots—and the Lord of heaven and earth—on the other.

WHAT DOES "WHITE" HAVE TO DO WITH WHITE CHRISTIAN NATIONALISM?

Race has everything to do with how Christian nationalism is constructed and lived out. In a study on attitudes toward racial inequalities, Perry and Whitehead make it clear that there are Black Christian nationalists, too, but that they view the nation and its history in a starkly different way than their White counterparts. In contrast to White Christian nationalists, who largely attributed racial inequality to laziness and lack of motivation on the part of Black people, Perry and Whitehead found that "Black Americans who affirmed being a Christian was very important to being truly American were more likely to attribute black-white inequality to racial discrimination and educational opportunities." This means, Perry and Whitehead maintain, "that connecting Christian and American identities does not necessarily bolster white supremacy, but for black Americans it may in fact evoke ideals of racial justice and structural transformation."

On the whole, Black Christian nationalists view Christianity as a means for uprooting unequal and unjust political and social systems. Raphael Warnock, who preaches from the pulpit once occupied by Martin Luther King Jr., was the first Black Democrat elected to the Senate from the Deep South since Reconstruction. Warnock frames it this way: "I've been trying to point us toward the highest ideals in our humanity and in the covenant we have with one another as American people—that all of us deserve an opportunity to create a prosperous life for us and our families." For most Black Americans who view the United States as a nation in covenant with God, the goal is not to maintain the status quo or return the country to a mythical past. Rather, this version of Christian nationalism means pushing the nation forward to reach its potential and to more fully embody the view that all people are created equal with the right to pursue life, liberty, and happiness.

It's a different story for White Christian nationalists. In general, the goal for them is not to push the United States to live up to its ideals for the first time but to return the country to a supposed idyllic period when it was flourishing. While Christian nationalism isn't limited to evangelicals, as we saw, the latter make up a significant percentage of the group, and they have been formative in the development of White Christian nationalist rhetoric (more on this in chapters 3 and 4). In her 2018 work on evangelicals and immigration, Dr. Janelle Wong shows that White evangelicals are extreme outliers with regard to opposition to the Black Lives Matter movement, national apologies for slavery, taxing the wealthy, and immigration. White evangelicals are more than twice as likely—and sometimes three times as likely—to oppose these issues as their Latinx, Asian, and Black counterparts. In essence, data shows how the White in "White evangelical" makes this group a unique subset of extremists on a range of political and social issues.

This leads Wong to conclude that evangelical support for Trump originated in a fear of losing status, socially and politically. She points out that White evangelicals perceive themselves to be the victims of discrimination. As I discuss throughout the book, I am a biracial person who experienced firsthand how the "White" in "White Christian nationalist" is definitive. The "White" in the "White Christian nationalist" train is, and always has been, the engine. In fact, Whiteness is more than that—it is both engine and fuel, both wheel and track for the locomotive of Christian exceptionalism. While the logo on the side of the train car might say "Christian," Whiteness—and the fear of losing racial status—is what propels the train down the track toward cultural and political supremacy in the United States.

WHY DIDN'T WE SEE IT COMING?

Almost two decades after leaving evangelicalism, I have no way of knowing if I would have taken part in these events. But there is a more relevant and, I think, urgent question to ask than my own personal musings on whether I might have been there. In light of the modern history of White Christian nationalism that helped get Trump elected, and then provided an integrating force for the insurrection he inspired, we must ask: Why didn't we see this coming? And what else are we missing? What further outworking of the MAGA movement will develop in the coming years? In what follows, I attempt to answer these questions.

While pastors and political operatives are the central players in this tale, one of the founding figures of the modern movement was a cowboy from the American West—a man full of animal magnetism and a brusque masculinity, a person born into privilege who somehow made himself out to be an everyman by eschewing book-learning and East Coast elitism, and one who led a successful political career with no major setbacks, only to become the biggest loser in American presidential history.

Chapter 2

EXTREMISM IS A VIRTUE

THE PRAYER MEETING WAS at six in the morning. It's not easy for even the most pious nineteen-year-old to get up before dawn to pray with a couple dozen folks twenty-five to fifty years their senior. But as a youth pastor at Rose Drive Friends Church in Yorba Linda, California, I was expected to show up to "Early Christians," the prayer meeting on Tuesday mornings as often as possible.

Early Christians took place in the "Fireside Room," a quaint room with a fireplace (seemingly unnecessary in the Southern California desert) adjoining the gymnasium of the church. When we arrived, everyone would fill in spots at the eight round tables, each with six chairs, set up throughout the room. In front of each chair there would be a ten-page packet of typed-up prayer requests, which congregants had submitted during Sunday services two days prior. Most Tuesdays, it was hard to keep my eyes open as each person at my table took their turn reciting one of the prayer requests on the page. Sometimes an elder would have to nudge me awake when it was my turn to pray.

Rose Drive is part of the Evangelical Friends denomination. Friends are often referred to as Quakers, who are historically known for their emphasis on social justice, pacifism, and a simple way of life devoid of luxury or extremity. Many Friends communities continue to cultivate these virtues. You would have never known these were Quaker priorities, though, by looking at the prayer requests we received from the Rose Drive congregation. The most common were for personal health issues, and after that came those for the military:

"Please lift up our troops, who protect our freedoms from evil forces."

"Pray for our military that protects the greatest country on earth."

"Please ask that God would vanquish our enemies and keep our boys safe."

In my seven years of attending the prayer meeting, I cannot recall one person asking us to pray for peace. We prayed for the armed services and law enforcement dozens of times every week. We "lifted up" requests to God for physical healing and family issues and job promotions. We even prayed for election outcomes: "Lord, please let your will be done in this election, so that abortion might finally be outlawed in this land." "We pray that your people would rise up and take back their country!" But never for peace. Never for systematic change related to racism, violence, or poverty. Never for our "enemies" in Iraq or Afghanistan.

The congregants requesting the prayers—and the faithful remnant who rose early on Tuesdays to pray—were affluent White folks. They had nice houses with pools and three-car garages as well as boats and cabins. Some were small business owners. Others were defense-industry engineers. There were judges and lawyers, contractors and CEOs. From the pulpit, there were never sermons about the dangers of wealth. Instead, the pastoral team adhered to a silent code surrounding money: "Don't bedevil it, because we need it in order to make this megachurch go."

If you listened to the prayers on Tuesdays and the sermons on Sundays, you'd think that Christianity is about individuals and families, about military might and victory. You'd think that it is a force for conservative politics and candidates and a friend of the wealthy and the powerful. In my mind as a nineteen-year-old, this was Christianity. These facets appeared ahistorical. In fact, they didn't *appear* at all. They were the cultural and religious air I breathed—standard, ubiquitous, and thus unapparent. This set of religious-cultural principles was so normalized that it was hard for me or anyone else to notice them.

But as I turned my attention to church history, theology, and philosophy in the ensuing years, I began to realize they were the products of modern politics and culture. Our theology and practice weren't the result of God's revelation to humanity. They were the product of decades of political and cultural backlash. A faith defined by culture wars more than the Bible or Quaker teachings. In this chapter, I recount the origin story of how my church, and much of White American Christianity as a whole, became part of a Christian nationalist conflict waged to halt the expansion of the civil rights and prevent the mainstreaming of religious, racial, sexual, ethnic, and other minority groups in the United States. This is as much a political history as it is a religious one.

Like many megachurches in Orange County, California, and around the United States, Rose Drive Friends Church was founded in the mid-1960s. While it has never been known as an overly political congregation, it was birthed in the midst of the culture wars that set the groundwork for the war White Christian nationalists in particular—and MAGA Nation in general—are currently waging against the rest of the country. It wasn't a historical accident that my church community prioritized individual success, prosperity, conservative politics, and the military might of the United States. It wasn't an aberration that we looked on those who opposed these things as enemies of God, bent on destroying his people and his chosen nation. It was the result of a conservative political-cultural-religious movement designed to keep White Christian landowners at the top of America's political and economic hierarchies.

What this means is that the prayers we received for our Tuesday morning meetings at Rose Drive were the fruit of political and legal battles, Supreme Court cases, presidential elections, and identity politics. Religious communities never develop in a vacuum. They comprise political actors and cultural agents. Thus, to understand why we prayed and what we prayed for on those Tuesday mornings, it's necessary to consider the political and cultural contexts that formed the soil from which the church grew.

My Christianity was shaped by the politics of the 1960s, when White people, especially White Christians, felt like they were losing their country to minoritized groups who had no right to it. In response, they developed a radical political agenda to stop the tides of history. Their staunch libertarianism was a means of preventing the government from making things more fair by expanding the civil rights of those who had been marginalized and excluded. Militarism and rabid anticommunism were ways of envisioning the goodness of God's United States in contrast to the godlessness of communist China and the Soviet Union. Individualist and procapitalist theologies were ways of shirking concern for the underprivileged at a systemic level. The nuclear family became the first principle for defending America, growing good citizens, and promoting individual prosperity.

Christian identity wasn't a later addition to this set of cultural wars, an awkward add-on to a political movement. It was the integrating force. Christianity was the mechanism holding all the components of what would become a 1960s counterrevolution into a cohesive whole.

A WHITE CHRISTIAN NATIONALIST COUNTERREVOLUTION

Modern White Christian nationalists point to the 1960s as the era during which the country really lost its way. While some may point to the abolishment of slavery as the first American downfall (more on this in chapter 3), for many, the sixties were the time when numerous serpents tempted Americans away from the bedrock values of faith, family, and freedom and toward a new social order, a sexual revolution, and an abandonment of the nuclear family.

"We have to remember that it's not just the Judeo-Christian tradition where the country was founded, but in the social and in the moral revolution of the 1960s and '70s," said Timothy Goeglein, an executive at the prominent evangelical parachurch organization Focus on the Family, in early 2020. In his view, the 1960s were "a frontal assault directly on the Beatitudes, on the Ten Commandments, on the whole body of ethics that forms the Judeo-Christian foundation of the United States of America."

It's important to decipher what he means by associating the cultural transformations of the sixties with an assault on Christianity. The 1960s witnessed a sea change in the way American society was ordered. The civil rights movement started in the previous decade, with events like the Birmingham bus boycott, and spread to Atlanta, Memphis, and then throughout the South. In 1964, Martin Luther King Jr. and Lyndon Johnson shook hands and posed for the camera after the landmark Civil Rights Act was signed into law. While imperfect, the law was the federal government's attempt to ensure that Black Americans would be treated equally to their White counterparts when it came to schooling, public services, and rights under the law. In 1967, the Supreme Court's ruling in *Loving v. Virginia* led to the legalization of interracial marriage, paving the way for people like me—a kid with a White mom and a Japanese American dad—to exist as the result of a legal union. Though this may seem like a historical blip, the Supreme Court ruling signaled to White conservatives that the ability to maintain "pure" bloodlines and separation from people of color would no longer be guarded by rules surrounding marriage. Many feared a nation of "mongrels," or mixed-race people.

Throughout the 1960s and beyond, women fought for the Equal Rights Amendment, though it was never ratified, in the name of equal protection under the law at home and at work. Betty Friedan published *The Feminine Mystique* in 1963, the same year President Kennedy signed the Equal Pay Act. In 1965, President Johnson signed Executive Order 11246, providing provisions against sexual harassment in the workplace. Divorce rates skyrocketed as new forms of family became normalized and women entered the workforce *en masse*. Women marched, chanted for equal pay, and lobbied Congress for the right to divorce without penalty. About the same time, the Sexuality Information and Education Council of the United States (SIECUS) began working with public school districts to provide comprehensive sexual education for teenage students. Antiwar protesters raged against what they saw as a senseless conflict and the travesties of American imperialism. And in 1969, the Stonewall uprising changed queer history forever, marking a turning point in the quest for recognition and protection of LGBTQ individuals under the law.

In response to these events, since the 1960s conservative Christians have deputized themselves the guardians of the "traditional" family and its patriarchal structure. They envision a familial unit in which the husband-father is the head of household and breadwinner, the wife-mother is a submissive companion who orders the domestic space, and obedient children are raised to think of their dad's voice as the voice of God. This family patriarchy is then superimposed on a vision for society wherein abortion is banned, the LGBTQ+ community is stripped of rights, women are homemakers rather than professionals, and similarly ordered patriarchal churches teach God's people the gospel all across the land.

There were other changes too, of the type that might go under your radar if you aren't part of a certain subculture or religious community. In 1962, the Supreme Court took on *Engel v. Vitale*. The case concerned the constitutionality of school prayer in public school settings where students were required to participate. It was brought by Steven Engel and other parents from Hyde Park, New York. The parents took issue with the school prayer that was read over the school loudspeaker every morning: "Almighty God, we acknowledge our dependence upon Thee, and we beg Thy blessings upon us, our parents, our teachers and our Country."

The court ruled 6–1 in favor of Engel. This meant banning official prayers in public school settings, particularly in mandatory participation contexts.

Potter Stewart was the dissenting justice. "With all respect, I think the Court has misapplied a great constitutional principle. I cannot see how an 'official religion' is established by letting those who want to say a prayer say it," Stewart wrote. "On the contrary, I think that to deny the wish of these school children to join in reciting this prayer is to deny them the opportunity of sharing in the spiritual heritage of our Nation."

The Christian nationalist rhetoric is subtle but present in this passage. Stewart references "the spiritual heritage of our Nation," as if it is a given and something that all Americans would presumably want to take part in. There is no recognition that praying to an "Almighty God" would alienate nontheists, most polytheists, and those wanting to keep their religious practice separate from school rituals. There is also no recognition that the Constitution guarantees the separation of church and state—and the freedom from religion.

A year later, in 1963, the court ruled the same way in a similar case. In *Abington v. Schempp*, the court considered the matter of required Bible reading in schools. The case originated in Philadelphia. The Schempp family claimed that the law requiring schools to begin each day with the recitation of ten Bible passages was unconstitutional. Lower courts sided with them. Even when the state changed the law to allow students to opt out of these readings, the lower courts ruled that such readings violated the constitutional prohibition against the government promoting religion or a specific religion. Eventually the Supreme Court ruled 8–1 in favor of Schempp, creating a situation where it was permitted to teach *about* religion but not to teach such lessons *for* religious purposes.

It should be noted that neither the Engel decision nor the Schempp decision prevented public school students from praying or practicing their faith voluntarily. As a high school student in the nineties, I often prayed with other students before school, held Bible studies at lunchtime, and walked around with a Bible in my arms. I was free to practice my religion. So, too, were Muslim and Jewish students and students of other faiths. But, the court ruled, public schools were not free to impose any type of religion on students or promote religion in general. This protected the non-Christian students, since it prevented school administrators from enforcing or promoting Christianity by praying over loudspeakers or teaching the Bible religiously. In other words, it ended Christian supremacy in favor of the freedom of religion (or no religion) for all students in public schools.

The Engel ruling in 1962 was not well received by the American public. There were protests, letter-writing campaigns, and calls for justices to be impeached. Though it did nothing to outlaw the *practice* of religion, the barring of the *imposition* of religion touched a nerve in the American body politic. The attacks on the court (and the families who filed the case) were malicious and persistent. While mainline Protestant—nonevangelical Protestants who, on the whole, take a more liberal approach to faith, politics, and morality—and Jewish leaders praised the decision, many Catholics and evangelicals viewed it as a sign of the nation's growing godlessness and decay.

Eventually the backlash subsided. But evangelicals, particularly in the South, never forgot when "God was taken out of public schools." "They put the Negroes in the schools and now they've driven God out," said George Andrews, a congressperson from Alabama, soon after the decision. The court decisions that "took God out of public schools" would remain a rallying cry for White evangelicals and a marker of when the country turned its back on the "spiritual heritage" on which it was founded.

THE SOIL OF EXTREMISM

While the work to expand civil rights for all Americans is unfinished, there is no doubt that these movements and policies reshaped the public square and forecasted a future in which racial and religious minorities, along with women and members of the LGBTQ community, would have an increased stake in the development of American democracy. They also portended a time when "Christian" would no longer be a privileged religious category. Many of us recognize these changes as welcome steps toward realizing the American ideals of equality and freedom for all. But as my *Straight White American Jesus* cohost Dan Miller says, not everyone wins through equality. Those who have benefited from inequality lose their privileged place. They don't see a level playing field as a positive. They see it as taking away their power and influence. It feels like persecution.

Thus, it's unsurprising that from the throes of sixties progressivism came the seeds for a conservative counterrevolution—one that fought, and is still fighting, the tides of history in order to "make America great again." This countermovement was cultivated by White Christians who felt as if their country was being stolen from them by people of color, women, LGBTQ people, and other interlopers upsetting the social and political orders.

In the face of the revolutionary transformation of the structure of American society, family, and gender roles, conservatives felt powerless. Between 1933 and 1968, Dwight Eisenhower was the only Republican to occupy the White House. And Ike, who was president from 1953 to 1961, was a moderate whose "dynamic conservativism" moderated fiscal stringency with a liberal approach to government services and the social safety net. In the wake of the New Deal, Eisenhower became the president of the "Middle Way." Representative of what some considered to be his liberal tendencies was his infrastructure plan. He transformed car travel by transforming the nation's roads. The highway system we take for granted today was the result of a Republican president's willingness to spend—and spend big—on government programs.

While the government was doing a lot at home, many conservatives felt as if it wasn't doing enough abroad. Working with his secretary of state, John Foster Dulles, Eisenhower felt the best strategy to battle communism was diplomacy and containment rather than embroiling the United States in another conflict (he was already dealing with the fallout from the Korean War). As the Cold War developed, conservative fears led to the demonization of any form of American collectivism as communist or socialist. Invoking the external bogeyman became a way to attack any internal opponent.

By 1963, many on the political right were fed up with compromise. To them it felt as if the country was not stepping forward into a more just and equal society but degenerating into chaos. What they needed in order to take the country back was not a moderate who would further concede to liberals, elites, and negotiate his way around communists. They were tired of Eisenhower's Middle Way. They wanted *their* way. In their minds, they needed a hero who would halt the nation's "progress" and return to its core values. They needed a cowboy.

As historian Heather Cox Richardson outlines clearly in *How the South Won the Civil War*, the cowboy—especially the on-screen cowboy such as John Wayne—became a mythical figure in twentieth-century America. The cowboy was imagined as a rugged White individualist who was self-reliant and never asked the government for a handout. Usually envisioned as a military veteran, the cowboy thwarted enemies of the state—such as Mexicans, Chinese, and Native Americans—without compromise or apology. This paradigm ignored, of course, the large numbers of people of color in the American West and the role of women in frontier society—not to mention the White supremacist violence that maintained notions of a "frontier" in the first place. It also operated as a model for the no-nonsense leader who didn't need fancy degrees or an army of bureaucrats to take sides, draw lines in the sand, and act decisively.

A COWBOY FOR PRESIDENT

All these factors created the perfect storm for an unlikely Republican candidate for president in 1964. Barry Goldwater was the "cowboy senator" from Arizona who promised to reverse the country's waywardness without hesitation or apology. Like Donald Trump half a century later, Goldwater was never supposed to be the GOP nominee. Conventional wisdom said that Nelson Rockefeller, governor of New York, was next in line to challenge the Democratic stronghold on the White House. Heir to the family fortune, Rockefeller was a country club Republican who had previously served as assistant secretary of state under two Democratic presidents. In line with Eisenhower's centrism, he promised fiscal belt-tightening, coupled with a moderate social program that would be open to debate and compromise when it came to the culture wars. Alongside him were figures like Michigan governor George Romney, father of Utah Senator Mitt Romney.

By contrast, Goldwater was viewed as an ideological bully from one of the far corners of the country, part of the rightward fringe of the Republican Party. The northeastern elites of the party didn't take him, or his southern and southwestern supporters, seriously. It was a grave mistake.

Despite his everyman image, Goldwater was born into privilege as the son of a successful Phoenix merchant in 1909. Yet he projected the aura of a self-reliant frontier man. Handsome and square-jawed, with a booming baritone voice, Goldwater oozed a cowboy mystique that resonated with those who considered themselves old-fashioned American individualists who relied on hard work and determination to pull themselves up society's ladder. According to his sister, Goldwater may have never read a book cover-to-cover. He dropped out of the University of Arizona after one year, when his father died, and then took over the family business. But his appeal to voters was instinctual. He emanated a raw magnetism that drew both men and women into his orbit. His campaign put up advertisements with his pictures and the simple caption: "THE MAN." One of his staffers explained that on the campaign trail Goldwater appealed to men and women through an aura that was "personal, animal, sexual, magic." In the Arizona senator, the masses saw the opposite of a northeastern elite more at home in a tuxedo or behind a desk than out on the range. They saw the MAN who would fight every battle and thwart all their enemies.

In many ways Goldwater's strategy became the blueprint for Republican success in the late twentieth century and beyond: deemphasize one's economic privilege, foreground individualist capitalist success and self-reliant manhood, and throw in a good dose of anti-intellectualism and antielitism. This is the perfect mix for a GOP frontrunner who can appeal to "real Americans" and their "old-fashioned values" of individualist capitalism, anticommunism, and de facto racial segregation—even if, like Goldwater, you grew up wealthy, or, like Donald Trump, have a golden toilet in your penthouse apartment.

It was those values that Goldwater tapped into to best Rockefeller, the prototypical aristocrat, for the Republican nomination. Whereas many Americans viewed the New Deal and Eisenhower's "dynamic conservatism" as the keys to mid-twentieth-century American prosperity, a vociferous minority viewed the vast and wide government spending programs as an unjust redistribution of wealth that favored those who didn't deserve it—namely, racial minorities and women— and left landowning White men behind. This, coupled with the Cold War and the perceived threat of communism, gave rise to a renewed effort to curb the role of government and institute a libertarian vision of society.

"Throughout history, government has proved to be the chief instrument for thwarting man's liberty," Goldwater wrote in *The Conscience of a Conservative*. "Government represents power in the hands of some men to control and regulate the lives of other men. And power, as Lord Acton said, corrupts men. 'Absolute power,' he added, 'corrupts absolutely.'"

According to Goldwater and his libertarian followers, government's role was to maximize freedom by keeping foreign threats at bay, administering justice, and enabling the exchange of goods and services. Beyond that, it should allow citizens to exercise their conscience when it comes to issues of individual morality. Social safety nets were for socialists. Government programs were an oxymoron. The best government was the least government—especially if the government was going to be in the business of creating laws to redistribute wealth and change the rules of the public square.

Libertarian ideals also proved to be a convenient way to formulate opposition to the Civil Rights Act of 1964 and the active desegregation of schools. While Goldwater maintained that racial integration was important, he refused the right of government to implement laws that would ensure it happened in communities and states. He maintained support for integration as an idea while railing against desegregation through law. Goldwater said on the campaign trail that the 1954 *Brown v. Board of Education* Supreme Court case that led to school desegregation was "not based on law." He also argued that the integration of schools should not happen by force but by choice. Goldwater would preface statements like this by assuring the crowd and the press that he thought that the races should live side by side in an integrated society. "I am not prepared, however, to impose that judgment of mine on the people of Mississippi or South Carolina," he would pivot. "That is their business, not mine. I believe that the problem of race relations, like all social and cultural problems, is best handled by the people directly concerned."

As the historian David Farber notes, by taking this line Goldwater was signaling to White segregationists that he would not get in their way in the battle to halt school integration in particular and government-backed laws and programs to end White supremacy in general. It was a classic libertarian move: claim that the government should have no hand in changing culture or society without recognizing that it was government that had stacked the deck against certain people in the first place. It was not a matter of not wanting the government's intervention; it was a matter of who would benefit from it and how.

While Goldwater was against government trying to help improve certain people's lives at home, he was blunt about its duty to take overreaching action abroad. In the early 1960s, he bemoaned the diplomatic foreign policy positions Eisenhower and then Kennedy took with regard to the Cold War. He wanted the United States to admit it was at war and then act accordingly. This is how he put it in *The Conscience of a Conservative:* "Either the Communists will retain the offensive; will lay down one challenge after another; will invite us in local crisis after local crisis to choose between all-out war and limited retreat, and will force us, ultimately, to surrender or accept war under the most disadvantageous circumstances. Or we will summon the will and the means for taking the initiative, and wage a war of attrition against them."

On the campaign trail in 1964, the Arizona senator claimed nonchalantly that he thought Ho Chi Minh and the Vietcong in Vietnam could be stopped if the military was willing to use low-grade atomic weapons to clear the forest. This set off a firestorm in the press, which framed the senator as a hawk who would embroil the nation in atomic warfare. While many were outraged, Goldwater's supporters were overjoyed to have finally found a fighter they could believe in.

Though he was not an overly religious man, Goldwater wrapped his cowboy libertarianism in a Christian myth of the nation. According to him, the difference between real conservatives and socialist-leaning others was that the former understood that each person is a unique spiritual creature. Emphasizing both individualism and a religious conception of the human being, Goldwater used the Christian mantle to tie together the libertarian, anticommunist, and anti–civil rights threads of his platform. In his acceptance speech at the 1964 GOP convention, he proclaimed that it was time to return to "proven ways—not because they are old, but because they are true. We must, and we shall, set the tide running again in the cause of freedom . . . under a government limited by laws of nature and of nature's God." He even said that if communists refused to believe in God, there could be no coexisting with them. One side would have to go.

One of the ingenious moves that Goldwater made was linking freedom, individuality, and capitalism to religion and labeling their opponents as the opponents of God and the United States. "Those who seek to live your lives for you, to take your liberties in return," he wrote. "This Nation was founded upon the rejection of that notion and upon the acceptance of God as the author of freedom."

God, nation, freedom: the holy trinity in the Christian nationalist theological pantheon. What's critical to notice in Goldwater's approach is that the politics come first. The foundations of the belief system are not Christian love or neighborliness but individualism, capitalism, and Whiteness. The *political* shapes the *theological* to its needs, forming a Christianity in line with nationalist and racist priorities. Religion is the vehicle. Politics is the engine.

THIS IS THE GOSPEL

By the time I converted to evangelicalism in 1995, these ideals had become the shadow doctrines of White American evangelicalism. While they weren't outlined in church handbooks, they were the unspoken cultural joists holding up White evangelical practice, as ubiquitous as they were invisible.

Every Tuesday at the early morning prayer meeting, we prayed for the military but never for peace or for our enemies. We asked God to protect our families but did little to protect the poor, vulnerable, and marginalized in our community. Our congregation was overwhelmingly of European descent. Becoming an evangelical actually made me *more* White because my mentors, my elders, and all the cultural contours of my life were White. My Japanese American family and customs became *other*, a foreign add-on largely incompatible with my new life in the Rose Drive community. The Japanese American element of my identity was not a part of me to celebrate but one to suppress into the background. The message was that it was okay to be a person of color, just one who didn't disrupt the church's mission by calling attention to racial identity or the need for racial justice.

Affluence was celebrated in our church through silence. No one spoke of it. No one dared denounce it. When I took the youth group to swim parties in the summer, they were at houses with trampolines, swimming pools with waterfalls and fancy slides, and full-court basketball setups in the backyard. On Sundays, the American flag was displayed proudly in the worship sanctuary, just to the side of the stage where the choir sang and the pastor preached. On the Fourth of July we sang both patriotic ballads and hymns as if they were one and the same.

Moreover, we viewed "other types of Christians" as neither really part of the kingdom of God nor real Americans. Any perspectives on the gospel that prioritized social justice were viewed as a slippery slope to communism and as diminishing Jesus from a divine savior to be worshipped to a social reformer to be admired. One youth group mom told me once that she sent her kids to a private Christian school because she wanted an environment that taught "zero tolerance" when it came to other religions. Even *learning* about other religions, neutrally, was not something she wanted for her kids. Tolerance, in her mind, is not a Christian virtue.

But she hadn't come up with this idea on her own. Her zero-tolerance policy for other religions—or at least for her children even learning about them—belonged to a whole universe of White Christian nationalist ideas about education and how to raise a new generation of real Americans.

MODERATION IS A SIN

Goldwater won the Republican nomination for president on the promise of conflict. In his acceptance speech, he vowed to fight the culture wars surrounding civil rights, foreign policy, and the role of the federal government with ferocity and without compromise. "I would remind you that extremism in the defense of liberty is no vice," Goldwater boomed to a raucous crowd in San Francisco. "And let me remind you also that moderation in the pursuit of justice is no virtue."

These infamous words from Goldwater's 1964 acceptance speech remain as jarring today as they were when he delivered them. As soon as he uttered that pithy sentence, his followers knew they had chosen the right man for the job. His defense of extremism and castigation of moderation stood in stark contrast to Eisenhower's "Middle Way" and put the Democrats on notice that a great battle was on the horizon.

What neither the noisy convention crowd in San Francisco nor Goldwater himself knew at the time was that the appetite for extremism—as well as the allergy to moderation—would characterize the spirit of the GOP and the White Christian nationalism that fueled it for the next sixty years.

And it just so happened that the epicenter of this counterrevolution was in my backyard.

Chapter 3

THE NEW SOUTH RISES

IN 1958, MY GRANDFATHER Noah Bradley told his family that they were moving to California. "Brad," as everyone called him, was a cotton farmer. He'd had his crops wiped out by flooding enough times that he was willing to call it quits and head West to try something new. A short while later they left Portageville, a farming town in the boot heel of Missouri, to make the trek to the Golden State. My mom, who was eight at the time, and her younger sister were scrunched in the back of the family station wagon, along with all their worldly belongings. They left behind dozens of family members and the only place any of them had ever known. After an arduous journey, they settled in the San Gabriel Valley, east of Los Angeles, and about forty miles from Orange County.

Eventually, Mom moved to Orange County, where she met my dad. When Grandpa died in 1978, just before my birth, my grandmother relocated too. By the time my brothers and I came along in the early eighties, Mom fit seamlessly into the Orange County landscape. A short blonde with blue eyes, she had, by then, only a charming hint of her southern drawl. Southern California had become home. Yet it wasn't because my mom and grandma had left the South behind. It's because they, and many others, had brought it with them.

Mom and her family were not the only ones on the road headed West. Between 1930 and 1960, six million southerners left home to relocate to major cities across the country, including Los Angeles and Orange County. Some of them were part of the Great Migration, which saw Black southerners leave Dixie in monumental numbers between 1917 and 1975. But that is not the whole story. Many White southerners left too, in what historians call the Sunbelt Migration. By 1970, more southerners lived in California than in any state in the South. This movement continued over the twentieth century, as economic growth in many Sunbelt cities after World War II stimulated migration from the Northeast and the Rust Belt. By 1990, Los Angeles, San Diego, and Phoenix were among the ten largest cities in the United States.

Orange County was one of the biggest winners of the Sunbelt Migration. Between 1950 and 1970, Orange County gained 1.2 million people. Between 1950 and 1960, 85 percent of the population growth was due to migration from other parts of the country. It was, in essence, a new gold rush made up of newcomers from the Midwest and the South. They were all flocking, like my mom and her family, for well-paying jobs, affordable housing, and Southern California's great weather.

The economic impetus for this migration was the Cold War, which fueled defense spending by the federal government and stimulated the economy in the process. The resulting windfall disproportionately benefited Southern California. By the early 1950s, California was at the top of the list for military contracts awarded. In the 1960s, the Golden State won twice as much money in such contracts than any other state. Before the Cold War, Orange County was a farming region, but it quickly transformed into the nation's hub for defense production. In 1950, very few Orange Countians worked in the defense industry. By the early 1960s, more than twelve thousand workers were employed by defense contractors such as Hughes Aircraft and Ford Aeronautics.

The establishment of the defense industry laid the foundation for other sectors. As migrants made their way to the Southland, they needed places to live, leading to a construction boom. Well-paying jobs at aeronautics and electronics factories provided the income for new single-family tract homes. Then Disneyland set up shop in 1955, making Orange County a year-round tourist destination.

While migration patterns and the reshaping of Southern California may seem tangential to a history of White Christian nationalism, the Sunbelt Migration is key to understanding the counterrevolution of the 1960s, the Goldwater rush in 1964, and eventually the White Christian nationalist movement that helped birth MAGA Nation. For many White people in both the South and the New South—Southern California, to which southerners had relocated—the rapid changes to American life as a result of various civil rights and freedom movements in the 1960s were unwelcome. The majority of White people, from Atlanta to Los Angeles—including my grandfather, who moved his family west in 1958—viewed the burgeoning civil rights movement as a threat to the God-ordained social order. They viewed policies and direct actions to integrate schools as an overreach by the federal government. Most of all, they saw on the horizon a future in which their children would be forced to attend the same schools and play on the same playgrounds with Black, Asian, and Latino kids—which in their minds was absolutely unacceptable. While Orange County was extremely homogenous—less than 10 percent of the county was non-White in the 1960s—these views weren't totally out of step with the rest of the country. A 1963 Gallup poll found that 78 percent of White people said they would move if many Black families moved into their neighborhood. As for the famous March on Washington organized by Martin Luther King Jr. and others, 60 percent of White people viewed it unfavorably.

As we saw in the previous chapter, this coincided with what many conservative Christians perceived as God being "taken out of public schools" and prayer being "outlawed." In the face of the perceived communist threat, they thought the United States was becoming more like Soviet Russia than the city on a hill the Puritans envisioned. In its place were new sex education curricula that taught young children things they should only learn about at home. Soon anticommunist organizations began peddling conspiracy theories to help provide a shortcut explanation as to why and how all these changes were happening in American society. The John Birch Society, for example, claimed that fourth-grade teachers were exposing themselves to students in order to teach anatomy and encouraging the practice of bestiality.

When they turned to their churches, some White Christians were faced with progressive action campaigns and messages about social justice. One often forgotten component of American religious history is that, from the end of the nineteenth century to the mid-1960s, mainline or "liberal" Protestantism was the predominant form of American religion. Since the end of the nineteenth century, there had been a division between evangelical and mainline Protestants in America. The former rejected the theory of evolution, argued that the Bible was the errorless Word of God and should be read literally, and emphasized individual salvation over social change. This is the tradition I inherited at Rose Drive Friends upon my conversion. By contrast, the mainline churches saw the possibility of cohering the theory of evolution with biblical teaching on creation, made room for critical approaches to the Bible, and viewed the gospel as a commission to help the vulnerable, feed the poor, and fight for justice and inclusion in every way possible.

It may be hard to imagine now, but it was this latter tradition that dominated American Christianity throughout the first half of the twentieth century. Many Baptist, Methodist, and Presbyterian denominations, especially in the Midwest and Northeast, were committed to causes like ending poverty, fighting for labor rights, and even working for racial justice. Their theologies lined up with the ideology of the New Deal: government can be a great equalizer that enables more Americans to experience the benefits of a free and prosperous nation. For those in these mainline denominations, individual wealth was not something to celebrate or flaunt. Individualism was seen as a vice—a turning away from collective responsibility. And for mainline Christians, especially in the wake of two world wars and the fresh wounds of the war in Korea, militarism was not part of the gospel.

In response, White Americans along the Sunbelt mingled Christian nationalist mythology infused with libertarian economics and the sacralization of the individual. This laid the foundation for a new grassroots political movement aimed at toppling the GOP establishment through a different brand of American Christianity. As the historians John Compton, Darren Dochuk, and Lisa McGirr have shown in groundbreaking works, Southern California was the epicenter of the burgeoning new conservativism. It was the perfect petri dish for a movement that mixed old-time Christian revivalism, libertarian economics, cowboy individualism, and—it must be said—a militant White identity.

AN UNZONED LAND

When southern and midwestern migrants first made their way to Orange County, going back to the early 1900s, they found a place out of reach of the mainline denominations' vast networks of churches. Their influence had not extended that far south and west. In religious terms, it was largely unclaimed territory.

Evangelical preachers quickly filled the religious vacuum in Southern California's religious marketplace. From the time of the first Sunbelt migrations, evangelical preachers found a friendly audience in the Southland. R. A. Torrey, Dean of the Bible Institute of Los Angeles (now Biola University), edited *The Fundamentals*, which became a foundational text for twentieth-century Christian fundamentalism, in 1915. Charles Fuller broadcast his fiery sermons from Placentia, a northern Orange County hamlet. In the 1950s, Bob Wells grew Central Baptist Church in Anaheim from a revival tent to a proto-megachurch in the matter of a few years. These White evangelical ministers envisioned themselves as missionaries reaching the lost. And they combined their missional outlook with an entrepreneurial spirit.

Robert Schuller's Crystal Cathedral, which started out as Garden Grove Community Church in the mid-1950s, exemplifies this. When Schuller moved to Orange County from Illinois in 1955, the only property he could find to lease and eventually buy to start his new church was a drive-in movie theater parking lot. When he signed the agreement, the owner had no idea Schuller was going to stand on a makeshift stage in front of congregants attending church in their cars. Away from the tradition and bureaucracy of his denomination's headquarters in the Midwest, Schuller was able to unleash his entrepreneurial instincts to their fullest in order to build a congregation from the gravel of an empty lot.

Soon hundreds of people were attending "drive-in" services every Sunday at Schuller's makeshift church. Schuller adapted well to his people's needs. Everyone could stay in their cars for church if they pleased. There was no strict dress code, which was a welcome feature for new Southern Californians who were getting accustomed to wearing T-shirts and jeans for any occasion. He kept the sermons short and thus family friendly. If you didn't want to do more than attend the fifty-five-minute service, there was no pressure to join a committee, campaign, or anything else. And all were welcome, regardless of denomination or even faith. The goal was to pack the house and worry about the doctrinal details later.

When attendance skyrocketed, it seemed that Schuller had proved a stunning point: Orange County was an unzoned land. Its drive-in movie theaters could become churches. And Methodists and Baptists and Presbyterians could all become one family in a church retrofitted for their needs.

The innovations didn't just come in the form of venue. Like other preachers in the Southland, Schuller played to his recently migrated audience—one filled with federal defense-industry employees who were rabid anticommunists and who saw capitalism as part of a God-ordained system in the greatest country on earth. Orange County, and Southern California as a whole, had become a national locus for anticommunist grassroots activism. The soaring rise in defense-industry jobs correlated to a population that was as outspokenly anticommunist and pro-America as any region in the country. Like pastors everywhere, Schuller and his White clergy counterparts mirrored back to their congregations their hopes, dreams, fears, and delusions.

In 1961, Fred Schwarz headquartered his School of Anti-Communism in Orange County. Fifteen thousand middle-class, mostly White Americans signed up for courses at the makeshift institution. The backbone of the curriculum was the idea that American democracy and "biblical Christianity" were the only hopes humanity had against the communist threat.

Orange County pastors like Schuller incorporated anticommunism into their sermons and teachings, as scholars Gerardo Martí and Mark Mulder outline in their work on the Crystal Cathedral. Schuller even developed a sermon series on the communist threat in local neighborhoods and what American Christians could do "to defeat worldwide communism." In Southland churches, American nationalism and anticommunism were raised to the level of doctrine. To be a good Christian in Schuller's church and many other Sunbelt houses of worship meant vehemently defending the "greatest country on earth."

In step with this philosophy, Schuller communicated a vision of Christianity as a privatized, individualist endeavor—a relationship with Jesus that happened in your heart and had little to say to the industry in which you worked or social issues such as racial discrimination, poverty, or homelessness. Unlike progressive mainline pastors, Schuller did not ask his congregants to join in letter-writing campaigns for progressive causes or goad them to attend a rally for labor rights. Instead, Schuller preached a morality of individual choice and responsibility. "His migration to Orange County to plant a congregation for his denomination, the Reformed Church in America, serendipitously coincided with the larger tilt of the country to the Sunbelt in Southern California," write Mark Mulder and Gerardo Martí in *The Glass Church*. "Schuller found a recently migrated, economically aspiring, and white middle class eager to hear his messages based on possibility thinking and his theology of self-esteem."

In ways that foreshadowed the rise of megachurches all over the nation, Schuller implemented a model built for the individual consumer. It was comfortable. It was uplifting. And it didn't require personal buy-in. There were few barriers to membership in the church. And parishioners were rarely asked about their politics, aside from the anticommunist messaging they heard from time to time. For Schuller and other evangelical preachers across Southern California, Christianity was not about reforming economic systems or toppling inequalities of the social order. It was a matter of taking care of oneself and one's family and defending one's country. Personal salvation and individual responsibility usurped the common good and systemic change.

Finally, with individualism, American nationalism, and the nuclear family—something I discuss at length in chapter 5—in place as the bedrocks of their churches' theology and politics, Schuller and other evangelical preachers added a procapitalist message to the gospel. "You have a God-ordained right to be wealthy," Schuller writes in *God's Way to the Good Life*. "You're a steward of the goods, the golds, the gifts, that God has allowed to come into your hands. Having riches is no sin, wealth is no crime. Christ did not praise poverty. The profit motive is not necessarily unchristian."

Schuller was teaching the prosperity gospel, a brand of Christianity that promises material and worldly blessings to those who obey God. According to this way of thinking, calamity, sickness, and even poverty are the result of a mix of disobeying God and not trying hard enough. Those who are blessed with material goods are seen as spiritual scions. Those who are not are seen as spiritual failures.

Messages like these were a welcome permission slip for those in the pews and watching on TV. They could enjoy the new affluence many in the region were experiencing as a result of well-paying government-funded jobs in the defense industry and the booming real estate market. There was no reason to feel guilty about one's material blessings. Financial success was increasingly seen as a marker of spiritual commitment, as the free market became the totem of White Christians in Southern California and beyond. In the 1964 election, this translated into furious support for Goldwater's antitax and anti-regulatory libertarianism and opposition to the legacy of the New Deal. In this way, sociologist of religion Gerardo Martí told me in a 2020 interview, "Big business began to align themselves with conservative Christians," in order to create a brand of Christianity that celebrated hard work, entrepreneurship, and financial risk.

Unsurprisingly, these components also cohered with a militant White identity. In the 1960s, only about 10 percent of Orange County's population was not White. The dearth of people of color in Orange County was the result of policy decisions designed to maintain segregation between White middle-class families and the Mexican Americans who were forced to attend segregated schools and the very few African Americans in the area. The large majority of Orange Countians owned single-family homes. This fact, coupled with the stunning White majority in the county, led to the development of what many have called "not in my backyard politics" (NIMBY) that entrenched racial segregation and prevented affordable housing from being built. Historian Lisa McGirr, in *Suburban Warriors*, recounts the extent to which White people went to keep their neighborhoods White. Dr. Sammy Lee was a world-famous Korean American athlete and two-time Olympic gold medal winner. In 1954, he tried to purchase a home in Garden Grove, a northern Orange County town on the border of Anaheim, but was prohibited.

Culturally, Orange County was a kind of open lot: a land free of the traditional authorities who had often directed people's energies and influenced their politics. It was not dissimilar to Schuller's drive-in church, in its independence from tradition and denominational oversight. This vacuum of religious and cultural authorities created a mass of White Christians who were ripe for political participation in a grassroots conservative movement buttressed by Christian rhetoric and built through neighborhoods, small groups, churches, social hours, and coffee breaks for stay-at-home moms while the kids were at school.

Orange County was the ideal setting to incubate this type of movement because there was a void of civic and social groups. There were few unions, few mainline churches organizing social justice drives or campaigns, few ethnic communities that directed people's politics. The Kiwanis and Lions Clubs didn't have generations-long footholds in these suburban enclaves. There was no minority religious group—a Jewish neighborhood or Buddhist enclave—that had been anchored in the region for generations. In Anaheim, California, as opposed to Pittsburgh, Pennsylvania, there were no Italian or Polish or Irish neighborhoods or rooted civic organizations that provided community and cultural influence. Orange County's midwestern and southern migrants were unmoored from the Main Streets of their old towns and installed into a sprawling suburban nexus. Any community to be built would happen through neighborhood small groups and church attendance. The lack of structure left a gap that became filled by extremist politics and conspiracy theories.

CONSPIRACY AND COMMUNITY

Robert Welch founded the John Birch Society as an anticommunist organization in 1958, and Orange County became the epicenter (more on this in chapter 8). From the beginning, it was marked by a fierce libertarianism and vehement stance against taxes, government welfare programs, and civil rights reforms. It was also based on the idea that Christianity and American democracy go hand in hand. The society used homegrown cells to cultivate and spread the movement. Members hosted small groups in their homes and were encouraged to invite friends and family to learn about the society's Christian libertarian principles.

In ways that parallel the more recent rise of QAnon, the John Birch Society went well beyond libertarian economics, though, and into the dangerous territory of conspiracy theories. It seduced members through claims that Dwight Eisenhower and Chief Justice Earl Warren were, in fact, communist agents who were trying to take down the government. Welch saw communism as a tactic of the Illuminati, a group he said was secretly controlling the world's governments from the shadows.

The John Birch Society published numerous reports that accused civil rights organizers of communist sympathies while alleging that people of color and immigrants were plotting to divide the country and control the world. In ways that were popular across the southern regions of the United States, Welch and other leaders used the bogeyman of communism as a way to delegitimize Martin Luther King Jr. and other Black leaders by claiming they were Soviet agents trying to overthrow the government. According to the Birchers, civil rights legislation and new proposals for fair housing represented a government takeover of American life, one most likely directed by Soviet agents at the highest level of government.

As libertarianism and racism collided in the cosmos of conspiracies that was the John Birch Society, the conservative political movement gained momentum. Now viewing themselves as part of a high-stakes political battle, conservative White Christians had come solidly into the orbit of a cosmic war between good and evil.

The Sunbelt migrants were not expatriates ready to adjust to the cultural values of a new place. They were implants, not transplants.

Rather than forming a new wave of outsiders ready to adapt to their new surroundings, they were a critical mass ready to reshape the area's political, cultural, and religious makeup. In Orange County and in Southern California as a whole, they were entering a proverbial empty parking lot ready for development. It was a chance to create the community—and the country—they had always wanted. As the historian Carey McWilliams observed way back in the 1940s, the new migrants to Southern California sought to re-create the sense of culture and values they left behind in the South and Midwest. Nostalgia has a way of twisting the past and thus creating an alternative present, however, and their longing for a past America was in many ways a longing for one that never existed. Their desire to make America great rested on an illusion of what it used to be.

But there was nothing and no one to stop them from these labors, and they kept trying to create from scratch the ideal form of what they left behind. So when the Arizona senator with the booming baritone voice and square jaw emerged as a viable presidential candidate, it seemed too good to be true. Barry Goldwater's opposition to civil rights, fierce libertarianism, rugged individualism, and Christian nationalist mythology were custom-made for the Southland's new arrivals.

THE GOLDWATER RUSH

It was fitting that the 1964 GOP convention took place in California, because it was a grassroots army of Goldwater supporters who helped the Arizona senator win the state and, ultimately, the GOP presidential nomination. With Orange County as its epicenter, the "Goldwater rush" spread throughout Southern California, from San Diego to Ventura. White libertarian Christians, organized in cells under the influence of the John Birch Society, knocked on doors, handed out pamphlets, and stood on street corners in order to do what seemed impossible: make Goldwater the nominee for president.

The historic parallels to the 1964 Goldwater grassroots campaign and Trump's unexpected rise in 2015 are too striking to ignore. Goldwater himself was viewed as an outsider and an extremist who said the quiet part out loud when it came to war, race, and civil rights. Like Trump, he had no interest in drafting detailed policy plans or listening to bookish advisers. Most importantly, the Democrats and most of his party viewed the Arizona senator as a candidate with no real chance of making a national splash. After all, his supporters were organizing in home "cells" to read John Birch Society conspiracy pamphlets. They were openly against civil rights legislation, in favor of atomic warfare, and convinced that everyone from Martin Luther King Jr. to Dwight Eisenhower were communist agents leading a worldwide conspiracy against the United States. Their tactic was all-out warfare, not carefully delineated plans or principles. Goldwater's volunteers felt as if they were part of an American counterrevolution— or, as one supporter said, a "revolving back" to America's values in order to save the first Christian republic in history.

Nonetheless, Goldwater won the nomination. When he took the stage in San Francisco at the GOP Convention, he stared down the moderates of his party and boomed out a warning. "This is a party, this Republican Party, a Party for free men, not for blind followers, and not for conformists," Goldwater announced. "Anyone who joins us in all sincerity, we welcome. Those who do not care for our cause, we don't expect to enter our ranks in any case. And let our Republicanism, so focused and so dedicated, not be made fuzzy and futile by unthinking and stupid labels."

If you didn't get on board, you'd be considered a faux conservative, at best, and a communist-collectivist Democrat sympathizer, at worst. The message was clear: In or out. One or the other. Pick a side, because there are no moderates in war.

In her groundbreaking work on how Southern Californian conservativism in the 1960s transformed the American political landscape, Harvard historian Lisa McGirr concludes that the Southland was the birthplace of modern conservatism, and Orange County was its nucleus. For McGirr, the formation of Orange County during the middle decades of the twentieth century is a prism for understanding the emergence of what historians now call the New Right and the "reconfiguration" of American politics throughout the rest of the millennium. While support for Goldwater and the new conservatism weren't limited to Southern California, the region is the clearest distillation of the religious, economic, political, and cultural ideals guiding them. It was the possibility model for a new movement. The paradigm for unapologetic nostalgia and political and cultural conflict. This brand of conservativism—based on free-market libertarianism, individualism, and staunch American nationalism, all held together by a Christian myth of the nation—quickly entrenched itself along the southern corridors of the United States.

FROM THE ASHES OF DEFEAT

Barry Goldwater lost to Lyndon Johnson in humiliating fashion in the 1964 election. In a historic defeat, the Arizona senator carried only six states: his home state of Arizona and five states in the Deep South. Northern Californians ensured he didn't win the Golden State. None of the counties in the Bay area or near Sacramento went for him. But if it had been up to Southern California, Goldwater would have been president. He won a majority in Orange and San Diego counties, and he performed well in several others. In 1964, the Southland voted like the South.

The newspapers and pundits announced the end of both the Goldwater cause and conservativism as a whole. They eulogized the grassroots extremism that galvanized new voters and frightened most of the nation. Despite the humiliation of defeat and the confident proclamations of the pundit class, Goldwater had inspired a movement. His candidacy was a window into the future of the GOP. The celebratory laughter roaring from Democratic spaces only exacerbated the resentment that Goldwater's supporters felt for the mainstream politicians, both Republican and Democrat. In their minds, the political elite of both parties had left them and most of the country behind in the name of civil rights, equality, and progress. More than anything, the Goldwater campaign signaled a tide change in American conservatism. The young campaign volunteers and staffers across the Goldwater movement had been formed politically by the language of war, radicalism, and takeover. Their training was not in dialogue or debate; it was in conflict and the will to power. Their mission was not to reform the country or to run a winnable race against the Democratic stranglehold on national politics. It was to destroy the opponent in order to take the country back from those who didn't deserve it.

THE MASTERMIND AND THE AD MAN

Paul Weyrich was one of Goldwater's foot soldiers in 1964. Despite the fact that he was barely old enough to buy beer when he joined the campaign, the Wisconsin native found in Goldwater the type of militant conservatism he felt the country needed in order to right itself. Weyrich's politics mirrored his religious views. In the wake of Vatican II, a landmark event in the Catholic Church that in many ways modernized and liberalized its doctrine and practice, Weyrich left the Roman Catholic Church for the ultraconservative Melikite Catholic Church, where he found a sufficiently traditional bastion of hierarchy and tradition.

"It is basic to my philosophy that God's truth ought to be manifest politically," he proclaimed in 1973. Later he added this clear articulation of Christian nationalism: "Ours is a war between truth and untruth. It is one facet of the war between good and evil. . . . This Nation was founded upon and more closely followed Christian principles than any other."

Goldwater's defeat did nothing to dissuade Weyrich from the mission. Soon after the election he became a congressional staffer.

At a fortuitous moment in 1969, he happened to walk into a Democratic planning meeting in the Capitol. Weyrich saw there what he felt conservatives lacked: a grassroots organizing machine that worked on multiple levels and from different angles to mobilize voters, shape policy messages, and cultivate public opinion in their favor. This was a lightbulb event for Weyrich. It was when he realized how to transform the charisma and collective effervescence of the Goldwater movement into a political machine that would blanket the country in conservative messages and ideals. Rather than relying on the magnetism of one person, and rather than fighting the moderate establishment in the GOP, Weyrich envisioned a political network that would operate as the nervous system of the Republican Party.

In contrast to Goldwater, who was an irresistible presence on the campaign trail but had no real interest in policy or organization behind the scenes, Weyrich was a natural-born institution builder. In 1973, he founded the institutions that now define Republican policy on the national and state levels. Weyrich launched the Heritage Foundation as a counterpart to the Brookings Institute; he launched the American Legislative Exchange Council (ALEC), the conservative state-level policy machine that formulates bills and policies for state legislatures to propose and ratify. Perhaps most importantly, Weyrich teamed up with two other Goldwater campaign soldiers, Richard Viguerie and Morton Blackwell, to found the Council for National Policy, a secretive network that to this day acts as the connective tissue linking the main arteries of conservative politics in the United States: the National Rifle Association, the Susan B. Anthony List, the Family Research Council, the League of the South, and the Liberty Counsel, which has tried to criminalize homosexuality, among many others.

"Weyrich was really the master strategist and the intellectual architect," journalist Anne Nelson, author of *Shadow Network: Media, Money, and the Secret Hub of the Radical Right*, told me in a 2020 interview. "And he had this ferocious vision. I found it quite overwhelming when reading his work, because his theoretical documents were basically: we have to create a movement that will overthrow the federal government and turn American culture on its head."

If Paul Weyrich was the mastermind, Richard Viguerie, with whom he cofounded the Council for National Policy, was the messenger and ad man. He obtained the Goldwater campaign's mailing list and then did the same with GOP donors on the state level. The result was an innovative direct-mail strategy that reached out to voters directly, often targeting the issues they were passionate about. "Viguerie's big idea was applying mass-mailing marketing techniques to politics," Anne Nelson told me. "Beginning with the Goldwater era, he started assembling mailing lists in ways that people really hadn't done in the political sphere before."

Remember: there was no Fox News in the early 1970s. No internet or widespread cable television. Viguerie's direct-mail campaigns were the forerunners of right-wing media's lascivious, targeted messaging that played on the resentment and fear of their recipients.

Despite being Catholic, Viguerie, the son of a Texas oil magnate, cut his teeth working for the segregationist evangelical preacher Billy James Hargis. He helped Hargis reach millions of readers and listeners through campaigns and crafted messages about the downfall of America at the hands of godless communists and race mixing. He knew that a recipe of resentment, political victimhood, and racial animus would entice this religious bloc to join what was becoming known as the New Right on its quest to retake the country.

By the early 1970s, Weyrich, Viguerie, and their New Right cohorts were making inroads in their quest to retake the country for God and White Christians. But despite their organizing efforts and political machinery, they simply needed more votes. All the calculations, messaging, and research weren't going to change this fact: they needed millions of American citizens to vote en masse with the radical new ideology they wanted to implement. The question remained: Which American demographic would come on board in order to push the GOP to the extreme right? Where could they find the hidden voters ready to transform the Republican Party on all fronts?

In order to find more votes, Viguerie flirted with George Wallace, the segregationist former governor of Alabama, who had run as a third-party presidential candidate in 1968 on a segregationist platform. Viguerie realized Wallace was too much of a firebrand to be an effective coalition partner for the New Right. While a long-standing alliance never formed, he learned something valuable about Wallace's segregationist voters: they were all White evangelicals. "The next major area of growth for conservative ideology and philosophy," he said in 1976, "is among evangelical people."

Viguerie was absolutely right. What started in Southern California and the South with the Goldwater revolution was, a decade later, poised to spread across the nation.

Chapter 4

SEGREGATION IS A RELIGIOUS RIGHT

WE USUALLY WENT ONCE a year. Some years we didn't go, but in those years, they came to us. The arrangement was a big deal for our church, a sign that we weren't racist. Friendship Baptist was a majority Black church just up the road from ours. It was as big as or bigger than our two-thousand-person megachurch, so when the two church bodies got together for our annual joint worship service—one Sunday afternoon in the spring—it felt like two entities of the same size meeting for a yearly hug. Some 98 percent of the people at Friendship Baptist were Black. A similar percentage of the folks at Rose Drive were White.

I have no idea how a Black church started in this hamlet of Orange County. Not only was the region devoid of any major Black populations; it had a serious history with racial prejudice and exclusion. In this part of Southern California, it was something of a miracle that Friendship Baptist even existed.

If it was at our place, our choir and pastor led the ceremony; if we met at Friendship Baptist, theirs did. I was fifteen when I first attended the annual service at Friendship Baptist. Though we professed the same faith and the same savior, it felt like I had been transported to a different realm altogether. The choir roared and swayed, and the minister moved and shouted in front of them, improvising his message as he called out and the congregation responded in turn. Their robes were majestic—tassels and waves and bright colors. Women in the pews would pull tambourines from their purses in order to join in the music making. The foot stomping. The clapping. "Yes, Lord" and "Thank you Jesus!" coming from all sides.

The White folks from Rose Drive tried to keep up with the beat and make themselves look comfortable. Trying unsuccessfully to clap and tap my foot to the Gospel music, I would notice embarrassed smiles and overeager displays of approval on the faces and bodies of the Rose Drive faithful. Despite being thoroughly out of our element—and no doubt in the presence of more Black people in one building than we had been all year—we wanted to show everyone how great we thought this was. If we could get through it, it would be a whole year before we had to do it again.

A few weeks after one of those services, I learned that there was a Christian bookstore affiliated with Friendship Baptist just a few blocks away. I was ecstatic. A Christian bookstore in bike-riding distance of my house? For a nerdy future professor, this was a dream. On my first visit, the clerk gave me the side eye. I realized later that not many high schoolers came in to browse the apologetics section. She may have also wondered what a White-passing boy was doing in a shop clearly designed for her Black congregation.

As I paid for my books and headed for the exit, I noticed it hanging over the doorway: a picture of Black Jesus looking over the entire shop. Later that week I met up with a friend for a Bible study and told him about it. "Why would they have a picture of Jesus as Black?" I asked him. "Everyone knows Jesus wasn't Black."

"I don't know," he said with a shrug. We opened our Bibles to start the study. On the inside cover of our versions was another picture of Christ. Only in this one he was neither Black, nor Jewish. He was Nordic. A blond, blue-eyed man who looked like he was from Sweden, rather than Palestine.

We thought nothing of it. That was Jesus, after all.

During that same period in my teenage years, I made a habit of taking pamphlets filled with gory images of aborted fetuses and partly formed body parts to school. I'd pass them out and share with anyone who would listen. Abortion was at the forefront of the culture wars, and as a teenager in 1990s evangelicalism, I was fired up. It was a common topic in Sunday sermons, in youth group curricula, and in the teen devotional literature we read alongside the Bible. One of the reasons Christians had to be involved in politics, I was told, was to combat the holocaust of unborn babies. While issues like war and foreign policy and tax law were also important, fighting abortion was the cause everyone—including teenage zealots like me—could support. It was a binary issue with no gray area. It was the reason, the story went, that God's people were involved in politics at all.

This is a common narrative among White evangelicals. "The abortion myth," as scholar Randall Balmer calls it, has become the popular origin story of evangelical involvement in the public square. Evangelical Christians became politically active in the mid-twentieth century because of the abortion issue, the myth suggests. But the reality is that racism, not abortion, was the central factor that motivated White evangelical Christians to get involved in American politics in the twentieth century. Regardless of how the "abortion myth" is told, the historical record shows that White evangelical politics in the 1960s and early 1970s were centered on the fight against racial integration—not the fight for the unborn. The thing that motivated them was race—and the right to remain segregated from people of color—not preventing abortion. In fact, racism is the foundation of

White Christian nationalism, the load-bearing portion that supports the structure and weight of the entire project.

NOTHING IS CERTAIN BUT DEATH AND RACISM

In chapter 1, we looked at how the 1954 Supreme Court decision in *Brown v. Board of Education*, which led to the desegregation of public schools, served as a precursor to opposition to the Civil Rights Act in the South and in the Sunbelt a decade later. This was the period when Jim Crow laws were under increasing scrutiny and the de jure segregation of the South's public square was coming to an end. Part of the reason Goldwater won the Deep South was his insistence that the government shouldn't play an active part in the integration of American society. He signaled to White Christians in the South and along the Sunbelt that he would not support policies demanding the integration of schools or any other public space.

What he didn't know at the time was that this passive resistance to the extension of civil rights to Black Americans and other people of color would unite the New Right, led by Paul Weyrich and Richard Viguerie, with the millions of White evangelical Christians whose votes Weyrich and Viguerie needed in order to revolutionize the Republican Party. By bringing children and schooling into the mix, Weyrich, Viguerie, and the New Right touched on the central nerve in the White evangelical system: race. In other words, the brain trust behind the New Right seized on the desegregation issue in order to recruit White evangelicals (and many White Catholics) to their movement. This led to the formation of the New Religious Right.

THE RACIST ORIGINS OF EVANGELICAL FAMILY VALUES

In the wake of the 1954 *Brown v. Board of Education* decision, White southerners removed their children from the public school system en masse in order to avoid enrolling them in institutions with Black students. They created private Christian schools and flooded them, creating White flight from the public school system. Between 1970 and 1980, attendance at Protestant private schools quadrupled in the South. The Virginia public school system in Prince Edward County actually shut down in order to resist desegregation. One report from the early 1980s stated that roughly 25 percent of southern private schools enrolled only White kids and another 50 percent had fewer than 3 percent students of color.

In essence, evangelical day schools served as a way for White southerners to bypass the integrated education system. White southern Christians were willing to do anything necessary to keep their children away from people of color. For them, the social order—especially when it concerned impressionable young ones—depended on the segregation of the races.

It is not surprising that White evangelical churches were the outlets for avoiding racial integration. Since the antebellum period, such southern churches had not only been complicit in anti-Black racism; their theologies had provided a powerful justification for the institution of slavery. In essence, White evangelical churches had provided the divine rationalization for the South, and eventually the Confederacy, to defend slavery as part of God's ordained plan for society and for the family.

While the time frame separating the Confederacy and the integration of schools may seem long, it was a matter of only a few generations. Only a few decades separate them. In many cases the grandchildren of the White Christians who defended slavery became the civic warriors who fought to keep their local schools segregated.

FAMILY VALUES FROM 1860 TO 1970

The evangelical obsession with education and family values didn't begin in the 1960s. It goes back to before the 1860s, when White southern evangelicals claimed that enslaved people were part of the family, the family was ordained by God, and thus to usurp its structure would be to go against God's plan for humankind. It is not hard, after all, to find passages in the Bible that seem to condone slavery—whether in the Law of Moses, comments from the Apostle Paul, or even in the references to biblical patriarchs owning slaves. In line with their reading of these passages, White southerners envisioned a patriarchal family that included slaves at the bottom of the hierarchy. This was the model for what the anthropologist Sophie Bjork-James calls the "divine institution" of the godly family.

But as the historian Elizabeth Jemison points out, it wasn't just that southern White Christians condoned slavery by biblical means; they took it a step further. By enslaving people of African descent, they saw themselves as *better* Christians than their northern counterparts. Patriarchal masters were God's earthly surrogates for their biological children, and Black people—who they believed could never become more than grown children—they "benevolently" provided for and guided. In a popular tract in 1857, Presbyterian minister Frederick Ross proclaimed slavery "ordained of God" and traced the authority structure of the patriarchal and racially ordered family all the way back to the book of Genesis. Just as it was good for women and children to submit to the male head of house as a wise and divine household figure, Ross's tract outlined, it was good for slaves to submit to their masters. In this model, freedom came through surrender to God-ordained authorities. For Black people, this meant accepting the headship of the White master as part of God's design. God the Father was embodied in their White father-figure.

For many White Christians in the antebellum South, slavery was a mandate from God. To question it, according to the historian Luke Harlow, meant to question the very order of society. Doing away with slavery might lead to the downfall of civilization. White southerners wondered if there wasn't a slippery slope to other forms of nonhierarchical family structures and societal organizing. Thus, when the Civil War began in 1861, White southern Christians across denominational lines—from Methodists to Baptists to Presbyterians to Episcopalians—imagined themselves as fighting not only for economic, patriotic, and cultural reasons but in order to defend God's mandated societal order. In other words, they saw themselves as defending Christian family values by enslaving other humans.

This continued throughout the era after the Civil War known as Reconstruction. The Southern Methodists claimed, about slavery, that "the position of Southern Methodism on that subject was scriptural. Our opinions have undergone no change." The Southern Baptists wrapped their proslavery theology in the language of the Lost Cause—the myth that the South fought a just war defending a Christian civilization against the greedy and power-hungry North. The Southern Baptist Seminary started in 1846 under the auspices of a proslavery theology. After the war, it used the Lost Cause to continue to defend the "benevolent" form of enslavement that had been abolished in the wake of the South's surrender.

Anti-Black racism—along with anti-Asian, anti-Indigenous, and anti-Latinx racisms and the religious foundation that justified them—hardly dissipated as the nation entered the twentieth century. The best example is the prevalence of the Ku Klux Klan from 1915 to the Great Depression. The KKK started in the years after the Civil War but was eventually extinguished by the end of the nineteenth century. However, in 1915 the second iteration of the Klan formed and began to spread its message of hate. By 1924, it had at least four million members—and that number likely does not capture those affiliated with the Klan who were not official members, including wives who supported their husbands' membership but were not members themselves. In the 1920s, mayors, congressmen, and pastors were all part of the Klan. For White families in the South, belonging to the Klan was normal—as normal, even, as joining the Boy Scouts or Rotary Club today. It was seen as a sign of patriotism and, as always, a commitment to the American family. It was also a way to be part of a Christian organization full of good American boys who put God and America first.

The Klan is the most well-known White supremacist hate group in the history of the country. What is less well known is that it was founded on—and sold itself—as a thoroughly Christian organization, whose goal was to take America back for God. The Klan's identity rested on a tripartite list of enemies: religious minorities (mainly Jews and Catholics), Black people, and immigrants. It combated these foes not only in the name of patriotism but also for the sake of Christ. Klan members displayed crosses as a reminder of the character on which their organization was modeled, as explained in the Klan newspaper in 1923: "sanctified and made holy nearly nineteen hundred years ago by the suffering and blood of the crucified Christ, bathed in the blood of fifty million martyrs who died in the most holy faith, it stands in every Klavern of the Knights of the Ku Klux Klan as a constant reminder that Christ is our criterion of character."

Kelly J. Baker, a preeminent scholar of the Klan's White Christian nationalism, maintains that the Klan's goal was to "re-conquer" the nation as a Protestant, White, and 100 percent American nation. Like slavery-defending Christians before them, Klan members' vision of the country was inseparable from both their Christianity and their White supremacy, because their Christianity and their White supremacy were entangled all the way through. The fiery cross that the Klan lit during ceremonies and left on the lawns of Black neighbors and other enemies, Baker argues, was both a light to the world and a warning to enemies. Seeing their nation as a city on a hill, White Christians viewed the nation's identity as being founded on the cross, which serves at the same time as a warning. "Perhaps Christ's light did emanate from the burning cross," Baker says, "but lifting up the fiery cross as a central symbol of the Klan was also an attempt to 'rally the forces of Christianity' to take back the nation. Conquering required purging the 'hordes of the anti-Christ' and the 'enemies' of Americanism from America. The cross served as beacon and warning. For Klansmen, its glow provided comfort, but for those 'enemies,' the fire terrified."

Though it never went away, the Klan dissipated by the early 1930s due to sex scandals and shady financial dealings on the part of its leaders. But its cultural ubiquity from 1915 to the Great Depression provides a clear lesson for anyone who thinks that racism and proslavery "family values" were isolated in the South. The Klan had members in all forty-eight contiguous states. It was a presence in big cities like Boston, in small towns from Kansas to Idaho, and in growing suburban enclaves—including Anaheim, California, the eventual home of Disneyland in Orange County. The Klan's Christian nationalism, built on the foundations of racism, xenophobia, and hatred of religious minorities, reflected the family values of White America from sea to shining sea.

WHITE VICTIMHOOD

Viewed in the context of proslavery theologies and the Christian nationalist agenda of the KKK, White Christians' reactions to the 1954 *Brown v. Board of Education* Supreme Court decision are not surprising. In the years after the 1954 decision, White southerners removed their kids from the newly integrated school systems in order to uphold the "family values" that had prevailed in the South, and in most of the country, since before the Civil War. The story of mid-twentieth-century America is often framed as one of ever-increasing equality and liberty for Black Americans and other people of color. And the middle decades of the century did witness the end of Jim Crow, the passage of the Civil Rights Act, and the implementation of the Voting Rights Act. But the story of backlash to this progress is vital to understanding the dominant presence of White Christian nationalism in our current political and cultural landscape.

While *Brown v. Board* was a landmark moment for these parallel American stories, it was another court case that activated White evangelicals politically in the South and the Sunbelt. In 1969, fifteen years after *Brown v. Board*, Mississippi's schools were finally set to be desegregated after many appeals and legal blockades. The only problem in places like Holmes County, Mississippi, was that when the Black students enrolled in the previously Whites-only schools, almost none of the White children remained. Only a few dozen of roughly eight hundred students in the county were left. Their parents had seen the integrated future of the schools and had enrolled them in private Christian academies. By the following year, 1970, there were no White children enrolled in the Holmes school district. There was, however, a bustling nexus of church-affiliated, White-only private schools, which were accepting all the self-exiles from the public system.

Two related lawsuits ensued. In the first, *Green v. Kennedy*, the court decided that the segregation academies should lose their tax-exempt status because the Civil Rights Act forbade racial discrimination. While the first suit resulted in just a preliminary injunction, the following year the DC circuit court's decision in *Green v. Connally* solidified the ruling. Institutions like segregation academies that engaged in active segregation would no longer be eligible for tax-exempt status under the law.

In 1970, Bob Jones University, an evangelical university in Greenville, South Carolina, received a letter from the IRS asking if it had a segregation policy. If it did, according to the Civil Rights Act's segregation provisions the university would be in danger of losing its tax-exempt status. The university, led by Bob Jones III, answered plainly, admitting that it did not admit Black people, because the Bible mandated segregation. The battle waged on for several years, but by 1976 the IRS had revoked the university's tax-exempt status.

This created the backlash Weyrich and Viguerie needed to rouse White evangelicals to political action. They seized on the IRS's threat to tax a Christian university to rally evangelical ministers such as Jerry Falwell of Lynchburg, Virginia, Tim LaHaye of San Diego, California, and others in a new coalition bent on protecting what they called family values and religious liberty. While Falwell and his fellow evangelical ministers told their congregations to stay out of politics during the civil rights movements, they now changed their tone. Good Christians, they argued, needed to organize, vote, and protest in order to make sure that their rights weren't trampled and God's United States of America didn't slide into godless chaos. This movement became known as the Religious Right.

FORMING THE RELIGIOUS RIGHT

As Bob Jones's standoff with the IRS carried on in the 1970s, Jerry Falwell, Tim and Beverly LaHaye, and several other prominent White evangelical ministers began to meet to discuss how to take back American culture and politics. In the 1960s, Falwell was a segregationist who would not allow Black people to attend his church. In line with the times, he opened his own segregationist academy school in conjunction with his church. Throughout the 1960s Falwell railed against the civil rights movement and Martin Luther King Jr.; he preached to his congregation that ministers should win souls, not march in the streets or get involved in social or political causes. But by the early 1970s, the desegregation issue, along with the war in Vietnam and the proposed Equal Rights Amendment, was enough to draw him out of the pulpit and into political organizing. Falwell already had a television show, *The Old-Time Gospel Hour*, that reached millions of listeners each week. At one point, Falwell claimed he had a bigger audience than Johnny Carson. He wasn't alone. Evangelical preachers had been leveraging radio and television for decades as a way to reach audiences directly. They had a ready-made apparatus primed for political messaging and voter mobilizing.

Falwell would go on to become one of the faces of the Religious Right, along with the LaHayes, Pat Robertson, James Dobson, Ralph Reed, and a few others. It's worth noting that the alliance between the LaHayes and Falwell was an alliance between the South and Southern California. Falwell's Liberty Church and segregation academy were in Lynchburg, Virginia, and the LaHayes were headquartered in San Diego, where they led a megachurch and Christian school. Their alliance cemented the connections between Southern California and the South.

In the turmoil of the tax-exemption fight, Falwell and his cohorts convinced their evangelical followers that it was time to fight back; and they knew that the best way to fight was to play the victim. Instead of framing the issue in racial terms—which they knew would sink their cause just as soon as it left shore—they instead sold the IRS's enforcement of the Civil Rights Act's segregation provision as an attack on family values and religious liberty. The IRS's revocation of Bob Jones University's tax-exempt status was an example of egregious government overreach, White evangelical leaders argued to their people, and they'd all better watch out for what might come next.

In terms of the family, Falwell and the budding leaders of the Religious Right said that they should have the right to educate their children as they saw fit—especially in a religious setting according to the contours of their faith. They complained about new sex education curricula in schools and the fact that corporate prayer was no longer allowed in the classroom. In ways endemic to Christian nationalism, they used the cover of the family to hide the racial issue at the core. Falwell encouraged anyone who would listen to take their kids out of the "damned" public school system. "I hope to see the day when, as in the early days of our country," Falwell says in his 1979 book *America Can Be Saved!* "We won't have any public schools. The Christians will have taken over them and will be running them." It was a bob-and-weave strategy. If he and his peers could make the desegregation issue into an attack on the family, they could sell it to their congregations and White Christians all over the country.

In addition to family values, Falwell and other leaders claimed that the tax issue made them victims of a tyrannical government. One Orange County man put it this way: "There is an inherent right there of people that our society and our Congress has decided is tax exempt. They are not granting anything, and it isn't a question of [the IRS] granting anything." A young congressman from Georgia named Newt Gingrich also weighed in to ask why the IRS was acting like Congress in trying to enforce laws. Their job, he opined, is to collect taxes, not right social ills.

The issue came to a head in 1978, when President Jimmy Carter's administration advised the IRS to begin enforcing the law in earnest. Even though the policy was put in place under Nixon, the New Right (led by Weyrich and Viguerie) and the Religious Right (fronted by Falwell) joined forces in order to bring the issue to the forefront of American political consciousness. In 1976, Weyrich approached Falwell to propose forming a new political organization, one that would leverage the power and influence of White evangelical clergy and parachurch leaders in galvanizing the tens of millions of conservative people of faith in the South, the Midwest, and the Sunbelt to vote Republican. They could use their pulpits and media outlets, Weyrich pitched, to change the course of American politics. In turn, he offered Falwell and his coalition a political party that would prioritize their "family values," their American nationalism, and, most of all, their Christian identity. The GOP would become the host that housed the budding Religious Right in a symbiotic political alliance.

In 1979, Falwell, Weyrich, and a few others merged the New Right and the Religious Right. Their goal was to fight for an agenda that was protraditional family, pronational defense, pro-Israel, and prolife.

Their first move? Wage all-out war on the sitting president—who happened to be a Southern Baptist, Georgia-born, Bible-toting, evangelical Sunday school teacher named Jimmy Carter.

POLITICAL MIDWIVES AND THE VALUE OF SEGREGATION

Before moving ahead with this story, we need to notice two aspects of the formation of the New Religious Right. First, there is a through line: from proslavery theology, to the Christian nationalism of the

KKK, to the White evangelical reactions against the *Brown v. Board* decision, to the IRS tax controversy of the 1970s. Christian nationalism is an ideology that sees the United States as a nation built for and by Christians. *White* Christian nationalism adds a racial layer to the mix by claiming that White Christians deserve to be at the top of the racial, economic, and political hierarchies. They reserve the right to make decisions about schools, taxes, and elections even if they are the minority and even if their proposals are racist and exclusionary.

The family values agenda that has been touted throughout Christian nationalist spaces since the 1960s is a direct descendant of a proslavery, White terrorist, segregationist lineage. The birth of the Religious Right as part of the New Right in the 1970s was the result of a repackaging of racist ideologies in the form of family values and protests against taxation. When Christian nationalists don't get what they want, they claim victimhood. Donning the mantle of traditional values in the face of an increasingly "secular" and "sexualized" society hides the insidious core of the movement: a centuries-long desire to maintain the United States as a White, Christian, patriarchal nation.

Second, the birth of the New Religious Right and the sweeping Christian nationalist movement that eventually took hold of the country during the Trump presidency wouldn't have come into being without the help of midwives. Paul Weyrich, Richard Viguerie, and their New Right cohorts were, as the historian Daniel Schlozman calls them, the political "entrepreneurs" and tacticians who exploited evangelical concerns about race, taxes, and the family in order to transform this religious voting bloc of tens of millions of people into Republican stalwarts. The New Right merged with the Religious Right through the issues of race, segregation, and "family values." Weyrich and Viguerie were political operatives bent on taking America back for the White, landowning men to whom God had granted it. The evangelical cavalry was the surest way to achieve their goals. Therefore, they did everything possible to court, contour, and mobilize them in the 1970s and beyond.

By doing so, they institutionalized the extremism Goldwater cultivated in the 1960s into a viable nationwide movement in the seventies. "We are different from previous generations of conservatives," Weyrich said in 1978. "We are radicals, working to overturn the present power structure."

White Christians were the perfect audience for this message. Told they were losing their country and the free exercise of their faith, terrified by an out-of-control federal government and cultural revolutions swirling all around them, the Religious Right accepted—and cultivated—the message of extremism. It is now, half a century later, the calling card of the contemporary GOP.

WHITE JESUS AND WAKING UP TO THE LONG CON

When my friend and I met for Bible study that day, the White Jesus in our Bibles was the "Head of Christ," an image created by painter Warner Sallman in 1940, but originally sketched in 1924. There's a good chance you've seen it, since it is the most widespread artistic image in American history. It has been replicated and disseminated over a billion times—in family Bibles, in Gideon Bibles placed in hotel drawers, and on mantles and refrigerators and guest bathroom walls all over the country.

Sallman's Christ is a Nordic-looking figure who looks more like a man from Sweden than a brown, Palestinian Jew from Nazareth. His fair skin, blue eyes, and wavy dirty-blond hair reflect a European savior. The work is neither a historical representation of Christ nor meant to be one. It is a projection of what Sallman and his White contemporaries imagined as properly representative of the country's faith. And it is a decoder ring for understanding both why I assumed as a teenager that White Jesus was the real Jesus and how the New

Right merged with White evangelicals to form the New Christian Right in the 1970s.

For many White Americans, particularly in the South (and Southern California), Jesus is, and always has been, a White savior. This is not an accident. Representations of Christ as a White man indicate a larger theological, social, and racial matrix of White supremacy justified by religious means. White Jesus is a projection of White desire—a model of how the United States should be ordered: A White patriarchal savior at the helm, shepherding his flock and guiding them toward their manifest destiny.

Before leaving the evangelical movement, I made two stark realizations: the Jesus pictured in my Bible was the product of White supremacy, and my faith-based political activism had been shaped by political mercenaries rather than by the gospel. White Jesus was a tool used by politicos to activate people of faith in the mid-twentieth century. Our obsession with abortion was a front for racism and patriarchy. A sinking feeling plagued me when I learned how a political insurgency shaped the politics of family values I had adopted as a teenager and young adult. If our morals, our politics, and our culture had been formed by outside forces, I wondered, what was the real motivation for evangelical political action? What was the point of all this work to reform the country?

As I soon realized, it came down to one thing: power.

Chapter 5

THE CROSS AND THE FLAG

IN 1912, A SMALL group of farmers and business owners started Yorba
Linda Friends Church thirty miles from Los Angeles in what was then
agrarian Orange County. The "Friends" refers to the Society of Friends,
more commonly known as the Quakers. Southern California may
seem like a strange place for Quakers to settle. But in 1912, Orange
County looked more like central Pennsylvania, where Amish, Menno-
nite, and Quaker communities dot the landscape, than the suburban
sprawl it is now. It was farmland, with a population of orange trees
and other fruit crops that far outpaced the number of people. Frank
and Hannah Nixon were among the founding members of Yorba
Linda Friends Church. It is where they would first introduce their son
Richard—who would become thirty-seventh president of the United
States—to the Christian faith (although neither the pacifist elements
of Quaker teachings nor the ethics of honesty seem to have stuck).

In 1918, Cecil Pickering, a friend of Hannah Nixon, wanted to
put up an American flag in the meetinghouse in order to honor the
soldiers returning home from World War I. Taking initiative without
consulting others in the community, she hung the Stars and Stripes
on a wall where notices and bulletins were often posted. Soon after

worship started that Sunday, William Marshburn, the first doctor and most prominent citizen of the tiny town, turned his chair and came face to face with the flag.

"Who dared put that thing up here?" he asked, right before ripping it down. A lifelong Quaker, Marshburn held the principle that Christian worship should be kept separate from nationalist devotion. In his mind, associating the flag with the cross was the path to idolizing the nation over the kingdom of God. The good doctor's sentiment didn't prevail in Yorba Linda—or the nation at large.

A generation later in the early 1960s, the Marshburn family helped plant a second Friends Church in Yorba Linda, just a few miles from the original. The pastor, C. W. Perry, was married to Mary Marshburn. Mary and other members of the Marshburn family, including her brother Don, helped found the new church: Rose Drive Friends. Rose Drive Friends Church is where I converted to evangelicalism in 1995 and served in ministry from 1998 to 2005. By that time, it had grown to a megachurch of roughly two thousand people. Gone were the days of agrarian Orange County. By the early 2000s, shows like *The OC* glamorized the region as the glitzy suburban alternative to Los Angeles. Gone, too, were the days of the fledgling Friends community in Yorba Linda. When I arrived, Rose Drive was a sprawling complex with baseball fields, youth rooms, and a middle school campus spread across acres of land. There were more than a dozen pastoral staff and an annual seven-figure church budget.

Dr. Marshburn's heirs didn't inherit their forefather's qualms about mixing nationalism and faith. From the time I began attending in 1995 to when I left in 2005, the American flag was always present in the worship hall. It was posted alongside the Christian flag on one side of the sanctuary stage. I remember wondering, as a teenager, if it made sense for us to worship God with the American flag hovering nearby as a part of our religious devotion. If we were meant to glorify God, why would we also revere Old Glory?

In 2015, a new music minister removed the American flag from the worship stage. While I had been absent from the community for a decade by then, old friends from Rose Drive told me that as soon as the American flag was taken out of the sanctuary, Leon, a member of the congregation, proclaimed it was his last Sunday at Rose Drive. While a number of issues were leading him out the door, the flag was the last straw. Leon refused to enter the sanctuary—or even to step foot on the church campus—if the American flag wasn't reinstated.

Leon wasn't just any member. A slim, cantankerous man of few words but of many opinions, Leon had been at the church since the beginning. He was the lifeblood of the place—the guy who drove the bus on youth group outings, fixed up the chairs and stage and pews when they needed repair, and ran the sound system for Sunday services. His life had been spent in service to Rose Drive Friends Church. But as soon as the American flag was no longer part of worship, he vowed never to attend there again.

So between 1918 and 2018, the Friends community in Yorba Linda went from tearing the American flag out of its worship sanctuaries to being a place where its most prominent and devoted members refused to enter them—the sacred spaces where they worship God—if the American flag wasn't present.

Not being able, or willing, to separate cross and flag is Christian nationalism in a nutshell. It's about more than theology or doctrine. Christian nationalism is a cultural identity built around the myth that the United States is a Christian nation. For many Christian nationalists, who believe that political power is a sign of God's favor, the Bible should be a governing document of the republic, alongside the Constitution. And many Christian nationalists are willing to topple and overtake anyone or anything that gets in the way of enacting this vision of the United States. Even if it means ousting one of their own.

A SUNDAY SCHOOL TEACHER FOR A PRESIDENT

Jimmy Carter was born in Plains, Georgia, on October 1, 1924. Plains is a tiny place in the southwestern part of the state. It's closer to the Florida Panhandle than to Atlanta. Jimmy's family were peanut farmers. He grew up running around the rural property with both Black and White playmates, a rarity in that time and place. Though his family were devout Southern Baptists, Jimmy didn't mark his conversion experience until his early teen years, when he felt God's call on his life. From that point on, he determined to dedicate himself to serving the Lord and his people. In good evangelical fashion, Jimmy went on to marry a childhood friend and sweetheart—Rosalynn Smith—in 1946. Soon after leaving school, Jimmy joined the military and quickly became an officer in the navy. He and Rosalynn moved all over the country, carting their young family with them.

When Jimmy's dad, Earl, became ill, however, Jimmy returned to the Carter peanut farm in Plains to be at his father's bedside. The visit changed Jimmy's path forever. Here is how Randall Balmer, who wrote a critically acclaimed biography of Carter, explained it to me in a 2020 interview:

Carter went back to Plains to be at his father's bedside as he was dying. And it just made a powerful impression upon him because as he was there at the bedside, various people from the community would come in to pay their respects to Mr. Earl, as they called him—to thank him for various kindnesses that he had demonstrated toward them very quietly in that community. For example, when he had extended credit at the Carter store for people who were facing financial difficulties, when he provided new clothes for a family so they could attend their daughter's graduation and be proud of themselves—for doing that sort of thing. And as these stories began to mount, Jimmy Carter was profoundly affected by that.

After moving his young family back to his home in Plains, Jimmy took over the family peanut farm and determined to help his community, like his father had before him. As he rerooted himself in Plains, Jimmy ran and won a seat on the school board. This role exposed him to the vast disparity between the White and Black schools in the region. Though Jimmy's father was not a progressive by twenty-first-century standards, Jimmy grew up playing with Black children. He was taught by his mother and influential teachers in his life to see all people as equal. When he took over the family farm, Jimmy refused to join the White Citizens League—a modern-day offshoot of the KKK—despite warnings from his neighbors that he and his family would be outcasts in the community and that there would likely be a boycott of the Carter peanut business. He was one of the only White men in Plains not to join the "League." Thus, when Jimmy noticed the stark racial inequalities that marked the school system, he knew that as a person who had dedicated his life to serving God and people, he had to act. He advocated for school integration despite the segregationist majority all around him.

Wanting to do more to transform the school system and other issues, he decided to run for statewide office. In our 2020 interview, Randall Balmer told me the story: "On his thirty-eighth birthday—October 1, 1962—he gets out of bed and he puts on his church clothes rather than his work clothes. And he informs Rosalynn that he's going down to the Cook County courthouse to file to run for the Georgia state senate."

Jimmy's political flight took off from there. After a few terms in the Georgia senate, he became governor of the state in 1970. In a capstone to a lightning-in-a-bottle political career, he won the presidency in 1976—seemingly coming from nowhere to take the most powerful political office in the world.

Carter's ascendance to the White House coincided with the rise of the Religious Right, and its merger with Weyrich's and Viguerie's New Right—what I am calling the New Religious Right. So much of the national press were unfamiliar with evangelical Christianity during the presidential election that they reported on Carter and his family as if they were aliens from another planet. *Time* declared 1976 the "Year of the Evangelical" in recognition of the growing visibility of conservative Christians all over the country and in reference to Carter's surprise presidential victory.

One might surmise that Jerry Falwell, Paul Weyrich, and their colleagues on the New Religious Right would have been ecstatic to have a White, Bible-carrying, Sunday school–teaching Southern Baptist farmer making his way to the White House, with scripture on his lips and the Lord in his heart. Yet while on paper it seemed a match made in heaven, it was not a partnership that worked on earth. The story of why it didn't is worth the telling.

THE DIVINE FAMILY

While Jerry Falwell and Paul Weyrich didn't officially launch the "Moral Majority" until 1979—an official political organization set up, among other things, to stop Carter's reelection and ensure Ronald Reagan would be the next president—their feud with Carter and his administration traced back to the beginning of Carter's presidency.

In 1976, Carter earned 54 percent of the Catholic vote and 47 percent of the Protestant vote. The latter marked a 7 percent increase in the number of Protestant voters the average Democratic presidential candidates normally received. In the wake of Watergate and Vietnam, the country was in the mood for a candidate whose folksy old-time values and religion conveyed a sense of trust, integrity, and honesty—factors sorely missing from American politics over the prior half decade. One factor in Carter's surprise victory was his ability to retain much of the Catholic majority, despite his overtly evangelical identity, while simultaneously increasing the Protestant vote. In one sense, Carter was a bridge candidate, whose Christian values seemed to offer a way forward for a Protestant-Catholic political alliance. Over the course of American history, Protestants have persecuted Catholics culturally and politically. The KKK was an explicitly anti-Catholic organization, as was the Know-Nothing party of the 1850s before them. The election of John F. Kennedy to the presidency in 1960 was, in fact, a minor miracle, given the formidable anti-Catholic sentiment that prevailed in American society.

It's not hard to see how Carter appealed to White Christian Americans—both Catholic and Protestant—at this point in the country's history. Still reeling from the cultural and sexual revolutions of the sixties and recovering from the shock of Nixon's betrayal and the brutality of the Vietnam war in the early seventies, many saw in Carter a man who emanated old-time family values: a small-town boy who married his childhood sweetheart, a military officer who quoted scripture as much as the Constitution and who didn't bring the baggage of corruption to the office. Carter sealed the deal by promising to convene a conference on family issues if elected to the White House.

After the election, however, Carter's identity as a born-again Christian was not enough for the burgeoning evangelical-Catholic bloc that composed the core of Falwell's and Weyrich's New Religious Right—and the eventual White Christian nationalist heart of MAGA Nation. By the mid-1970s, Weyrich and Viguerie had already approached Falwell and his evangelical cohorts about forming a political organization that would enable conservative White Christians to take the country back for God and themselves. While Falwell didn't agree to form the Moral Majority until 1979, he and Weyrich had already keyed in on the grand strategy for the reconquest of America: the family.

In the previous chapter, we traced the line from proslavery theologies in the 1800s to the KKK of the 1920s to the reaction to the *Brown v. Board* 1954 decision and finally the call to desegregate schools in the late 1960s. By the 1970s, Falwell, Weyrich, and their colleagues had all framed the issue of school desegregation as an attack on the traditional family and the God-given right to parent one's children as they see fit. Realizing the potential of using the family as a symbol in the war to reconquer America, Falwell and his colleagues on the Religious Right began to expand "family values" discourse into other domains, including abortion, feminism and the Equal Rights Amendment, and the movement for LGBTQ rights. It was an ingenious if insidious strategy: Use the family to sell White Christians as victims of cultural persecution rather than as the perpetrators of prejudice. Reframe their opposition to civil liberties and protections for people of color and the LGBTQ community as staving off assaults on God's traditional family structure rather than as out-and-out racism.

Jimmy Carter was collateral damage in this culture war. As we have seen, the decision to revoke the tax-exempt status of segregationist schools and churches came from the Supreme Court in *Green vs. Connally*. The IRS began to enforce the rule under Nixon. By the late 1970s, churches were beginning to fear they would be next in the IRS's line of fire. And so, to many White evangelicals, Jimmy Carter's administration became the face of the government's "attack" on religious communities. Not only was this an issue of keeping the government out of how parents decide to educate their children; it was a matter—according to the New Religious Right—of an infringement on religious liberties.

"The education system has been taken over by secular humanists," argued San Diego megachurch pastor Tim LaHaye. According to him, Carter was "establishing a religion and giving the high priest a position on the cabinet." The revocation of tax-exempt status of segregationist schools also served to bolster the evangelical-Catholic alliance, albeit in this instance against Carter. As Falwell himself explained, the tax issue "worried Catholics as much as us."

In response, many evangelicals began homeschooling their children. Since the 1980s, homeschooling in the United States has grown exponentially, with conservative Protestants funding and fueling the push. While evangelical homeschool families claimed that the public school systems were polluting their children's minds with ideologies such as feminism, communism, and environmentalism, many now see Christian homeschooling as the front line of the culture wars. The most popular curricula in Christian homeschooling circles unabashedly promote Christian nationalism as a way of training the next generation to fight God's war. In some lessons, students are taught that African Americans were better off under slavery and that Nelson Mandela was a "communist agitator."

While this new and unexpected religious-political bloc fought the IRS, it also waged conflict against the Equal Rights Amendment. As the historian J. Brooks Flippen has shown, evangelicals (and many Catholics) viewed the ERA as a threat to the nuclear family. They maintained that the Bible prescribed certain roles for men and women, and they believed the new amendment, which would have ensured legal protection against gender discrimination for women, would usurp God's vision for the structure of the family and society.

By far the most influential opponent to the ERA was Catholic activist Phyllis Schlafly, an antifeminist organizer from Illinois who opposed the ERA in the name of family values and argued for the maintenance of patriarchal gender roles. Schlafly maintained that the ERA was a dangerous step toward a society where the "traditional" family would be abandoned and chaos would reign. A skilled organizer, Schlafly compiled extensive mailing lists to build a grassroots movement to stop the amendment from passing. She claimed that if the ERA passed, women would lose their children in divorce proceedings, homosexual marriage would be legalized, and women would be sent to the front lines of combat. Her scare tactics, coupled with her extraordinary ability to reach her audience directly through well-organized mail campaigns and public events, helped stop the ERA from ratification.

In many ways, Schlafly and other proponents of the traditional family employed the same argument used in proslavery theologies, just recycled for use in the 1960s rather than the 1860s. Despite the shift in issue from slavery to women's rights, the argument stayed the same: God envisions the family as a hetero-patriarchal unit. A change to the laws would upset God's plan.

Catholics and evangelicals also mobilized against any progress on the front of LGBTQ rights and protections. In 1977, Falwell became personally involved in the campaign to stop legislation in Florida's Miami Dade County that aimed to protect LGBTQ individuals from discrimination in the workplace. Standing alongside Anita Bryant, a beauty queen turned antigay activist, Falwell once again decried the attack on "traditional" family values and the malice of the "homosexual" community.

Then there was the issue of abortion. Abortion had been a priority issue for American Catholics for decades. As we saw in the previous chapter, it was not a Protestant issue even in 1973, when the *Roe v. Wade* decision came down. But by the late 1970s, many evangelical leaders began using the abortion issue as another means of employing the family for political purposes. Abortion was sold as another attack on the family and the "sanctity of life." Given the dizzying changes wrought by the sixties, evangelical luminaries such as Falwell and the theologian Francis Schaeffer didn't have a hard time using abortion as a strategy to portray secular humanists and non-Christians as part of a large plot to persecute and marginalize conservative people of faith.

Carter explained publicly that he personally opposed abortion but that he did not believe that the government should legislate a woman's right to control her own body. He drew on his Baptist heritage in order to argue that a clear separation of church and state means this: Christians can strive to create the type of society they envision as resonant with the kingdom of God, but they cannot expect government policy to effect the change for them. He believed Christians should work to embody God's justice and peace on earth but that this meant protecting the liberties of people of all religions—and people of no faith at all—rather than just their own. In essence, Carter was too Protestant for his Christian nationalist counterparts. His position was drawn from a long tradition of Baptist nonconformists who view freedom *from* religion as the basis for freedom *of* religion.

On the other side, Weyrich, Falwell, and their evangelical and Catholic audiences prioritized American nationalism over the separation of church and state. Their goal was dominance, politically and socially. So even if Carter upheld a stringent Christian personal ethos, and even if he personally opposed abortion, they railed against his unwillingness to take the antiabortion stance in policy and legislation.

All of this came to a head at the long-awaited conference for families that Carter had promised on the campaign trail and finally convened in June 1980. If this was the moment that the embattled president thought he could win back White evangelicals and Catholics, he was sorely mistaken. Carter's goal was to examine "the strengths of American families, the difficulties they face, and the ways in which family life is affected by public policies." The organizers who led the conference took this as a mandate to explore how "nontraditional" families, including single-parent and LGBTQ households, were navigating the social and professional landscapes. By this point, Falwell and Weyrich had officially launched the Moral Majority, a political organization aimed at mobilizing conservative Christians to vote and rally behind various issues, including opposition to abortion. Instead of participating in the conference on families, Falwell and his cohorts protested it. The Moral Majority labeled the gathering "the Anti-Family Conference," while Alabama governor Fob James decided not to deploy delegates "because the conference appears to oppose Judeo-Christian values."

IF YOU CAN'T PROTECT THE FAMILY, HOW WILL YOU SECURE THE NATION?

There was one more issue that drove a wedge between Carter and the New Religious Right. Despite his status as a military officer, Carter displayed an unwavering commitment to diplomacy and negotiation in matters of foreign policy. He emphasized human rights in his criticism and attacks on the Soviet Union, he gave control of the Panama

Canal back to Panama in an effort to create goodwill between the United States and countries in the region, and, perhaps most damning, his handling of the Iran hostage crisis led to a disastrous rescue attempt. For Carter, the responsibility of the United States as a world power was to exemplify patience, diplomacy, and humility. While the success of his foreign policy can be debated, it's clear that these approaches were born from his deep personal piety. They were the policy expressions of a Christian trying to live out Christ's command to love your neighbor.

By contrast, figures like Jerry Falwell clearly preferred a commander in chief who would emanate a tough-guy persona in interactions with the Soviet Union and other foreign powers. The Weyrich-Falwell coalition viewed Carter as too much of a dove when it came to the Soviet Union and foreign policy in general. "If we would substantially reduce or totally eliminate most of our foolish welfare programs at home and abroad, we would have ample funds to defend this country and provide for the people within it," Falwell wrote in the magazine *Faith Aflame* in 1976. "As Christians, we are certainly in favor of providing for the aged, the sick and the helpless. But we certainly need to get away from these giveaway programs which are producing a generation of 'bums' in our society. Paul said 'if a man will not work, neither shall he eat.'"

Falwell's call to end "foolish welfare programs" and a call for a candidate who would "defend this country" coincided with his I Love America Rallies, a series of 1976 events celebrating the nation's bicentennial and highlighting the "old-time" religion that supposedly made the country great. The altar calls at the rallies were dubbed "Last call for America." A gospel choir would sing patriotic songs to accompany the throngs of Americans coming down to the stage to devote themselves to saving the country from ruin.

All the base elements of Christian nationalism were front and center in Falwell's "I Love America" tour: the conflation of the flag and the cross into an entangled symbol of the nation as chosen by

God to carry out a special mission in the world; the transposition of the call to accept Christ into a call to transform America's politics before the country is supposedly lost. And the symbolism—gospel hymns played before and after patriotic ballads, coupled with the patriotic accoutrements of the state—reflected Falwell's belief in the inseparability of the nation and the kingdom of God.

Falwell's approach could not have been more different from Carter's, even though both men came from the Baptist denominations, were lifelong southerners, and professed the same faith. Despite their shared identity, Falwell, along with the stalwarts of the New Religious Right, viewed Carter as too weak to protect either the family or the nation. It was like an enemy was occupying the White House. Their goal became to elect someone who shared their Christian nationalist priorities, if not their Christian piety.

A HOLLYWOOD STAR FOR PRESIDENT

It's easy to think of Ronald Reagan as an affable, handsome Hollywood actor who used his stage presence and on-camera persona to woo conservatives and independents. Though his policies were conservative through and through, he had the power to charm and magnetize his audiences in ways that escaped other Republican candidates, including Barry Goldwater. His appeal, the tale goes, was as much likability as it was policy.

The standard story about Reagan and the New Religious Right is that the latter abandoned Carter the Evangelical for Reagan the Actor in a bid to see their political agenda advanced by the White House. There's no denying the truth of this narrative. As the 1980 election approached, the new bloc of Christian nationalist evangelical and Catholic voters that formed the heart of the New Religious Right turned away from Carter and threw their support fully behind the former governor of California. "There's no question that Moral Majority and other religious right organizations turned out millions of voters," Falwell proclaimed after Reagan's victory.

In many ways, the shift from the Southern Baptist to the Hollywood actor was unsurprising. Evangelicals and Catholics were unhappy with Carter's approaches to abortion, the ERA, gay rights, and the Cold War. They wanted a nationalist more than a Baptist, and political power more than religious solidarity. Despite the fact that Reagan was a divorced man who made his living in Hollywood—a den of sin, according to many conservative Christians—and despite the fact that he had supported abortion as governor of California and had tense relationships with his older children, the New Religious Right viewed him as more "Christian" than the evangelical sitting in the Oval Office. "We have to make a choice between a person who may be less than perfect but who supports the values we believe in," said Paul Weyrich. "In that case, we come down on the side of Ronald Reagan."

But the story goes back further than the Carter administration, to the Goldwater campaign of 1964. As Election Day approached in 1964, Ronald Reagan gave a famous speech on behalf of Goldwater. While Goldwater would ultimately lose the election, the speech, "A Time for Choosing," propelled Reagan to the national spotlight as the next great hope of American conservatism. "This is the issue of this election, whether we believe in our capacity for self-government or whether we abandon the American revolution and confess that a little intellectual elite in a far distant Capitol can plan our lives for us better than we can plan them ourselves," Reagan said. "You and I are told increasingly we have to choose between left or right. What I'd like to suggest is that there is no such thing as the left or right. There's only an up or down."

As Randall Balmer noted in a 2021 interview with me, Reagan's first foray into politics was to support the repeal of a California housing act that had been designed to eliminate racial discrimination in real estate transactions. Like Goldwater, he opposed the Civil Rights Act and the Voting Rights Act.

Only two years after the failure of the Goldwater campaign, Reagan became governor of California. His campaign was based on, among other things, restoring "law and order." He was reelected to a second term in 1970. By that time, the whispers of his presidential run were turning into shouts all over the country.

Twenty years before he ran against Jimmy Carter, through an extremist libertarianism and Christian nationalism that began with a grassroots movement in Southern California, Ronald Reagan was building and cultivating support. Nothing changed when Reagan ran for president. He was the same candidate who had been formed by racial animus and libertarian ideals in the 1960s.

"I think the crowning moment that showed Reagan for what he was, was the fact that he opened his general election campaign in 1980 with an address at the Neshoba County Fair—in, of all places, Philadelphia, Mississippi, on August 3, 1980," Randall Balmer told me in our 2021 interview. "Philadelphia, Mississippi: the place where sixteen summers earlier, the Ku Klux Klan had abducted, tortured, and murdered three civil rights workers. And lest one miss his meaning . . . Reagan on that occasion invoked the timeless segregationist battle cry of states' rights."

When Ronald Reagan won the presidency, it represented more than just conservative Christians supporting a candidate who promised to give them political power. It represented the mainstreaming and nationalization of a Sunbelt faction of the Republican Party that was once considered extremist. It injected the radical views of the John Birch Society's Robert Welch, along with Goldwater, Weyrich, Viguerie, and Falwell, into the heart of the GOP. If Goldwater lost the battle in 1964, a decade and a half later his heirs won the war.

Viewed through this long lens, the choice of Christian nationalists of the New Religious Right—Reagan over Carter—is less surprising. Reagan's election in 1980 was the result of two decades of Christian nationalist organizing, coalition-building, and campaigning on the part of the New Right and the Religious Right, who never wavered in their mission to retake the country for their God and for themselves. It developed in Southern California and in the South. Then it took the nation by storm.

POWER TRUMPS PIETY

In retrospect, the evangelical breakup with Jimmy Carter was the result of numerous complex issues. But all the details lead back to a central theme: though Carter was one of them, his policies didn't fit their agenda. His faith was unquestionable. He was born and raised a Southern Baptist, served as a missionary, supported his church at every turn, and married his one and only love. Carter's politics, on the other hand, were not aligned with the vision Weyrich, Falwell, and the others had for the United States. They felt he didn't represent the power of the nation. In essence, Carter was Christian enough but not nationalist, or patriarchal, or warmongering enough for their tastes. The man who embodied family values was characterized as hating the traditional family. The man who was an officer in the navy was castigated as unpatriotic when it came to foreign policy. We could say that he brought the cross into the White House but that, according to his critics, he left the flag out of the sanctuary.

Thus, in the 1980 presidential election, the Christian nationalists of the New Religious Right supported a divorced Hollywood actor, with a mixed record on issues surrounding "family values" and a history of supporting abortion, over the Southern Baptist Sunday school teacher who married his high school sweetheart, served with distinction in the armed forces, and often took his Bible with him when leaving the house. It was the election that made clear that the cross wasn't enough. For Christian nationalists, the cross must always be accompanied by the flag.

This leads to one final lesson to be learned from the Carter-Reagan election. When it came to voting for Donald Trump, Christian nationalists had a precedent for prioritizing politics over morals and policies over identity. In the wake of Trump's 2016 election, in which he gained the support of 81 percent of White evangelicals and 60 percent of White Catholics, many claimed that conservative Christians must have had to hold their noses in order to vote for a thrice-divorced television star who talked about God at opportune moments but seemed, by all accounts, to have no relationship *with* God. Yet viewed through the lens of the Goldwater-Reagan heritage, as it was cultivated by the likes of Weyrich, Falwell, and others, voting for Trump was likely a gratifying, once-in-a-lifetime opportunity for many Christian nationalists. If Reagan's two-term presidency was the culmination of Goldwater's extremism, then the election of Trump was an unforeseen triumph. A man who mixed the unhinged rhetoric of Goldwater with the civil war mentality of Weyrich and Falwell and the camera-ready persona of Reagan, Trump was not an imperfect candidate who somehow managed to garner the votes of White Christians. He was the prototype of the candidate White Christians had been searching for since the early 1960s.

GOING BACK TO CHURCH

When Dr. Marshburn threw the flag out from the worship room in Yorba Linda that day in 1918, he was trying to send a message: the United States and the kingdom of God are not one and the same; their missions and values are distinct; and the glorification of God should not take place alongside the adulation of Old Glory. This, in essence, was Jimmy Carter's approach. He wanted to be a Christian and an American, but not a Christian nationalist. In other words, he did not believe the country was built for and by White Christians, and he did not think it was the government's job to protect or privilege them.

This wasn't good enough for the White evangelicals and Catholics on the New Religious Right. When I reflect on how their alliance helped turn the tide of American history by ushering Ronald Reagan into the White House, I'm brought back to all those Sundays at Rose Drive when I was a teenager and young adult. Since I was a convert, I hadn't grown up in the church like many of my peers sitting near me in Sunday services. It meant I would take in the scenery like a tourist visiting a new country for the first time. I noticed the maroon color of the choir's robes, and the way the pastors held their Bibles with a special tenderness. When they prayed in church, I soaked up their peculiarly gentle cadence. During sermons my mind often wandered, so I flipped through all the hymnals in the pew rack, learning the lyrics for the first time. My eyes scanned the room, the enraptured faces of adults and fidgety kids looking at the pictures in their Bibles. It also meant that I saw something that for others just blended into the background. At the front of the sanctuary, to the left of the stage, the American flag stood so close to the Christian flag that the two were often touching. In the White American Christianity to which I converted, there was no question that the flag and the cross belonged together. They were the twin pillars of our faith.

At this point it's clear why we took this as a given: By the time I became an evangelical, the New Religious Right had cemented its stronghold over the GOP and White American Christianity. The Christian Americans like Jimmy Carter were relegated to secondary status. The Christian nationalists held power. But political victory wasn't enough. They still needed to take back American culture.

Chapter 6

THE PURE AMERICAN BODY

THERE WAS A LOT riding on that kiss. More than usual for the first inti-mate moment of a high school romance. We knew it, too. Our rela-tionship depended on it. Our families' futures depended on it. More than anything, the fate of our nation depended on it.

One of the benefits of being a zealous teenage convert to evan-gelicalism is that your parents stop worrying about what's happening behind your closed bedroom door when your girlfriend comes over. After dozens of Bible studies, prayer groups, and Christian concerts, they kind of just turn off the normal teenage-radar and let you do your thing. So when Alexis and I went up to my room at eleven that Friday night—me a high school senior, her a freshman in college—no one in my family even blinked. We'd been dating for almost three years by then and had done little more than hold hands and hug goodbye. Like me, she was a convert who took her faith to the extreme. We were an even match when it came to our devotion to God, to evangelism, and to cultivating a life marked by godly virtues such as patience, integrity, and, most of all, purity.

Though we planned to marry soon after I graduated high school, we decided that it would be best to have our first kiss intentionally, in a planned and disciplined way rather than a spur-of-the-moment temptation that could lead us down a lustful path.

According to the historian Sara Moslener, in April of 1993 the first True Love Waits Pledges were taken at a Southern Baptist conference at a local church in Texas. This was the Southern Baptist Convention's test pilot of the program. It soon spread to other local churches throughout the denomination. The first rally was in 1994 in Washington, DC. At the gathering, evangelical luminaries delivered message after message to the teenagers in attendance that the most important part of their personal walk with God was remaining sexually "pure" before marriage. At the end of the rally, there was an altar call—a standard feature of evangelical meetings, going back to the Second Great Awakening. But this one was different. The call was to pledge oneself to a life of purity. Those who answered the call signed cards that were later delivered to the National Mall in Washington, DC.

My *Straight White American Jesus* podcast cohost Dan Miller pledged his purity on a True Love Waits card at his church in Colorado. For him, it was a promise to keep his mind and body free of sexual sin and to be part of a generation who would turn American culture around. His card was delivered to the National Mall in 1994. There was a clear message behind sending hundreds of thousands of cards to the nation's capital: the pledge to develop and maintain pure teenage bodies was a pledge not only to obey God's commands but to build national strength and integrity. Somehow, there was a connection between nation-building and the sexual abstinence of teenagers in Milwaukee and Tucson and Baton Rouge. By the time the cards were delivered in July 1994, more than two hundred thousand teenagers like Dan had pledged their commitment to be part of a new generation of young people willing to stand up for God, rage against the cultural tides, and say no to sexual licentiousness.

When I converted soon thereafter, the currents of purity culture, as manifest in the True Love Waits movement, were sweeping through evangelical churches. On the surface, the message was straightforward. It went something like this: Since the 1960s, we have lived in a culture that celebrates sexual freedom in destructive ways. By obeying God and committing yourself to abstinence before marriage, you are a countercultural rebel who is going to have a loving, intimate, and healthy sex life once you enter the bonds of marriage.

The emphasis, as usual in evangelicalism, was on individual piety. We were warned that sex outside of God's plan would destroy us spiritually and physically. The inflictions would be swift and ferocious—depression, anxiety, low self-esteem, not to mention AIDS and syphilis. And unlike other sins, which God washed away as soon as we confessed, sexual sins would wreak permanent damage on ourselves and our marriage.

"See this piece of tape?" one of our youth leaders would say in front of the crowd at Bible study. "What happens when I put it on Jesse's arm?" He would put the tape on Jesse and then rip it off, leading to a yelp from the poor volunteer and roaring laughter from the crowd. "Now, when I put the same piece of tape on Ben, it has lost its grip." The sequence would continue down a line of volunteers on stage until the tape was mangled and thrown into the trash. "This is what your sexuality is like. If you keep attaching yourself physically to people, eventually you will be used up and thrown away."

These lessons made me afraid. Unlike other sins, which would be forgiven and washed away by Christ, it seemed that sexual sin had lasting effects even after you repented. I had already experimented with sex before my conversion. In order to be right with God and ready for marriage, I decided that antisex militancy was the only path that would work. Alexis and I decided early on in our dating relationship that we wouldn't kiss until marriage. In our minds, kissing would lead to more kissing, which would lead to temptations we didn't want to have to face.

But as time went on, it became clear that there was more to the purity message than not giving in to bodily lust. Keeping our bodies pure was the way to renewing the purity of other bodies. Both Alexis and I had divorced families—"broken homes," as they were known in evangelical circles. Few, if any, of our relatives were born-again Christians like we were. If we wanted to turn the generational ship around in order to create a family tree of God-fearing people, the first step was maintaining our relationship's purity as the foundation for a pious genealogical legacy. The family is the vessel of godly instruction and formation, we learned. If the tree's roots were rotten, how could we expect our children and their children to ever love God and find eternal salvation?

As young people, we knew that the stakes of individual purity extended even beyond the fate of our families to the fate of our nation. If we wanted to restore America's glory, it would take a generation of godly families rooted in the pledge to purity. It would require seeing a connection between the purity of our teenaged bodies and purity of our body politic. As those massive mailings of purity pledge cards to the National Mall from that first rally suggest, True Love Waits was more than a movement to get kids to stop fooling around at Inspiration Point or prevent teen pregnancy. The organizers sent a clear message to our generation: sexual purity is the road to national renewal. It's the frontline of the culture wars. And you are the soldiers.

VICE PRESIDENTS AND SINGLE MOTHERS

According to evangelical leaders during the eighties and early nineties, in order to see the rot creeping into American culture, all you had to do was turn on the television. While family-oriented programs like *The Cosby Show* and *Family Ties* still dominated the airwaves, these years also saw new representations of gender roles, sexual identities, and family types on the small screen. *Three's Company* portrayed a supposedly gay man living with two women in the same apartment, and *My Two Dads* challenged conventional notions about healthy families and parental guidance. But the program that caused the most controversy was the ratings bonanza *Murphy Brown*, a show about a woman who decided to raise a child on her own while managing a successful career.

In 1992, then vice president Dan Quayle criticized *Murphy Brown* in a speech about family values: "Ultimately however, marriage is a moral issue that requires cultural consensus, and the use of social sanctions. Bearing babies irresponsibly is, simply, wrong. Failing to support children one has fathered is wrong. We must be unequivocal about this. It doesn't help matters when prime time TV has Murphy Brown—a character who supposedly epitomizes today's intelligent, highly paid, professional woman—mocking the importance of fathers, by bearing a child alone, and calling it just another 'lifestyle choice.'"

Quayle links what he takes to be the decay of American culture to the breakdown of the nuclear family. He suggests that if single mothers who refuse partners and raise children without a male figure in the household are allowed to proceed without sanction, then the country will decline. By sounding this alarm, the vice president was tapping into a cultural current of the decay of White sexual ethics. In 1993, the libertarian author Charles Murray caused controversy when he published "The Coming White Underclass." Murray begins the essay with a racist caricature of the Black American family characterized by out-of-wedlock children living in fatherless homes. He then paints with broad strokes to create a picture of Black life in urban areas as akin to "Lord of the Flies writ large," where "the values of unsocialized male adolescents" are "physical violence, immediate gratification and predatory sex. That is the culture now taking over the black inner city." In Murray's mind there is a direct line between out-of-wedlock childbirth and social chaos. Even more frightening for Murray were the statistics that revealed that White Americans were having children out of wedlock at increasing rates. In Murray's analysis, there is a one-to-one correlation between the destitution of Black life and the percentage of children born out of wedlock. If the number of "illegitimate" White children reached the same level, he suggested, it would create a White underclass similar to that of Black America. His concerns about marriage, sexual ethics, and the nuclear family were rooted in racist tropes about Black people and Black families.

Dan Quayle was nowhere near as controversial as Murray, but his thinking followed similar pathways. For Quayle, the route to national renewal was the nuclear family. Americans must return to the family values, which, for Christian nationalists, are the locus keeping the country connected to God: "So I think the time has come to renew our public commitment to our Judeo-Christian values—in our churches and synagogues, our civic organizations and our schools. We are, as our children recite each morning, 'one nation under God.' . . . If we lived more thoroughly by these values, we would live in a better society."

The writers of *Murphy Brown* didn't take the criticism lying down. In the opening episode of the following season, the main character, who is a newscaster, says into the fictional camera: "These are difficult times for our country, and in searching for the causes of our social ills we could choose to blame the media, or the Congress, or an administration that's been in power for twelve years. Or we could blame me."

Murphy Brown was singled out because the character represented multiple aberrations from the family structure and sexual ethics that Christian nationalists view as essential to American prosperity. She is a professional who prioritizes her career. She is a single woman who has autonomy over her sex life. She is a single mother who is intentionally raising her child without a male partner. To top it off, in the show Murphy Brown is a role model to others—a newscaster whose life and work are showcased on national television.

The show's writers astutely identified the issue that Quayle and his ilk had with the character and the show. In Christian nationalists' minds, there is a direct connection between "impure" sexual practices and "broken" family structures and the fate of the nation. They condemn the likes of Murphy Brown because they see in her character a representation of the sexual and familial waywardness they blame for destroying the nation from within. The fate of the nation depends, for the Christian nationalist, on sexual purity and proper familial structure. Without those, their story goes, we will be a nation of fatherless boys lacking proper masculine virtues and a society overrun by violence, aggression, and chaos.

FROM SEXUAL PURITY TO NATIONAL PURITY

The election of Ronald Reagan to the presidency in 1980 signaled the political influence of the New Religious Right. Although Falwell, Weyrich, and other leaders eventually became frustrated with Reagan, electoral politics has never been the same. GOP candidates on the local, state, and national levels now cater—and some would say capitulate—to this bloc of voters to win elections and gain power. Political scientists debate whether the millions of conservative Christian votes actually swayed the 1980 election. But both the New Religious Right's leaders and the American public came to a clear conclusion: conservative White Christians are the new bedrock of the GOP. Any candidate who doesn't take them seriously will go the way of the Georgia peanut farmer who left the White House with his Bible between his legs. If they were willing to turn on one of their own, what do you think they'll do to *you*?

Yet as these stories go, success isn't always as fulfilling as one expects. Even if the New Religious Right was able to take national electoral politics by storm, throughout the eighties they got the sense that the war was far from over. Even if American politics seemed to be back on track, they concluded that American culture continued to suffer from the effects of the sexual revolution and the changing dynamics of family and childrearing it had engendered: Single mothers. The normalization of divorce. The acceptance of gay and lesbian individuals in mainstream society. The AIDS crisis, which they saw as God's wrath on the gay community. New sex-ed programs teaching teenagers about contraception. Not to mention the prevalence of abortion in the wake of *Roe v. Wade*.

If the seventies witnessed the use of the family by White Christian nationalists seeking to maintain power in the wake of the civil rights movement, the sexual revolution, the women's rights movement, and the queer rights movement, then the eighties and nineties witnessed the dissemination of the rhetoric of "family values" as the pathway to national renewal. Under this new strategy, the family wasn't simply a symbol that White Protestants and Catholics used to defend themselves against charges of racism and misogyny. The family, and by extension the movement for sexual purity, became a weapon, deployed in a multitude of situations to shore up the nation's values and, in turn, protect it from the attacks and influence of godless communism and secular humanism coming from the Soviet Union and China.

FOCUSING ON THE FAMILY

The idea of family values didn't start in Southern California, but it was centered there for a long time. Without a doubt, James Dobson was the most influential harbinger of the family values discourse throughout the eighties and nineties. Trained as a child psychologist at the University of Southern California, Dobson founded Focus on the Family in 1977 in Arcadia, California, about thirty minutes from where I grew up in Yorba Linda. Since its founding, Focus on the Family has been a parachurch organization that provides training materials and other resources for parents and spouses to cultivate a godly household and family structure. In line with Murray's and Quayle's concerns about fatherless families and illegitimate children, Dobson's attention focused initially on raising boys to become godly men. Eventually, this expanded into a comprehensive program for cultivating the entire family according to biblical values. By the turn of the millennium, Focus on the Family radio shows were broadcast on more than five thousand stations around the world and had an audience of approximately 200 million listeners. When I was a teenager, its presence felt ubiquitous within evangelical culture. A Focus on the Family segment on raising boys or developing the traits of a godly family seemed to be on the local Christian radio station every time we got in the car and tuned in.

But the influence of Focus on the Family went beyond radio to conferences, books, pamphlets, Sunday school curricula for parents and teens, and video series. While pastors had the attention of their parishioners on one or maybe two days a week, Focus on the Family threaded through their lives every day, sometimes every few hours. Focus on the Family built what scholar of religion Susan Ridgley calls "a cohesive conservative vision" that mixed evangelical theology with psychological approaches to family life and a healthy dose of American nationalist themes. This meant that even though James Dobson was not a minister, throughout the eighties and nineties he became, in essence, one of the most influential pastors in the United States.

For Dobson, the first building block for a godly family was the marriage relationship, which he viewed as the locus of the divine-human relationship. In other words, for Dobson marriage reflects the connection between God and human beings, so it must be structured and enacted accordingly. For Dobson this meant a complementarian model, wherein the husband is the authoritative head of household and the wife his submissive complement. Here is how scholar Sara Moslener describes his approach:

> Focus on the Family became known for its advocacy of a domestic ideology that reflected a desire to return to family life and gender roles that closely resembled the ideals of

nineteenth-century white, middle-class America. For Dobson, these ideals were more than a historical legacy: they amounted to an act of obedience to the order of creation established by God in the book of Genesis. Dobson translated his biblical lessons into an accessible formulation clearly demarcating gendered behaviors and relations. Men and women, he asserted, were created with different but complementary traits that, together, fulfilled God's design for human relationships.

According to Dobson, complementarianism was a barrier against the corrosive influences of feminism and the "gay lifestyle," as many White evangelicals call it. This ideology categorically excludes any deviation from the standard of a heteronormative couple entering into a lifelong relationship with the intent of reproduction. There was no way to make feminist or queer theologies work with what Dobson argued was the bedrock of biblical teaching—the heterosexual nuclear family. There are clear roles in marriage: men are the leaders, the CEOs of the family; women are their submissive partners. Complementarianism is now a litmus test doctrine in many evangelical churches and denominations. Even if the rules aren't always explicitly stated, there are lines one can't cross and, if you are a woman, doors you can't enter. As a woman in a typical White evangelical church, you can't be a pastor or an elder. And if you are a man who doesn't subscribe to this ideology, you have little chance of being a leader in certain communities.

Around the time Dobson's particular brand of family values was gaining influence in the 1980s, a group of evangelical families began what is often referred to as the Quiverfull movement. The name Quiverfull comes from Psalm 127, where children are portrayed as a delightful heritage from God. Quiverfull families see all forms of birth control as contrary to God's sovereignty over reproduction. With no birth control measures in place, women are expected to sacrifice themselves—and their bodies—to any pregnancy with which

God blesses them. The Quiverfull movement was made famous by the TLC show *19 Kids and Counting*. Although the family it focuses on, the Duggars, didn't claim to be Quiverfull, their lifestyle and family structure exemplified the Quiverfull approach: a heterosexual couple, a patriarchal authority structure, a woman limited to the roles of wife and mother, and a family of well over a dozen children.

In line with Dobson's ideology, the Quiverfull movement sees childbirth as a form of fighting the culture wars; it is, in its crudest form, a way of creating more child foot soldiers on one side of the battlefront. Vyckie Garrison was raised in a Quiverfull movement. Since leaving, she has been writing about her experiences. "You also have to remember the sense of purpose that accompanies the Christian Patriarchy and Quiverfull movement," she writes. "We were raised to fight the enemy, be that Satan or the environmentalist, socialists, and feminists, to come against them in spiritual warfare and at the polls. . . . Put simply, their goal is to take over the country, instituting godly laws ruling according to Christ's dictates." According to Garrison, one of the reasons movements like Quiverfull are attractive to evangelical families is that one doesn't have to be a theologian or a pastor to be a lieutenant in the war to take back the country for God. As long as you can have children, and keep having children, you can contribute to the cause in significant ways.

FAMILIES WITH GOOD GENES ONLY

Focus on the Family and proponents of Quiverfull claim that their approaches to family and marriage are taken straight from scripture. However, at least in Dobson's case, even if he touted the scriptural basis of his theology of marriage, it was actually undergirded by a sinister legacy, one inherited from the eugenicist movement. Eugenics is the study of human genetics with the intent of learning how to increase the occurrence of "positive" genetic characteristics and decrease the occurrence of "negative" ones. Eugenics has been used throughout modern history as a faux-scientific basis for defining certain racial groups as bearing positive traits while labeling others as the bearers of negative characteristics. It has been used, among other things, to justify the racist views that Black and Indigenous people are less intelligent than other races.

As the scholar and author Audrey Clare Farley demonstrates, before Dobson founded Focus on the Family, he trained with the eugenicist Paul Popenoe, whose work, along with that of other eugenicists, inspired Hitler and the sterilization program he implemented in Nazi Germany. Popenoe's fear was that White people, whom he viewed as superior to all others, would be replaced by other races who were outbreeding them. In 1930, he founded the American Institute of Family Relations in Los Angeles in order to formulate strategies for encouraging White couples to remain married and produce more children. By 1960, it was one of the biggest marriage counseling centers in the country.

Popenoe and his cohorts discouraged women from pursuing higher education or professional lives, and they gave stern advice against interracial marriage. In essence, Popenoe was articulating a vision of a racially pure society in order to ensure the dominance of the White heterosexual family in opposition to families of Black, Indigenous, and other people of color, as well as queer individuals and families. He mixed the quack science of eugenics with White supremacy and a regressive understanding of gender and sexuality in order to instruct White people—especially White women—that marriage and reproduction were of utmost importance to "saving" American civilization.

Dobson worked for Popenoe in the late 1970s, and Popenoe wrote the foreword to Dobson's first book. Here is how Audrey Clare Farley described their relationship to me in a 2021 interview: "As his assistant, he [Dobson] authored all kinds of publications, which were basically Popenoe's ideas for a public audience—about male, female differences and strict gender norms, the dangers of evil feminism and how it's going to lead to society's decay." Thus, in the years immediately before Dobson became a household name in White evangelical circles, he was a research assistant and public voice for one of the most influential eugenicists of the twentieth century.

And just like Poponoe, Clare Farley told me, Dobson "viewed homosexuality and feminism as grave threats to the family. He would dismiss domestic abuse. . . . He would sometimes accuse women of faking it, just to get attention, that sort of thing. Even where he believed abuse was real, he never really thought of it as a good reason for divorce. Everybody had to stay in their marriage."

Dobson discouraged his audiences from interracial marriage and warned against the prevalence of "welfare queens"—a thinly veiled reference to Black women living in poverty who, in his mind, were single mothers destroying society by living off the government and raising their children without fathers. Like many evangelical leaders of the mid- and late twentieth century, Dobson subtly discouraged interracial marriage by claiming that such relationships failed on the "grounds of compatibility."

Like Popenoe, Dobson wanted pure families and a pure society. Unlike Popenoe, who was a devout atheist, Dobson used the authority of religion and the power of sacred texts to give these ideas divine sanction. Thus, it's not surprising that Dobson's teachings were imbued with nationalist concerns. What was at stake were not only the development of godly families but the redemption of a nation given over to all sorts of "impurities": from feminism to homosexuality and mixed-race families. Viewed through the lens of the eugenicist legacy, it is clear that race played a role in Dobson's vision of "family values." The family is for him the locus of the divine-human relationship, and the proper family is patriarchal and founded on White cultural norms.

Dobson inherited his understanding of gender and its ties to civilization from another twentieth-century White conservative named

George Gilder, a staunch antifeminist and the founder of the Discovery Institute. For Gilder, men are sexually destructive beings who, without the soothing presence of a wife, will tear down society through their aggression and violence. "Men are naturally designed to be not just aggressive, but destructive," scholar Sara Moslener, paraphrasing Gilder's argument, told me in a 2020 interview. According to Gilder and Dobson, men are inherently powerful and authoritative, but they require sexual satisfaction and stability in order to harness their energies positively. Women are weaker, more passive, and without inherent authority. In marriage, women trade sex for stability, and men forgo societal destruction for sexual satisfaction. Gilder maintained that "marriage is the social institution whereby those destructive instincts are contained," Moslener said. "So it's a containment theory." For Gilder, marriage is a transactional relationship upon which society depends in order to avoid internal strife and instability.

Dobson molded this pseudoscientific theory into a theological frame, taking cues from Gilder and arguing that men and women are designed by God to engage in a complementary heterosexual relationship. Like Gilder, he saw marriage as important not only for personal fulfillment (man) and safety (woman) but also because harnessing the energies of men through wedlock is the only way to cultivate a functioning society. Any deviation from this model, by dint of queer sexualities, polyamorous relationships, or an abundance of unmarried people, would spell doom in the mind of Dobson for American—and, for that matter, any—society.

"In short, the biblical foundation of marriage and family is seen as a relic by liberal politicians and our popular culture," Dobson wrote in 2020. "And yet, the very future of this nation rests on the strength of our marriages and families. If our country is to survive and pull itself out of the current mire, we must learn and draw our strength from the cornerstone on which it was built—the family."

There is only one step from the basic tenets of purity culture to a racialized and nationalistic view of marriage, sex, and the family.

"Our culture, like ancient cultures that ultimately were destroyed in large part due to their own moral depravity, has been severely weakened," Dobson writes. "A stable family unit committed to the truth and precepts of the Bible was once the foundation and backbone of our nation. That model is now the exception, not the rule."

In Dobson's view, maintaining sexual purity and forming heterosexual nuclear families are a matter of staying true to God's design. It is what's good for us. But he goes a step further: our bodies are not our own. When you sin sexually, you misuse what is God's, since your body belongs to God. Not only does this anger the Creator; it threatens to destroy our country.

It is teachings like this that convinced Alexis and me that sexual impurity would have a permanent imprint not only on our relationship but also on our families' legacies and our nation. Dobson described the United States of the eighties and nineties as embroiled in a "civil war of values." In his mind, even if the political tides had turned when Ronald Reagan was elected, the threats coming from the ascendance of communities of color and LGBTQ communities were threatening to destroy the nation from within. It is a small jump from a racialized, patriarchal view of marriage as the bedrock of civilization to seeing children as the soldiers in the cultural civil war. "Children are the prize winners of the second great civil war," Dobson writes. "They will determine the future of the nation."

CHRISTIAN NATIONALISM: THE ORIGINAL PURITY CULTURE

The singular obsession of purity culture is, of course, the body. As a teenager, I was taught that disciplining my mind and flesh were of the utmost importance to remaining pure. Any sexual thought was considered "adultery in your heart," meaning that a lustful glance, a sexual urge, or even an extended hug could be on par with cheating on one's future spouse. Always the zealot, I ritually removed any sexually explicit images from our household, including bikini ads from surfing magazines and the yearly swimsuit edition of *Sports Illustrated*. Girls in our youth group were taught to wear modest clothing in order to prevent leading boys and men into sexual temptation. We were all instructed to avoid being alone together, to exercise regularly in order to expend energy and ward off arousal, and to do everything possible to avoid touching ourselves or others in any sexual way.

When I think of my own experience with purity culture in the context of Dobson's theology and politics, it leads me to a simple yet startling conclusion: *Christian nationalism is America's original purity culture.* It is the vehicle for constructing a "pure" nation and society. In its essence, purity culture is a projection of all the gendered, racial, and societal fears that White Christian nationalists harbor onto the canvas of teenage flesh. The wager is that if we can discipline the virile teenage body into submission to a patriarchal, heteronormative, and often racialized mode of being, then those bodies will be the foundation of a rightly ordered national body. By tracing the roots of Dobson's family values to Popenoe's eugenicist project and Gilder's patriarchal views of sex, marriage, and civilization, we can see that purity culture was cultivated in a decades-long culture war waged by White Christian men against people of color, women, and queer folks.

This is the argument my podcast cohost Daniel Miller makes in *Queer Democracy: Desire, Dysphoria, and the Body Politic.* Throughout the book, Miller shows that for millennia, the body has been a metaphor for how people groups and nations have envisioned their collective character and virtue. In other words, most countries and communities imagine their collective self as looking a certain way— as having a certain type of body. The nation-as-body metaphor is centuries old. Christian nationalists envision the American social body as straight, White, Christian, native born (and thus English speaking), and patriarchal. When White Christian nationalists imagine the "real American," they think of John Wayne or Donald Trump or Nancy Reagan, a woman who abides by patriarchal norms.

They do not imagine Barack Obama, Kamala Harris, or Alexandria Ocasio-Cortez, much less a trans teenager of color or a queer immigrant. Their model American looks a certain way and has a certain body. Its phenotype, sexuality, gender, and religious practice are rolled into a singular vision of the American anatomy.

"American Christian nationalism therefore expresses a desire for a return to a mythologized social and political order," Miller writes. In other words, White Christian nationalists want to reimpose on the nation a hierarchy in which "real Americans occupy positions of social and political authority while all other, merely nominal, Americans properly occupy subordinate places within it." It's not that people of color and immigrants aren't allowed here. It's just that they need to know their place in the American *corpus*. To extend the body metaphor here: they are subordinate members who take orders from the central nervous system, frontal cortex, and other executive organs and parts. If they try to topple this order and become a central part of the American physique—or worse, become the commander in chief of its armed forces like Obama did when he was elected president— the White Christian nationalist will view the American body as out of whack. It will "feel" like something is wrong—as if there is a sickness plaguing the nation.

Within the White Christian nationalist imagination, pluralism and multiculturalism, and the expansion of representation and civil rights to minoritized groups, writes Miller, "[represent] the American social body's monstrous and grotesque transmogrification." For White Christian nationalists, gains made by historically excluded constituencies don't represent the expansion of freedom but the ruining of the American body. Their goal becomes reshaping society into the model they feel is right. "Christian nationalism therefore represents a socially dysphoric effort to preserve or reinstate real Americans' position atop the American-national hierarchy," Miller argues.

Viewing themselves as the "real Americans," then, White Christian nationalists feel entitled to occupy the top of the social and political hierarchies throughout the country. They see it as "natural" that White Christians would maintain power up and down the political and social systems. This corresponds to the ways Dobson and his predecessors envisioned the "natural" family as a heterosexual, patriarchal unit designed by God. Purity culture, inspired by Dobson and the "family values" movements, maps directly onto Christian nationalists' understanding of the natural order of the American social body as a straight, White, Christian male who holds dominion over all aspects of the nation. "The historical privileging of those recognized as embodying the idealized prototype of the 'real' American is presented as a natural occurrence, giving the American national body its 'natural' shape," Miller writes. In that sense, he says, "contemporary departures from its normative contours can only be 'unnatural' and, therefore, pathological."

What happens when historically excluded groups such as BIPOC communities, LGBTQ individuals, and feminists begin to change the shape of the American social body by working toward greater civil rights and legal protections? Christian nationalists experience this as the pollution of the American body—the introduction of impurities into the national DNA in a way that will lead to its destruction. This is why Miller calls Christian nationalism a "socially dysphoric reaction to the queerness of the American social body." Any deviation from the straight, White, male Christian makeup of the national body image is felt and seen as social body dysphoria. In other words, it feels like the soul of the nation isn't lining up with its body. It also explains why White Christian nationalists often feel as if something is "wrong" before they can put words to their discomfort.

Seen through this lens, the purity culture movement that shaped my teenage years can be understood as an attempt to regulate the national social anatomy through the regulation of White teenage bodies. Our sexual purity was the road back to a pure America—the right America. Dobson consistently links the fate of the nation to the sexual regulation of teenagers because, in his mind, the next generation must be molded into the proper social form in order for he and other Christian nationalists to win "the civil war of values."

IT WAS ONLY A KISS

Thus far we have followed a thread that runs throughout the development of the New Religious Right. Following it reveals how White Christians from the 1860s to the 1960s and beyond have used "family values" to defend segregationist and homophobic policies, doctrines, and practices. This works according to a clear pattern.

White men such as Weyrich, Viguerie, Falwell, and others who believe that society should be ordered according to a racialized and gendered structure fear that they are losing their country. They want a United States where White Christian men control the social and political hierarchies and all others (women, immigrants, and people of color) know their place. The civil rights movement, sexual revolution, women's liberation movements, and queer rights movements threatened this order.

When accused of racism, misogyny, and other forms of prejudice, they turned to the family as the shield for their actions and beliefs. The family, they argue, has a God-given structure. God formed it to be led by a man, to be composed of a married man and wife, and for the parents—especially the father—to have control over their children's bodies, education, and moral formation. Thus, issues ranging from school desegregation to women's rights to abortion to queer rights can fall under the umbrella of threats to "family values."

When confronted about their exclusionary worldview, White Christian nationalists generate outrage by wondering why the "old-fashioned Christian family" is under attack in the contemporary United States. They transpose the charge of racism or misogyny into a frame of victimization whereby their faith, family, and freedom are infringed on by radical new ideas and revolutionary politics.

The traditional family is the perfect vehicle for this transposition, because it is difficult rhetorically to dismantle White Christian nationalism's exclusionary politics without having to skirt around, under, or over the barrier of family. At times their critics play right into the White Christian nationalist strategy, without even knowing it, by opening themselves up to being "antifamily" and "anti-Christian."

Once again, the example of Jimmy Carter highlights how this works. Jimmy Carter was the wrong kind of Christian and not enough of an American nationalist. Ironically, the military officer turned American president didn't emanate the nationalism required for the New Religious Right to support him. By appointing people of color and women to the federal judiciary, by opening the door for the recognition of queer families, and by supporting the Equal Rights Amendment Carter was, according to White Christian nationalists, allowing improper elements to penetrate the sacred structure of the American family and the American nation.

In this chapter, we have added another piece to this puzzle. The drive for "family values" is a drive to purify the nation. The purity culture to which I committed myself in the nineties, promising to remain abstinent until marriage, is an outgrowth of the family values discourse, and the family values discourse is an outgrowth of White Christian nationalism. According to the history we have traced, the ideal family for the White Christian nationalist is not mixed with other races, is composed of a man who works and provides and a woman who knows her place in the home as subordinate to her husband. The children are under the control of their parents. The father is the voice of God in the household. Finally, the United States is revered alongside the kingdom of God as deserving devotion and loyalty. White Christian nationalists are always Christian and American. Neither identity is separable from the other. They depend on each other. They inform one another. They prop each other up. They use each other in order to envision and create the "right kind" of national body.

In 2016, James Dobson went back on previous comments in which he expressed concern about Trump's character and publicly endorsed Donald Trump. "I am endorsing Donald J. Trump not only because of my apprehensions about Hillary Clinton and the damage she would inflict on this great country," Dobson said. "I am also supporting Mr. Trump because I believe he is the most capable candidate to lead the United States of America in this complicated hour." For some, Dobson's endorsement of the thrice-married television star was surprising. After all, Trump is famous for his liaisons with models and sex workers; he appeared in media for *Playboy* magazine; and by the time Dobson's announcement came, the infamous *Access Hollywood* tape, in which Trump explains how he grabs women "by the pussy," had already reached public ears.

Yet if we view Trump as the paragon of the national body White Christian nationalists envision rather than as an individual example of godly sexual ethics, Dobson's endorsement makes more sense. He wants a pure nation—a national social body that is modeled after a White, landowning, native-born man who is ready and willing to expel, abuse, and make war against intruders, outsiders, and anyone who threatens the proper order of the country. For Dobson, sadly, Trump fits this vision.

None of this story changes what I experienced kissing Alexis for the first time. When Alexis and I put our lips together that summer evening, the exhilaration of the moment was overridden by heaviness. It felt as if there were waves of pressure lapping into my back as I leaned over to bring my lips to hers. My body was weighed down by the need to contain my desire—pause it before it leaped forward and out of my control. On top of halting my teenage hormones, I felt as if our future—our family's future, our nation's future—were hanging over us, haunting that first moment of intimacy. There was no teenage levity. No living in the moment. Instead, we were two young people trying their best to save the whole world through a kiss—and only a kiss.

Chapter 7

KILLING DEMOCRACY TO SAVE THE NATION

IN LATE SEPTEMBER OF my first year of high school, just four months after my conversion to evangelicalism, I attended the "See You at the Pole" rally at the flagpole in front of my high school. Any fears I had about attending a public prayer rally were allayed when I saw the dozens of other kids who had gathered an hour before classes would start. While we envisioned ourselves as a persecuted minority, Orange County evangelicals comprised a sizable percentage of the population. In a school of 2,000 students, about 150 had turned out to pray that September morning.

When Mom let me out of her gray minivan in the parking lot, the early arrivers had already formed a circle around the pole, holding hands and bowing their heads. There was no program or leader. When someone felt led to pray, they did, "interceding for" our teachers, school, nation, and friends. At times we broke into song; at times there was silence. We carried on until the bell rang for first period.

"Why were you guys praying to the flag?" a classmate asked me later that day. Only then did it occur to me that it probably seemed as if we had gathered in some sort of patriotic ritual to honor Old Glory. Looking back, I see the kernel of truth lodged in his sense that we were praying not *at* the flagpole but *to* the flag. Switching out one two-letter preposition for another one, my classmate perhaps intuited something I did not yet see.

See You at the Pole is a yearly event that gathers evangelical students at their respective institutions to pray at the foot of the American flag. Having been started in 1990 by students in Texas as an offshoot of the National Day of Prayer, See You at the Pole was a time to "lift up their friends, families, teachers, school, and nation to God." By the next year, reportedly over a million teenagers across the nation gathered at their schools' flagpoles. The rally has taken place on the fourth Wednesday of September ever since, with millions of young Americans participating every fall.

As a zealot with a tendency to take things to the extreme, I went above and beyond during my senior year and committed to praying at the flag *every* Friday; I invited anyone to join me. Most Fridays I was alone when I stood there at the pole an hour before school. Sometimes there were three or four of us. We prayed for God to reign on our campus and in our nation. We asked him to combat the godlessness of our culture and to change the hearts of our teachers, administrators, and peers. Gathering at the foot of our country's national symbol each week, we asked the Lord of heaven and earth to retake what was rightfully his. We wanted our school and our country to be a shining light to the world—a place where the kingdom of God and the American nation were indistinguishable.

AMERICA, CITY ON THE HILL?

In 1630, John Winthrop proclaimed to his fellow Puritans that New England would be a city on a hill for all the world to emulate. He was drawing on Matthew 5, where Jesus extols his followers to participate in the kingdom of God in a way that will make them a shining light to all people. Winthrop envisioned his people as a "New Israel" and a "chosen people" who would shed light across a world made dark by sin and tyranny.

Americans have long conflated the kingdom of God and the nation-state. The notion that the United States is a shining city on a hill resounds throughout our history. The likes of John Kennedy and Ronald Reagan have called on it during times of war, hardship, and crisis to remind Americans that this great democratic experiment is not the easiest route but is the right one, that democracy is complicated and often painful but worth it in order to live in freedom, peace, and equity. The biggest proponents of the city on a hill metaphor have always been politicians and Christian pastors, two groups invested in forming an image of the American republic as a light to the world morally, civically, and religiously.

During my high school years in the late 1990s, however, many White evangelicals felt as if the country was slipping further and further away from its exceptional role as God's chosen land. Despite James Dobson's movement for family values based on the hetero-patriarchal nuclear family, and despite the purity pledges sent to the nation's capital, there were signs of godlessness all around. President Clinton was embroiled in an adultery scandal involving an intern. This was the era of fierce debate over same-sex civil unions and eventually the legalization of same-sex marriage. The American family was changing. Mixed-race couples were increasingly normalized in many parts of the country. Divorce rates stabilized, while the taboo surrounding divorce was evaporating. Single mothers. Single fathers. Blended families. Children with two moms. Children with two dads. These became standard figurations of American life. And the levers of democracy—elections, policies, and legislation—seemed powerless to stop them. But most of all, American culture kept moving forward in spite of White Christian nationalists' attempts to stop the progress. It seemed as if all the work to revolutionize electoral politics and stem the tide of cultural revolution in the seventies and eighties wasn't enough.

"I believe it should be the duty of every Christian to pray for repentance and revival in the land," Billy Graham wrote in 1993. "If I were not a believer in Christ, I might at this point in history succumb to total pessimism." While Graham urged Americans to pray to the heavens for renewal, some Christians began to look east for new political and cultural blueprints in Russia and eastern Europe. In order to effect the visions of a "pure" America and to realign the American social body, some White Christian nationalists became enamored of authoritarian regimes as the exemplars of morality and civic structure. They began looking to countries where there is no meaningful democratic governance or human rights records—countries ruled by autocratic strongmen without a free press, democratic processes, or even freedom of religion. In what would become an authoritarian turn within White Christian nationalism, adherents began to believe that preserving the holy trinity of family, God, and nation might be worth the sacrifice of democracy itself.

FROM THE GOLD RUSH TO PUTIN'S PUPPET

One night in 1964, Dana Rohrabacher was hiding in a tree, waiting for bandits to show up at the office below. His plan was to thwart their attack and protect the campaign and the candidate that had ignited in him a youthful zeal for politics. As a student at Palos Verdes High School near Los Angeles, Rohrabacher had become enthralled with Barry Goldwater after reading the Arizona senator's *The Conscience of a Conservative*. No vandals showed up that night to the Goldwater campaign offices that Rohrabacher was "protecting" from high up in that tree, but this story became an emblematic tale of his commitment to the Goldwater revolution in conservative politics. Like many others from the Arizona senator's failed presidential run, Rohrabacher used the defeat as the basis of his political calling.

Over the next decade, Rohrabacher made his way from Southern California to Washington, DC. After time on Capitol Hill, he became assistant press secretary to President Ronald Reagan, helping outline Reagan's foreign policy, which came to be known as the Reagan Doctrine, and build out the Gipper's anticommunist policies and message. After Reagan left office, Rohrabacher returned home to California and won election to the US House of Representatives for a district in the northern coastal region of Orange County. Rohrabacher would spend the next thirty years (1989–2019) representing this conservative Orange County enclave in Congress. As a Goldwater campaign alum and a Reagan administration official, he had the quintessential profile for the district, having cut his political teeth on staunchly libertarian policies and vehement anticommunist rhetoric. Below his surfer-dude persona and Christian lingo was a bulldog who wasn't afraid to represent the county's ultraconservative constituents even when others considered him extremist.

But then something strange happened. The man who had come up through the ranks warning the world of the threat of communism in the Soviet Union morphed into the most pro-Russia member of either house of Congress.

It began thirty years ago when he hosted the then vice mayor of St. Petersburg, Vladimir Putin, in Washington, DC. They played a game of touch football and then drunkenly arm wrestled to decide who should win the Cold War. From the turn of the millennium forward, Rohrabacher transformed into what some have dubbed "Putin's favorite congressperson." Over the years, he has compared Putin to Gorbachev and has said Reagan would want the United States to establish good working relationships with Russia. He tried to derail the Magnitsky Act, which prohibits certain Russian oligarchs from entering the United States and inhibits their ability to bank here. He also compared Russia's military invasion of Crimea to the Revolutionary War.

So how did the man who was once so devoted to libertarian ideals that he hid in a tree to protect the Goldwater campaign from vandals become the most vocal congressional advocate of Vladimir Putin, a leader who uses his autocratic powers in the least libertarian ways possible? Putin is known for restricting immigration, limiting free speech and the free press, controlling Russia's economy through a network of oligarchs with state business interests, and teaming up with the state church to wage violence against members of the LGBTQ community. Rohrabacher's pro-Russian platform became so pronounced that in 2016, Republican congressmen Kevin McCarthy, who became House minority leader a few years later, said in a private meeting with Paul Ryan and a few others that he thinks Putin pays two people: Donald Trump and Dana Rohrabacher.

While it's impossible to conclude decisively how and why Rohrabacher went from an anti-Soviet crusader to a pro-Putin cheerleader, one hint might be in what he told KPCC Radio in 2013 about his infamous arm-wrestling match with Putin. "He's a little guy, but boy, I tell you, he put me down in a millisecond. He is tough. His muscles are just unbelievable. He's a tough guy and he's supposed to be a tough guy. That's what the Russian people want." As a "tough guy," Putin doesn't abide by democratic institutions and processes. He acts with absolute authority and threatens those who challenge him with physical violence. His rule is based on force and might, not the will of the people. And perhaps surprisingly, this is exactly why religious luminaries on the New Religious Right now see him as the model global leader.

As we explored in the previous chapters, one of the foundations of the New Religious Right is American nationalism, fueled by "I Love America rallies" and the constant juxtaposition of the cross and the flag. Communism—particularly the Soviet type—has always been a go-to bogeyman for White Christian nationalists. Yet all it took for the movement to reverse its stance on Russia was for the former Soviet Union to transition to an autocratic regime led by one "tough guy." Allan Carlson, the former director of the Family and America Study Center and the founder and longtime international secretary of the World Congress of Families—organizations committed to defending traditional "family values"—put it this way in 2018: "There are great experiments in post-liberal political and economic life occurring right now in real places in Poland's law and justice party, in the Hungary of prime minister Victor Orbán, and yes, in the land of the great Russians led by Vladimir Putin."

Carlson's praise for these parties and leaders isn't an accident. Paul Weyrich, the godfather of the New Religious Right, began taking regular trips to Russia in the 1990s. There he trained activists and saw in Russia a chance to reraise Christendom. "Clearly it is in the American national interest to keep Russia on its side not only in the fight against radical Islamic fundamentalists but on a more permanent basis," Weyrich cowrote with Edward Lozansky in 2001. "And the Russian people must understand that being an American ally brings substantial dividends."

For Weyrich, remaking the United States as the city on a hill would require foreign help from Russia. Here's how Sarah Posner put it when I interviewed her in 2020: "In the early days of Putin, he kind of admired him and thought it was okay for a strong leader to dispense with some of the procedures and protocols of democracy in the service of advancing that kind of ideal of a Christian nation. This was not something that was really on the radar of many rank-and-file Christian rights activists until the Trump era."

Always the visionary, Weyrich saw, by the turn of the millennium, what his comrades on the New Religious Right wouldn't until a decade later: Russia is a model for the type of "pure" nation that White Christian nationalists want. Russia is not only one of the Whitest places on earth; under Putin's regime, it has also become openly hostile to outsiders, especially those coming from Muslim-majority countries. It has a Christian past rooted in the hierarchical and patriarchal Orthodox tradition, which in many ways matches up with the kind of authoritarian politics that does not wait for, or depend on, democratic mechanisms to process decisions about policy or governance.

Authoritarians like Putin have become the model leader for a segment of the American population who have lost their majority but want to maintain the purity of the American body. For them, democracy is not the ideal form of governance if it doesn't yield the political and cultural hierarchies they desire. If installing an authoritarian who will act on their behalf and against the will of the people is their best hope of retaining control, then, for some of them at least, so be it.

Sarah Posner, author of *Unholy: Why White Christians Worship at the Altar of Donald Trump*, summed it up in 2019:

> Indeed, many in the US Christian right believe America has failed as a role model for the rest of the world—that liberalism, unrestrained, has brought a once great nation to its knees. To them, the "illiberal" autocrats across the Atlantic are fast becoming the new standard-bearers in a global battle for traditional values, an antidote to what they see as rising decadence and moral relativism in the West.

What this means, on the ground, is a visible partnership between what is known as the Alt Right (short for the "alternative right"), made up of openly xenophobic and racist figures who want the United States to be a White ethno-state, and the heirs of the New Religious Right, religious communities that want the United States to be a Christian nation marked by patriarchy and Christian hegemony. Both groups mourn a mythological America they see as lost to the throes of pluralism, immigration, the expansion of civil rights for people of color and the LGBTQ+ community, and the changing racial demographics of the country.

It's worth noting that this is how Christian nationalism provides an umbrella for a diverse coalition of groups and movements. While many in the Alt Right may not seem religious in terms of their church attendance or daily Bible reading, they find in the Christianity offered by Dobson, Carlson, and others a resonant worldview. If White Christian nationalism is based on the foundations of racism, xenophobia, and queerphobia, then it offers Alt Right bigots a religious umbrella for their movement that can accommodate their core ideology without demanding adherence to particular doctrinal positions or church attendance.

This, of course, lines up with the history we have traced in previous chapters. The formation of the New Religious Right was founded on protecting segregation academies, a patriarchal nuclear family, and vehement nationalism. In this sense, it is easy to understand how the inheritors of Weyrich's and Falwell's visions of America not only find allies with the Alt Right abroad, but could look to Russia and other central and eastern European countries as paragons of how society should be racially ordered: with Whites at the top and everyone else in their proper place below them. What is most startling about the authoritarian turn in White Christian politics is how quickly the New Religious Right flipped its position on Russia.

Weyrich died in 2008, the same year Barack Obama won the White House. The election of the first Black president accelerated the process of White Christian nationalists' enchantment with authoritarian figures like Putin as the answer to the problem of the United States' liberalism. After Weyrich's death, other organizations and other leaders stepped in to fill the vacuum, cultivating relationships with far-right leaders and organizations abroad. The most important of these was the World Congress of Families, an international coalition dedicated to the "family values" ethos first cultivated by Dobson's Focus on the Family in the 1980s.

WORLD CONGRESS OF FAMILIES

A common refrain is that the United States no longer "makes" anything. We don't export many goods anymore; we import them from China, India, and other places. But one way to think about the World

Congress of Families (WCF) and similar organizations is as export-
ers of the American family values movement. Though it was formed
independently in 1997, the WCF is now part of the International
Organization of the Family, which according to their mission statement, "Unites and Equips Leaders Worldwide to Promote the Natural Family." In addition to the WCF, the International Organization
of the Family publishes a journal, runs a leadership institute, and
shapes policy initiatives. The International Organization of the Family uses the WCF to promote complementarianism and the nuclear
family as the bedrock of any healthy nation. The organization views all
nonheterosexual relationships and family structures as destructive and
harmful to children, labeling them a "gender ideology" that corrupts
individuals and countries alike. And they are patriarchal through
and through—the earthly father is seen as an extension of the divine
Father, and thus his authority is unquestionable and near absolute.
"The complementary natures of men and women, both physically and
psychologically, are evident throughout the course of human history
and in every society," writes WCF founder Allan Carlson and vice
president Paul Mero in *The Natural Family: A Manifesto*. "Deviations
from natural sexual behavior cannot truly satisfy the human spirit."

Seeing a bleak situation at home, the WCF has been in bed with
foreign leaders and organizations it believes can help bolster its movement and create an international synergy in the fight for the "traditional family" for almost two decades. It has exported the Christian
language of family values and, in turn, learned from authoritarian
leaders who share a similar patriarchal and heteronormative vision
of society. "They've had these conferences all over the world," Sarah
Posner told me in our 2020 interview. "But in recent years, they've
had them in coordination with far-right leaders in places like Italy,
Hungary, Moldova, Russia. And so in recent years, they've begun to
look at and partner with autocratic leaders, who they actually get to
officially cohost the conference. So it's not just that they had a conference in Budapest; it's that Orbán helped sponsor it. Or in Italy

they had a conference in Verona, and Matteo Salvini cosponsored it. The one that I covered was in Moldova, which was cohosted by the then president of Moldova, who was Putin ally Igor Doden."

The rhetoric coming from these conferences can be unnerving even for those used to operating within conservative Christian settings. Forming connections in countries like Hungary, Georgia, and Turkey means that public anti-LGBTQ hate speech can be in full bloom, with little fear of public outcry. As one speaker at a World Congress of Families gathering in the republic of Georgia in 2016 said: "Tell the LGBT tolerance tyrants, this lavender mafia, these homofascists, these rainbow radicals, that they are not welcome to promote their anti-religious and anti-civilizational propaganda in your nations."

In the previous chapter, we saw how Christian nationalism is the original purity culture. For White Christian nationalists, the goal is to foster a "pure" society based on the foundation of the patriarchal, heteronormative nuclear family. This, according to Dobson, Carlson, and their cohorts, is the pathway to national strength and vitality. Purifying the bodies of teenagers and ordering the family the right way will lead to an impenetrable national body, resistant to decay and decline. Authoritarian leaders like Hungary's Viktor Orbán and Russia's Vladimir Putin agree. Both men have used the rhetoric of Christian values and heritage to justify violence against LGBTQ communities and policies outlawing queer sexualities and gender identities. In 2020, Orbán criticized western Europe for "experiments with a godless cosmos, rainbow families, migration, and open societies."

The family values rhetoric doesn't stop there, however. "We think that the problems of Europe can be traced back to the denial of Christian roots. We see the misinterpretation of tolerance many times. Being tolerant should not mean that one gives up his or her identity," said Katalin Novák, Hungary's minister of state for family, youth, and international affairs, in 2019. She later gave a keynote address at the "Make Families Great Again" conference held at the Hungarian embassy in Washington, DC.

In 2018, Putin outlawed "gay propaganda" and defended this action by claiming that the family is the basis for a prosperous nation. He said, "We know there are ever more people in the world who support our position in defense of the traditional values that for centuries have formed the moral foundation of civilization."

These ideas and actions have garnered nothing but praise from the WCF. "And the homosexual propaganda—the law in the Russian Duma: it passed on first reading, it would ban propaganda to minors, preventing them [LGBT people] from corrupting children," wrote Larry Jacobs, WCF managing director, in 2013. "What a great idea and the rest of Europe is going the other way, legalizing LGBT propaganda."

While issues surrounding gender and sexuality are the stated reasons for the WCF's and other conservative religious organizations' liaisons with authoritarian leaders, their actions reflect a startling reality: many White Christian American nationalists now see autocratic regimes as the shining cities on a hill. They are the models of how to construct a pure society. Using the rhetoric of Christian heritage and family values, leaders like Orbán and Putin give transcendent authority to their antidemocratic, anti-LGBTQ, and antipluralist modes of governance. "They've made a kind of seamless transition from being anticommunist to supporting these autocrats," Sarah Posner told me in 2020. "And it seems that the reasonable conclusion to draw would be that they don't like totalitarianism when it's left-wing totalitarianism, but they're okay with it coming from the right."

Even if Putin and Orbán rely on undemocratic processes, physical violence, and various forms of corruption to achieve what they see as the proper order to their societies, White Christian nationalists favor their tactics over the slow-moving processes of a democratic republic. When the bedrock of your worldview is the will to power, all that matter is results. The goal is domination, not dialogue or debate— much less democracy.

TRUMP, PURITY, FAMILY VALUES, AND AUTHORITARIANISM

Given the New Religious Right's admiration of Putin, Orbán, and other autocratic strongmen, their unwavering support for Trump makes complete sense. In the opening to his presidential campaign, Trump uttered what are now infamous words about Mexican people. "They're sending people that have lots of problems at that. Bringing those problems with us. They're bringing drugs; they're bringing crime. They're rapists."

On January 27, 2017, just weeks into his presidency, Trump signed an executive order that banned foreign nationals from seven predominantly Muslim countries from visiting the country for ninety days, suspended entry to the country of all Syrian refugees indefinitely, and prohibited any other refugees from coming into the country for 120 days. "I think Islam hates us," he said. "There's something, there's something there that … that's a tremendous hatred. There . . . there's a tremendous hatred. We have to get to the bottom of it."

He then shocked the nation after violence erupted between White supremacists, including neo-Nazis, and counterdemonstrators at a 2017 rally in Charlottesville. "I think there's blame on both sides," he said. "You look at both sides. I think there's blame on both sides, and I have no doubt about it and you don't have any doubt about it either. And if you reported it accurately, you would say it. But you also had people that were very fine people on both sides."

In May 2020, Trump's former head of national security, John Bolton, released a memoir. In one episode, he chronicles Trump's response to President Xi's explanation as to why the Chinese leader needs to build concentration camps for Uyghur Muslims. According to Bolton, Trump said that building the camps was "exactly the right thing to do."

When he ran for the presidency in 2015, Trump made waves by calling the press the "enemy of the people." He repeatedly called for investigations into his political enemies, encouraged supporters to call for the jailing of Hillary Clinton, and used the Department of Justice as his own personal law firm. During the 2020 uprisings in reaction to the murder of George Floyd, Trump infamously ordered peaceful protesters be dispersed with tear gas so he could march through the Rose Garden to hold up a Bible in front of St. John's Church.

These are only a few examples of Trump's authoritarian tendencies. Predictably, they did little to scare off the White Christians who helped usher him into the White House in 2016. In fact, among White evangelicals, Trump's support rose 3 percent in 2020. Overall, in the 2020 election, 84 percent of White evangelicals, 57 percent of White nonevangelical Protestants, and 57 percent of White Catholics voted for him.

IT TAKES AN IMPURE MAN TO PURIFY THE NATION

If we want to gain a more expansive view of why White Christian nationalists have transformed Trump into an American savior, we have to combine our analyses of purity culture and family values with their infatuation with foreign strongmen. The first question to answer is what autocratic rulers do for a nation. History is clear that authoritarian leaders limit free speech, control the media, enforce draconian laws that inhibit personal freedoms, and ban or marginalize minorities and the LGBTQ community. For most of us, this spells bad news. Not only does autocracy belie the will of the people in favor of the rule of one (or a few), but it goes against the basic rights we associate with democratic societies: freedom of the press, of assembly, of religion, and of speech; the right to pursue life, liberty, and happiness; the right to transparency from our leaders; and the ability to vote them out when their policies and views no longer represent the majority.

By sacrificing civil liberties and human rights, however, strongmen autocrats are able to effect purity in ways democratic processes, like voting, and democratic institutions, like state and national legislatures, cannot. In the last chapter, we saw how this vision of the family grew from the eugenics and nationalistic models of Popenoe and Gilder and then was given a religious frame by Dobson through Focus on the Family. Viewed through this lens, we can conclude that in many ways purity culture and the family values discourse developed and spread by Focus on the Family and the World Congress of Families are in essence strongmen values stuffed into the shell of a theology of sex and the family. The shared foundation of authoritarian regimes and the family values ideology is a desire to order every level of society—individual, family, and nation—according to a White, patriarchal authority structure imbued with a transcendent authority from God the Father.

TRUMP'S FAMILY VALUES?

When I stood in front of my school's flagpole on those lonely Friday mornings, praying for my classmates and my country to come back to God, I never expected that my evangelical brethren would one day pin their hopes for national repentance on a thrice-married television star accused of sexual assault, corruption, fraud, and money laundering. When I kissed Alexis for the first time as a high school senior, using every nerve, muscle, and ounce of willpower in my body to avoid lust and temptation, I never expected that one day a man who had sexual encounters with a sex worker mere weeks after his third wife gave birth would become the candidate of choice for "family values" voters.

One of the peculiar aspects of the White Christians' love affair with Trump is the clear dissonance between their sexual ethics and his sexual abuses. It's perhaps the most glaring hypocrisy when it comes to conservative religious voters claiming Trump is an American messiah who will deliver the nation back to its founding—and back to God. Yet there is a way that Trump's sexual savagery actually reinforces rather than betrays the family values discourse and purity culture ethos we've been examining in this chapter and the previous one. And it ties directly to the White Christian nationalist admiration for foreign strongmen.

As we've observed, the foundations of these movements are White supremacist and queer-phobic in nature. Their visions of a pure society are based on the American social body as a straight, White, native-born body, living under patriarchal authority, who speaks English as their native language. Trump not only celebrates this model, but as president he did so as the leader of the American family. In Trump and Trump's family, White Christian nationalists saw the embodiment of the "pure" nation in terms of ethnicity, race, gender, and sexuality.

But it goes deeper than having a White family with Nordic genes in the White House. In *Compromising Positions*, Leslie Dorrough Smith, a scholar of religion, argues that White heterosexual men are often forgiven of sexual transgressions such as extramarital affairs, harassment, and even abuse because their aggressive sexual behavior is actually seen as a virtue for the leader tasked with protecting the nation from invaders and extending the American empire. In some sense, they transcend the call for sexual purity because their "hyper-masculine aggression is read by the public as a sign of America's own prowess and strength," Dorrough Smith writes. "In other words, the moral details of our leaders' illicit sex are not only irrelevant to whether he bears power but may actually be an indication that he deserves the power he has," Dorrough Smith continues, "precisely because his sexuality proves his masculinity, and thus his claim to authority."

Many Americans, including large swaths of White Christian nationalists, seem to accept that the figure who is asked to protect the purity of the national family may have to overstep the bounds of purity himself in order to do so. This transgression is viewed not as an unforgivable sin but as a sign of virility and power. As Kristin Kobes du Mez argues in *Jesus and John Wayne*, one of the clear lessons of the conservative Christian idolization of Trump is that certain "family values" Christians often want a leader who is unencumbered by Christian virtue in order to help them bolster and cultivate the family values they claim are the bedrock of civilization.

As I said before, Jimmy Carter was too much of a Christian to be a Christian nationalist, much less a protoauthoritarian in the vein of Putin or Orbán. His dedication to Christ actually hindered his manifestation of the types of viciousness that many White Christian nationalists see as requisite for protecting the nation from outside invaders and internal threats. Carter, in other words, was too Christian to be the kind of president many White Christians want. Instead, they prefer a self-styled barbarian, unhindered by the duty to be Christlike.

"They see him implementing his agenda against all odds. If the swamp gets in his way, Trump bulldozes over it," Miranda Devine wrote for Fox News in 2019. "Supreme Court, tick. Taxes cut, tick. Regulations slashed, tick. Jobs up, tick. Military rebuilt, tick. ISIS stopped, tick. Globalism challenged, tick. Paris climate treaty scrapped, tick. Borders strengthened, tick. Wall built, half-tick."

For his supporters, Trump's barbarism is a feature of the system, not a bug. "The American people chose a barbarian for president," Devine writes, "because they knew only a barbarian could drain the Washington swamp." As we will see in the next chapter, White Christian nationalists see the world as in a constant state of cosmic war, where all those opposed to them are God's enemies who will eventually be defeated. They see themselves as the true believers—and true Americans—charged by God to carry out his mission on earth. Trump has been viewed as the barbarian-king who is willing to fight this war without concern for civility or etiquette. Like a good strongman, he is seen as the head and protector of the American family—one who oversteps the bounds of purity in order to make it possible for a pure nation to exist. His transgressions are not only forgivable; they are signs that he is up for the job.

This is why White Christian nationalists often fly the Trump flag alongside the American flag at rallies, church events, and parades. This is why one now sees apparel that reads "Jesus Is My Savior, Trump Is My President." This is why Trump is often likened to a biblical figure chosen by God to lead his people out of exile and back to the promised land. And it's why, if the republic and the democratic institutions that uphold it need to be martyred in order to maintain their vision of the American body and American family, some White Christian nationalists will choose autocracy over the will of the people. They will erect gallows outside the Capitol, violently attack police officers, and vandalize chambers of Congress, instead of letting someone else become head of the national body.

In many ways it's no surprise that the group who believed—and still believes—it has an inherent right to power over the nation sees democracy as unfortunate collateral damage in their culture war. If the will of the people needs to be left behind in order to remake America as the city on a hill, then so be it. The goal is to retake the country for God, even if the republic has to be martyred in the process.

Chapter 8

REAL DELUSIONS

DURING MY SENIOR YEAR of high school, the youth group at Rose Drive started a new Bible study on Friday nights. Held at the Johnsons' house, it started at seven and often didn't end until around ten. Tony, who was in his early twenties and had just moved to Orange Country from Calexico, a town near the US-Mexico border, led the group. He was the high school assistant minister who worked part-time at Rose Drive while attending the Calvary Chapel Bible College. Calvary Chapel, as a denomination, started from the "Jesus People" movement in Southern California during the sixties. In what must be one of the most extreme examples of the way 1960s counterculture morphed into sold-out 1980s conservatism, the Calvary Chapel movement that started as mostly guitar-playing hippies and religious vagabonds became a denomination of dogmatism, with buttoned-up conservative theology. Calvary Chapel has a special focus on the end times—much more than Rose Drive. So on Friday nights Tony—a short, compact guy with a wrestler's build and a black ponytail—would lead us through Revelation, the infamous apocalyptic text at the end of the New Testament. While most biblical scholars agree it is a kind of mystical political commentary on the Roman occupation in Palestine, many evangelicals see it as the key to understanding when and how the apocalypse will happen.

The Friday night Bible study grew from a handful of kids to several dozen over the course of the school year. We packed the Johnsons' modest living room, squeezing in close to make sure everyone could find a place, and I'm sure it took most of the weekend to clear the house of the aroma of pizza and body spray. After half an hour or so of singing and prayer, Tony would hold us rapt for hours with his teachings about the end times. He would explain how the earthquakes, famines, and global tragedies happening all over the world were actually signs of the end times. The rapture—the event some Christians believe will lead to all the "saved" being instantly taken into heaven in the blink of an eye—was surely near. He took obscure passages from Revelation and shaped them into lucid blueprints of where the world was heading in the years to come, explaining that the antichrist would rise to power, most likely through a unified governmental structure such as the European Union.

Soon, Tony warned us, the mark of the beast would be introduced in some form of technology implanted into our bodies. That implant would act as a tracking device for the antichrist and his new world order. He mapped scriptural references to serpents and beasts and whores of Babylon onto the impeachment trial of Bill Clinton, the development of the new unified currency called the euro, and the push to study harvested stem cells through new technologies, a huge controversy on the West Coast at the time. All of these were indications that the end was near.

Tony wasn't the only person in my life making these types of proclamations. A few of my friends and I passed around books like Hal Lindsey's *Late Great Planet Earth* and the books of the Left Behind series by Tim LaHaye and Jerry Jenkins. We also listened to Calvary Chapel preachers like Chuck Smith and Greg Laurie on the radio, on our way to surfing trips and afterschool hangouts. My girlfriend, Alexis, and I would debate the meaning of passages in Revelation. In the tit-for-tat arguments over hermeneutics unique to evangelicalism, we'd use commentaries and books to back up our interpretations.

Learning about the end times always made me, and others, feel like we were gaining special knowledge—an initiation into cosmic secrets and techniques for reading the signs of the times. It was a fellowship of those-who-know. We felt select, even among the church community—the chosen remnant within the chosen remnant. Whereas many adults in our midst had forgotten the immediacy of our age in favor of golf games and nice dinners, mortgage rates and 401Ks, we huddled together on Friday nights to be vigilant in the face of the extraordinary. Unlike them, we were ready to give everything we had to play a role in God's secret plan for the cosmos.

And because we met on a Friday, our gatherings felt like a reprieve from the day-to-day godlessness of our schools and daily lives. I was used to people thinking of me as an extremist. I was the guy who led a Bible study at lunch and walked around with Jesus tracts to hand out at any given moment, the zealot who refused a letterman's jacket in order to give the money to buy Bibles in Nepal, the freak who stood alone on Friday mornings praying at the flagpole. While I took pride in being different, it was also exhausting. On Friday nights, I didn't have to swim up current. At the end of each week, the Johnsons' living room felt like a cocoon of belonging. Everyone there accepted that the world didn't understand us, didn't know the truth, and would carry on in its blind, fallen state until Jesus returned. For a few hours we could bask in the shared knowledge that we were among the few in the world who knew what was *really* going on—and knew how it would all end. There was a significance in the fact that not only did we all believe the same thing; we believed it *together*.

WHAT IS A CONSPIRACY THEORY ANYWAY?

The end-times theology that we learned and cultivated on those Friday nights resembles a conspiracy theory. According to anthropologist

Susannah Crockford in her work *Ripples of the Universe*, "what makes a 'theory' a 'conspiracy theory' is the surfeit of meaning and explanation, overextending the agency and intentionality behind complex socio-political situations." In other words, if you examine current events as part of an intentional scheme planned by evil agents, rather than accepting the apparent and simple answers afforded by logic and evidence, you are wading into the waters of conspiracy. These events might include political developments, such as elections or coups, or scientific advancements that require we change our daily lives, like wearing masks during a pandemic. For Crockford, some religious beliefs and conspiracy theories are similar in that they both make nonfalsifiable claims about reality and "grant agency to causation in a way that challenges assumptions of rationality." In other words, they make claims about what is real on the basis of divine authority with no regard for human rationality. Their stances are based on rumor and delusion rather than evidence, logic, or data. Not all religious beliefs fall under this category. Many religious communities make assumptions about the limits of rationality but are committed to using reason to its limits whenever possible.

When it comes to the true believers in fundamentalist religious communities and conspiracy theorists, however, both those inside and outside the religious movement or the conspiracy recognize the peculiarity of the belief system. Everyone knows what the conspiracy theorist or true believer adheres to is not part of the accepted normal. But the insiders, according to Crockford, "believe that in certain circumstances there are occulted dimensions to reality that only the initiated are aware of. Understanding is granted by initiation; the believer believes themselves to have access to knowledge that the unbeliever does not."

This type of worldview has the same effect for both conspiracy theorists and true believers (like those of us at the Johnsons' house on Friday nights). It teaches them never to trust what is front of their eyes. It instructs them to see invisible forces and hidden actors working to control the levers of power and the narrative of events while ignoring any explanation based in logic or evidence.

"The overall effect is the suggestion that what appears is not what is," Crockford writes. "There are invisible forces at work. Reality, especially as depicted in the mainstream media, is illusory because it is being consciously manipulated by those who hold power for their own gain."

While many religious traditions adhere to things unseen, they do not all instruct their devotees to ignore the apparent and the obvious, or to posit that their realities are being consciously manipulated by the powerful. Religious fundamentalisms and conspiracy theories do make such prescriptions, and this is what sets them apart. This is what the scholar of conspiracy theories Giovanna Parimigiani calls *dissensus*, or seeing differently. Though they are part of "private networks of belonging," the fellowship of those-who-know, members of conspiracy communities try to tear down the "partition" between their fringe worldview and what is held as acceptable forms of knowledge and authority in the public square. In other words, they want to take their fringe beliefs into the mainstream, turn the fantastical into the real and magic into science.

If you think you know the truth behind how the world functions, then you want to evangelize as many as will listen. There is a certain coherence to this impulse, which animates both current forms of White Christian nationalism in the United States and the White evangelical movement I was part of as a teenager. While part of the fun of those Friday night Bible studies was participating in a select group of initiates, the prevailing sentiment was the need to pull back the veil and enlighten as many people as possible to "what is really going on." This means not only spreading the word about the nearing end times but also working to legitimate your worldview in the public square. You become energized to change what is accepted as rational, true, and real. Unfortunately, conspiracy is now a mainstay in American politics.

The conspiracy theories driving MAGA Nation's war on America are multidimensional, and they have insinuated themselves into the everyday discourse of millions. The goal is to reshape what is real, rational, and true. Even if it has no basis in the facts.

WHITE CHRISTIANS AND QANON

It started with one post on October 28, 2017. A user on the online forum 4Chan, going by the handle "Q Clearance Patriot" and claiming to be a high-level official with access to top-secret information, posted that it was "the calm before the storm." Hillary Clinton would be arrested, the 4Chan user said, "between 7:45 and 8:30am EST on Monday morning, October 30th, 2017." From there, the web of theories spun out of control. Within months, followers of "Q" believed that then president Donald Trump was fighting a cabal of the global 1 percent who supposedly worshipped Satan, ran a global pedophile ring, and were working to topple the Trump administration before it could expose them. Scholar of QAnon Marc-André Argentino told me in 2020 that spin-off theories soon emerged: about space aliens, reptilian creatures masquerading as humans (Alex Jones famously said on his show "Infowars" that Hillary Clinton smelled like sulfur because she is a demon), underground military bases, and astral planes. The overriding frame of Q is the expectation that Trump will someday lead the "Storm," wherein the global network of elites, including his political opponents Hillary Clinton and Barack Obama, will be arrested and the shadow ring of conspirators will be brought to light.

Trump did nothing to discourage the conspiracies or downplay their delusory nature. In August 2020, when asked about QAnon conspiracists, the former president said, "These are people that love our country." When asked about the idea that he was saving the world from an elite cabal, Trump responded: "But is that supposed to be a bad thing or good thing? If I can help save the world from problems, I'm willing to do it. I'm willing to put myself out there."

He didn't stop there. In October 2020, Trump appeared at an NBC town hall. When asked about QAnon, he first claimed not to know anything about it but later added: "What I do hear about it is they are very strongly against pedophilia, and I agree with that. I mean I do agree with that, and I agree with it very strongly."

Before his Twitter account was suspended, Media Matters reports, Trump retweeted QAnon accounts 315 times. The conspiracy spread throughout the Republican Party. In 2020, forty-four candidates who espoused QAnon conspiracies ran for state or national office, and two won seats in the US Congress—Marjorie Taylor Greene and Lauren Boebert.

So how much overlap exists between QAnon conspiracies and the White Christian nationalist extremism at the center of our investigation? As we have seen in previous chapters, White Christian nationalists and the GOP are intimately entangled in contemporary American politics. So it's no surprise that many White Christians became ardent supporters of QAnon, supplementing their faith in Christ with their faith in Trump to rescue the world from a far-reaching satanic conspiracy. In a study by the sociologists Paul Djupe and Jacob Dennen, data shows that in 2020, 50.6 percent of nondenominational Christians believed in some aspects of the Q conspiracies.

"For most Evangelicals, there was some resonance," scholar of QAnon Marc-André Argentino told me in a 2020 interview. "It might bring them down into this path because these theories of QAnon—about satanic cults, the necessity of torture and killing of children for Satan, antivaccine and antiabortion narratives, baby farming for massive networks of satanic world leadership, spiritual warfare—a lot of these things echo what they've been told."

It might be tempting to try to separate QAnon Christians from Christian nationalism. After all, not all White Christians are Christian nationalists who believe the country was built for and by White Christians or that they should hold a privileged position in the country's political and cultural spheres. However, the data says otherwise.

"We found that Christian nationalism, support for QAnon, and anti-Semitism are linked," Djupe and Dennen write. "Among the 25 percent of our respondents who most strongly believed in Christian nationalism, 73 percent agreed with the substance of the QAnon conspiracy."

While the Christian dimensions of the QAnon conspiracy seemed surprising to some, deep historical precedents show the entanglement of White conservative Christians, conspiracy theorists, and GOP leadership since the 1960s. In every chapter of the New Religious Right's history, there has been a corresponding conspiracy theory that explains why their opponents are not just wrong about certain political issues but are actually malicious actors who are trying to destroy the country and its people of faith. Like the authoritarian tendencies we examined in the previous chapter, conspiracy theories are a bridge between White Christian nationalists and groups with resonant interests and worldviews. They are connective tissue in a network of movements that are connected by their belief that an overthrow of the current state of things is necessary to return the country—and the cosmos—to its natural order.

A LITANY OF CONSPIRACIES

In 1966, my father arrived on the mainland from Maui. He is a Japanese American guy who was raised in majority Asian communities. When he was growing up, White kids at his schools were the exceptions. His first home in California was a two-bedroom apartment in Los Angeles. He was a first-year college student at Cal State LA, but rather than living in a dorm with other people his age, he lived with his grandmother, mother, sister, brother-in-law, and two nephews. Seven people, four generations, all trying to make a life in a new place.

A childhood friend of my father's was attending Chapman University in Orange—the heart of Orange County, the overwhelmingly

White region where he would someday raise his family. Dad decided to visit her, making a thirty-mile drive from Los Angeles to the heart of Orange County. As he tells it, once he got off the freeway in Orange, he tensed up. After all, it was Orange County—not the kind of place you want to get pulled over if you're a person of color. To stay calm and focused, he kept up an inner monologue: Drive the speed limit. Don't swerve in the slightest. Keep your eyes forward.

My father had heard about the John Birch Society (JBS) and how they felt about outsiders. In his mind, Orange County was the epicenter of the JBS. He remembers wondering whether, if he got out of the car, they might jump out of the bushes to ambush him. Although he was new to the Southland, word had reached as far as Maui that Orange County was an extremely conservative place, one not so welcoming to those who looked a little different from most of the residents. Having grown up in a predominantly Asian American community in Hawaii, he was, for the first time, in a White-majority space, and he was afraid. My father didn't know the full history of the JBS as he drove that night. And even if he'd heard about their extreme politics, he surely didn't know the extent of the conspiracy theories behind them. But he intuited that their worldview made little room for someone like him.

John Birch was a Christian missionary to China who was killed by Chinese communist soldiers in 1945. For many, Birch became the face of a martyr: a faithful believer killed by communism's agenda to destroy both the United States and Christianity. A few years later, Robert Welch founded the John Birch Society as an anticommunist organization. From the beginning it was marked by a fierce libertarianism and vehement stance against taxes, government welfare programs, and civil rights reforms. It was also based on the idea that Christianity and American democracy go hand in hand.

"The John Birch Society is a group of Americans who have voluntarily joined together," Welch says in a grainy black-and-white promotional video from the early 1960s. He speaks with a peculiar cadence while sitting down and looking into the camera. He continues: "to restore with brighter luster and deeper conviction, the faith inspired morality, the spiritual sense of values and the ennobling aspirations on which our Western civilization has been built."

Members of the John Birch Society hosted small groups in their homes and were encouraged to invite friends and family to learn about the society's libertarian principles. In that sense, by using homegrown cells to cultivate and spread the movement, the society mimicked the growth strategies of the communists Welch despised so much.

Yet the John Birch Society went well beyond libertarian economics to dangerous conspiracy theories. Welch believed the Illuminati, a secret society, was founded in 1776 as a global puppet master, pulling strings behind the facade of national governments. This led him to conclude that communism and socialism were manifestations of the Illuminati's efforts to control the lives of every individual on earth through a united government. The society published numerous reports that accused civil rights organizers of communist sympathies. The JBS also, as scholar Christopher Towler notes, accused civil rights leaders of communist subversion while alleging that people of color were plotting to divide the country and control the world. Welch even suggested that Dwight Eisenhower and Chief Justice Earl Warren were communist agents trying to take down the government.

EXTREMISTS ARE THE NEW NORMAL

When we consider the hallmarks of GOP politics and White Christian doctrine during the Trump years, and particularly during the COVID pandemic, certain themes come to mind: denying science, not trusting authorities, blaming marginalized religious and racial communities for the country's problems, and decrying the "liberal agenda" in public school curricula. These political and cultural strains may have seemed to materialize out of nowhere, but they were planted in modern conservative politics half a century ago by the extremists of the John Birch Society and their allies. In ways that portended the conservative demonization of Black Lives Matter, Welch told JBS supporters that the civil rights movement was a communist conspiracy. Society members argued against the peaceful protests in order to support law enforcement. The JBS's attempt to build a campaign to impeach Justice Earl Warren was in some ways a harbinger of QAnon conspiracists' belief that high-ranking government officials are plotting against America. Finally, in ways resonant with so many strains of conspiracy and propaganda in contemporary American conservative spaces, the John Birch Society railed against the United Nations as a globalist institution ready to overthrow the American way of life through a one-world government.

Despite the fantastical nature of many of these doctrines and beliefs, the JBS had a tremendous effect on American electoral politics, just as QAnon had in the 2020 election and beyond. Many historians suggest that the Birch Society pushed Barry Goldwater to the Republican nomination in California. Though Goldwater detested Welch, he knew he needed rank-and-file Birchers in order to win the nomination—just as the contemporary GOP knows it needs QAnon adherents and other conspiracists now. Then and now, the party was willing to look the other way at some of the stranger aspects of extremism. "They believe in the Constitution, they believe in God, they believe in freedom," Goldwater said in early 1964. "I don't consider the John Birch Society as a group to be extremist," he added in April of that year.

The JBS drew on its network of homegrown cells, grassroots mobilization tactics, and a wide web of fearmongering messages to push the Arizona senator to California victory. Without the Golden State, Goldwater would have never emerged at the top of the Republican presidential ticket.

As we saw in chapter 5, the ascendance of Ronald Reagan was not a repudiation of the extremism of Goldwater's campaign. It was the outcome of the mainstreaming of the fringe in the GOP. Ronald

Reagan is now remembered in conservative circles as the modern standard of Republican politics: a class act whose legacy reverberates through the Bush dynasty and beyond, and the forefather presidential hopefuls mention as their hero. What's often forgotten is that Ronald Reagan, too, was profoundly influenced by the conspiracies of the John Birch Society. Rick Perlstein and Edward Miller report that Reagan claimed several fringe theories to be fact: that Gerald Ford faked assassination attempts to win votes and that the Soviet Union had moved twenty million people out of cities after nuclear fallout. One of his newsletters advocated for laetrile, a supposed wonder drug that Birchers claimed could cure cancer. And according to Perlstein and Miller, Reagan once told students at the White House that Lenin had espoused a grand plan to conquer America after rifling through the "hordes" of Asia—except Lenin never said it; Robert Welch did.

Reagan was not a conservative. He was an extremist who used his charm and carefully crafted rhetoric to convince the moderates in the GOP that when the time came, he would act like an adult rather than a rogue cowboy like Goldwater. Remember from chapter 5 that his presidency marked the crescendo of the New Religious Right's ascendance in American politics. They campaigned against the Southern Baptist Jimmy Carter in order to install the divorced Hollywood actor who used conspiracy theories to gain votes and win power, truth and reality be damned.

When Trump refused to denounce followers of Q, saying they "loved their country," he was taking a page from the Reagan playbook. When Trump regurgitated conspiracies about the Chinese government or millions of fraudulent votes, he was unwittingly mimicking the John Birch Society. And when, as the leader of the free world, he said at a White House press briefing that we should consider using bleach and ultraviolet rays "inside the body" to wipe out the coronavirus, he was echoing the quack advice not only of internet conspiracists but of the modern GOP's revered forefather: the Gipper himself.

SATANIC PANIC

The John Birch Society's network of conspiracies was not the only one prevalent in Reagan's America. In *Abusing Religion*, Megan Goodwin reminds us that in 1983, Reagan gave the infamous "evil empire" speech, in which he claimed the Soviet Union was diabolically trying to place the United States in a place of moral and military inferiority. Reagan, Goodwin observes, goes on to articulate the "crisis" facing the United States in a spiritual binary: "While America's military strength is important," the former president says, "let me add here that I've always maintained that the struggle now going on for the world will never be decided by bombs or rockets, by armies or military might. The real crisis we face today is a spiritual one; at root, it is a test of moral will and faith."

The speech was given to the National Association of Evangelicals, which explains the heavy use of religious imagery and references. While the Soviet Union is set up as the godless enemy threatening the country, Reagan's comments came in the context of what many took to be an internal spiritual struggle happening in small towns and suburbs all over the country. There was a heightened sensitivity among White evangelicals and other Americans to anything supposedly related to the occult, spiritual warfare, or New Age spirituality. It set the context for what became known as the "satanic panic."

In 1980, the same year Reagan ran against Jimmy Carter, *Michelle Remembers* became an instant best seller. It's a "memoir" by Michelle Smith, who supposedly worked with her therapist (and eventual husband) to recover memories of her captivity and abuse at the hand of satanists.

As I've chronicled in the foregoing chapters, those in the New Religious Right saw the 1960s as having ignited a set of revolutions in American politics and culture that had to be stopped. At the center of the culture wars were issues of sex and gender—the Equal Rights Amendment, women in the workforce, abortion, LGBTQ+ rights, and the sexual revolution. Falwell, Weyrich, and their cohorts had primed their followers for battle. They saw external threats to the United States, evil forces in the forms of communist China and the Soviet Union. They saw opponents to their agenda as internal threats trying to destroy their way of life. Thus, when *Michelle Remembers* appeared, it encapsulated the "spiritual warfare" facing a nation, one that the New Religious Right perceived to be falling away from God and its religious founding. For many, it was not a large step from viewing those who disagreed with them as un-American to imagining them as sexual abusers determined to capture young women for Satan.

I remember the church staff meetings in which the children's pastor presented her findings that the Harry Potter books became darker and darker as the series developed, eventually approaching the line of promoting the occult. I recall parents prohibiting their children from playing Dungeons and Dragons and debating whether or not they should be allowed to listen to Christian rock music because even that could be deemed a weapon in Satan's attacks.

But as Goodwin reports, the hysteria wasn't limited to evangelical church staff meetings. The panic reached beyond the walls of evangelical churches. "Nightly news programs warned parents about the dangers of hard rock and heavy metal music," Goodwin writes, "thought to contain 'backmasked' messages that, when played in reverse, would encourage listeners to hail Satan." And throughout the eighties and early nineties, the FBI, TV hosts, and members of Congress all investigated the claim that a ring of satanic actors were trying to corrupt American children and in extreme cases hold them prisoner as sexual slaves.

"The criminal investigation lasted almost a decade and was at its height, the longest and most expensive criminal trial in US history," Goodwin told me in a 2021 interview. "The FBI spent almost a million dollars trying to prove that some sort of global satanic conspiracy was attacking mostly white women and children. And millions were donated to organizations like Believe the Children."

The problem? There were no findings of widespread satanic abuse across the United States. The investigations were almost completely in vain. Despite hundreds of cases, dozens of book tours, and extensive Senate deliberation, it turned out that the satanic panic was built on a delusion. There was no Satan behind the panic.

FROM BIRTH CERTIFICATES TO PIZZA PARLORS

Andy Martin went to law school but never became a lawyer. His admission to the bar, according to the *New York Times*, was blocked because of a psychiatric report that described him as having a "moderately severe character defect manifested by well-documented ideation with a paranoid flavor and a grandiose character." By 2004, Martin had gotten involved in politics. After Obama's famous speech at the Democratic convention—the speech that vaulted him to the national stage and into widespread conversation as a potential presidential candidate—Martin wrote a press release at Free Republic. In the document, Martin states that "Obama is a Muslim who has concealed his religion." Martin also claimed falsely that when Obama swore in for office, he did so on the "Kuran," rather than the Bible. In his book *Obama: The Man behind the Mask*, Martin speculates about the former president's birth certificate. Martin wanted Obama's senate seat in Illinois and was trying to gain traction in the campaign—one of many failed campaigns for senate and president Martin has run in his adult life.

Martin's campaign for the Illinois senate seat went nowhere, and legitimate media outlets ignored his claims. But right-wing blogs and outlets picked them up. Soon the "Obama is a Muslim" falsehood became an underground chain-email sent around among family members, coworkers, and friends—the type of email that provides no real evidence but seems, to certain eyes, to be legitimate and based on real research. One person posted it on FreeRepublic.com and commented: "Don't know who the original author is, but this e-mail should be sent out to family and friends."

By the time Obama ran for president in 2008, Martin's insinuations about Obama's religion, birth certificate, and desire to overthrow the American government became a common talking point among the Illinois senator's opponents. In the years after 9/11, Islamophobia was dominating right-wing media. But when Obama ran for the highest office in the land, conservative conspiracy theorists set their sights on a new internal enemy. The son of a White woman from Kansas and a Kenyan-born immigrant, Obama was the perfect target for the xenophobia and racism that anchor White Christian nationalism.

In September 2008, Fox News aired "Obama & Friends: The History of Radicalism," a program that "investigated" the claims of the "birthers," who asserted—falsely—that Obama was not born in the United States and that therefore an Obama presidency would be unconstitutional. These were people who took Martin's questioning of Obama's birth certificate to a new level by questioning whether he was born in the United States. With Sean Hannity as host, the show featured a conversation with Andy Martin, in which he repeats the lie that he first propagated in 2004. He adds that Obama's community organizing work on the South Side of Chicago—during which Obama lobbied for the development of an employment center, demanded asbestos be cleaned up in public housing facilities, and worked to expand healthcare to low-income residents—was "training for a radical overthrow of the government." Neither Hannity nor anyone else on the program challenge Martin's claims. It was watched by nearly three million people.

The birther conspiracy only grew when Obama took office. In 2009, figures like Liz Cheney, Rush Limbaugh, and Lou Dobbs discussed in serious terms and in public whether the claims of the birthers might indeed be credible. One soldier even challenged his deployment overseas because he asserted that he couldn't take orders from a man born outside the United States claiming to be commander in chief.

Not to be outdone by politicians, soldiers, and pundits, Franklin Graham—son of Billy Graham and a prominent figure in White evangelical culture—said this about Obama in August 2009: "He was born a Muslim. His father was a Muslim; the seed of Muslim is passed through the father like the seed of Judaism is passed through the mother. He was born a Muslim; his father gave him an Islamic name."

Before long, the birther conspiracy and the claim that Obama is a Muslim had spread far beyond its origins in Martin's brain. By 2010, according to a CBS/*New York Times* poll, only 58 percent of Americans believed Obama was born in this country. One out of five believed he was born elsewhere.

Soon the real estate mogul and reality star Donald Trump joined the birther fray. In 2011, Trump revived the birther conspiracy by talking about it endlessly wherever and whenever possible. He gave interviews to Fox and other television outlets, called into radio shows to talk about it, and gave quotes to print journalists. Trump claimed that he had his people looking into the president's birth certificate, and in typical Trumpian fashion, he hinted—but never demonstrated—that there were shocking secrets to be revealed. When Obama released his long-form birth certificate in 2011, Trump claimed victory. "I've accomplished something that nobody else has been able to accomplish," he said. "He should have done it a long time ago."

Trump then quickly dismissed the form as potentially falsified and in need of more investigation.

THERE IS NO ANSWER

There was never going to be a satisfactory answer for Trump, of course, or for the conspiracy-believing public who rallied behind him. The goal of the birthers was not to discover the facts of the matter. Their mission was always, as journalist Michael Scherer says, to provide an "emotionally satisfying" explanation for White people as to how a Black man with a Black wife and a name like "Barack Hussein Obama" could become leader of the free world. As my podcast cohost Dan Miller says, Trump became the id of a White, and largely Christian, American populace that wanted someone to express their frustration about the country's "decline." They longed for a mouthpiece unafraid to point the finger at immigrants, people of color, and religious minorities. Obama became the canvas for this vitriol, a symbol that could hold all the vectors of rage in one focused target: the son of an immigrant and Muslim; a Black man; and a biracial child raised in Hawaii, that island state that, in the minds of many Americans, is barely part of the country, a kind of foreign entity somehow included in the Union.

When it came to faith, many White Americans doubted Obama's Christianity on the basis that his father was an immigrant and a Muslim and that he is a biracial person, a supposed socialist, and thus a traitor to the United States. His professions of Christian faith, church attendance, and hymn-singing did nothing to dissuade his opponents from calling Obama a seditious actor and a mole sent to destroy America.

Ultimately, the birther conspiracy was never about whether the forty-fourth president of the United States was born in this country. It was, as journalist Adam Serwer says, a "statement of values" and an expression of "allegiance" to a certain vision of the United States. It represented the desire of White Americans to return to a time when their power and authority were unquestioned—a time before the revolutions of the sixties transformed American culture by expanding civil rights and legal protections to religious, racial, sexual, and gender minorities.

Viewed through this long history of conspiratorial delusions, Trump wasn't something out of nowhere. He was *the* thing that many White Americans—and especially White Christian nationalists—had been looking for since Goldwater's defeat in 1964. The story of Trump's unlikely road to the presidency is well known by now. His ascendancy was made up of many moving parts: from the attacks on Hillary Clinton, to the Russian disinformation campaigns, to the failure of GOP leadership to disavow him like they did George Wallace in the sixties, and so on. But there is a key element that shouldn't be missed: His whole campaign was built on a conspiracy designed to enable White Americans, and particularly White Christian nationalists, to regain the privilege of determining the real, the true, and the factual in the American political and cultural systems. The story of birtherism became the basis for a movement based on grievance and malice. Birtherism, and the presidential campaign built on it, was a revenge tale not unlike a horror movie, where an aggrieved man takes out his rage on anyone in his path—especially the women and people of color who dare to challenge him.

RUNNING ON ALTERNATIVE FACTS

Nothing has stopped the conservative conspiracy engine that has been chugging since the 1960s and that Trump set into overdrive. The grievance and rage have been channeled into other conspiracies. When Russian hackers broke into John Podesta's emails in 2016, no one expected that they would be the basis for "Pizzagate." Podesta was then the head of Hillary Clinton's presidential campaign, and when his emails went public, conspiracists noted his communication with the owner of a Washington, DC, pizzeria called Comet Ping Pong. In one email Podesta proposes a fundraiser for Clinton at the restaurant. Soon some Trump supporters latched onto the idea that the owners of the pizzeria were working with Podesta, Clinton, and others to traffic children as sex slaves. Supposedly dozens of children were locked in Comet Ping Pong's basement.

The pizzeria doesn't have a basement, and even when the owner, James Alefantis, invited some protesters to come inside to see, they still didn't believe him. Within a year, a man had showed up at Comet Ping Pong, armed with a gun and ready to take down the ring of sex traffickers he believed were hiding children in the nonexistent cellar. One family's business was subjected to months of angry protesters and an armed invader because of a fantasy created from an email.

Things only got worse during the 2020 election. Like Goldwater had done in his treatment of the Birchers, Trump did nothing to thwart the QAnon conspiracy and welcomed the adulation of its adherents. This encouraged QAnon believers to make their voices heard by running for office. Dozens of QAnon candidates ran for local, state, and national positions. By December 2020, one poll showed that nearly one-third of Americans believed in some aspect of the Q conspiracy. Three of the candidates in California's 2021 gubernatorial recall election expressed support for Q in some fashion.

All of this means that Americans are living in separate realities. Many believe there is a global cabal of sex-trafficking, Satan-worshipping elites who run the world. Some still believe Obama was born in another country. Some adhere to the idea that the Illuminati are operating out of a pizzeria in an upper-class neighborhood in the District of Columbia.

But the most damaging falsehood is Trump's Big Lie: his claim that he won the 2020 election and that it was stolen from him through voter fraud and other tricks by Joe Biden and the Democratic party. In some ways the Big Lie is the progeny of all the previous conspiracy theories that envisioned some nefarious network secretly running the government. In other ways it gives legitimacy to the QAnon conspiracy and others, because the Big Lie gives ballast to the claim that a group of elites is running the government fraudulently behind the country's back.

THE PRAGMATIC FUNCTION OF CONSPIRACIES

Conspiracy theories are ways for groups at the margins—or who feel as if they are at the margins—to gain power and authority by changing the narrative surrounding truth and reality in the political realm. For some within end-times conspiracy communities, the theories about the end of the world and "what's really going on" are explanations for their sense of suffering and helplessness in a world that doesn't accept or understand them. Others take it a step further: If they can legitimate their claims about grand schemes by global elites and new world orders, they can flip the board, topple the system, and gain power.

Taken together, these components of conspiracy theories explain why so many White Christian nationalists have been prone to participating in them over the last half century. It makes sense that religious groups who believe that the media is "too liberal," that the government is out to get them, and that the antichrist is already walking among us are prone to conspiracies about election fraud, birth certificates, and pizza parlors.

But there's a special ingredient to White Christian nationalists' proclivity for conspiracy. This is the group who believes America was founded as a "Christian nation," and who thus believes it has the right to maintain the top spots of American politics and culture. When they feel their influence and power dwindling, conspiracies become a tool for reasserting their worldview as legitimate. In these instances, they are a group used to privilege, and they are trying to hold on to it by changing the standards of the real and true. They believe they have a God-given right to hold power in the United States. That belief extends beyond winning elections and making policy. It goes all the way to deciding what is real and what isn't. The details of the QAnon and Pizzagate conspiracies may seem comical, but they are insidious in nature. For those on the outside looking in, one of the hardest parts to grasp is comprehending that many people actually believe their core tenets. They are not playacting. They are not pretending.

When I listened to Tony exegete the book of Revelation as a high school senior, I didn't think we were just doing story time. His teachings about the antichrist shaped my worldview. They gave me the foundation to go out into my community and do what seemed like strange and awkward things—like walk up to strangers at public places and ask them if they knew where they would spend eternity.

Since 2020, the Big Lie has shaped the worldview of tens of millions of Americans. It is propagated by a man, Donald Trump, who many of them believe was anointed by God to rescue America. His words and actions give them the basis to do radical and extreme things—like overrun the US Capitol in order to stop an election.

Chapter 9

INSURRECTION

THE BATTLE OF JERICHO is one of those Bible stories you come back to often as a youth pastor because it pretty much teaches itself. So many passages of the Bible seem impossible to relate to modern life, especially when your audience is a hundred middle schoolers who have yet to figure out deodorant or shaving. What are you going to tell eighth graders about prohibitions against eating shellfish in Leviticus or pages-long genealogies in Genesis? The dirty secret of being a youth pastor is that you skip those parts of scripture in order to get to the stories that you can use to inspire a young generation to commit their lives to the Lord.

During my seven years in ministry, I must have expounded on the tale of Daniel in the lion's den a hundred times. The same goes for the story of Shadrach, Meshach, and Abednego, the three comrades who emerged unscathed after King Nebuchadnezzar threw them into a furnace. The easiest one was David versus Goliath. Anyone should be able to use that story to teach a kid some lessons about standing up for your community, not letting bullies get their way, or the underrated deadliness of slingshots.

The battle of Jericho is in this category of easily teachable Bible tales. According to Joshua 6, the Israelites were descending on the land of Canaan, which God had promised to their forebears. After forty years in the desert and four hundred years in Egyptian captivity, they were ready to take what God had granted them—a whole territory of land occupied by another people group. After some initial skirmishes with the Canaanites, the Hebrew people had their first major conflict: the battle for Jericho. As instructed by God, the Israelites marched around the city walls seven times, shouting the name of their deity and blowing horns as they repeated the circle. After the seventh time, the walls miraculously fell down, allowing the Israelites to enter and besiege Jericho, leaving little trace of the people who called it home.

When I taught this story, the easiest pedagogical strategy was to spiritualize it. The lessons were about obeying God even when the world thought doing so was crazy or trusting in God's commands more than secular logic. I encouraged the students to think about what "walls" in our lives God wanted us to allow him to knock down—pride, envy, lust, or anger. What sins were holding us back? Did we have the radical faith to obey him even when it appeared foolish to unbelievers?

We rarely spent time on the gory details of what happened once the Israelites entered Jericho: "When the trumpets sounded, the army shouted, and at the sound of the trumpet, when the men gave a loud shout, the wall collapsed; so everyone charged straight in, and they took the city. They devoted the city to the Lord and destroyed with the sword every living thing in it—men and women, young and old, cattle, sheep and donkeys" (Joshua 6:20–21). And even though I shied away from deliberating over what some have called an attempted genocide, there was always a kid or two who wanted to know why God would allow such a brutal destruction of life.

"Did the kids need to be killed?" they would ask. The first time it happened I looked at the kid blankly. Simultaneously impressed with the question and having no clue how to answer it, I stumbled around and probably tried to evade the implications of the question. Eventually, I turned to biblical commentators to help me make sense of it.

Here is how Andy Patton frames it at the Bible Project, a ministry resource guide that has over two million subscribers and more than 100 million views on its various video channels: "The conquest was more about ending the Canaanites' religious and cultural practices than ending their lives. The problem wasn't the people, but idolatry. . . . It could be compared to what the Allies set out to do during World War II. They were on a mission to end the Nazi regime, but that didn't mean they had to kill every German. . . . They were a part of God's plan to cleanse the land of evil practices and push back the dark spiritual powers that had enslaved the people of Canaan."

I am familiar with this type of exegetical gymnastics. I learned—and employed—such tactics as a pastor many times. For me, as for most evangelical leaders, the overriding goal was to make scripture relevant to everyday life. What's clear to me now, though, is just how blithe this type of explanation is when it comes to confronting the violence in the story of Jericho.

If God and the Israelites didn't want to kill all the Canaanites, why did they? If it wasn't about ending lives but abolishing idols, why did all the lives have to be ended? If the Hebrew people wanted to push back the spiritual powers enslaving the people, did they have to kill all the people in the process?

Ultimately, I doubt all of the inquisitive kids in my youth group found any of my attempts at answering their valid questions to be satisfactory. A literal reading of the Bible is less intellectually taxing than a coherent one. A few decades after I led those Bible studies, the story of the felling of the walls of Jericho would become a basis for Christian nationalist performance of grievance in ways that made the plain reading of the text—as the story of a God-ordained holy war against infidels—explode into national view.

FROM JOSHUA 6 TO JANUARY 6

On December 12, 2020, nearly a month before the January 6 insurrection, the first "Jericho Marches" took place across the country. Though there were events at numerous state capitols, the main march took place in Washington, DC. With pageantry and scripture and prayer, Christian nationalists reenacted portions of the story of Joshua and his troops as they marched around a pagan city.

The founders of the Jericho March represent the powerful Christian nationalist alliance between White evangelicals and White Catholics that has formed over the last half century. Cofounder Robert Weaver is an evangelical who identifies as a Pentecostal. The Oklahoma insurance salesman was nominated by Trump to lead the Indian Health Service in 2018 but withdrew his candidacy due to revelations about his misrepresentation of his supposed Native American heritage. He got the idea for the Jericho March in a vision from God, in which the Almighty told him that the election "is not over" and that he wants to "let the church roar!"

His cofounder, Arina Grossu, is a conservative Catholic who had a similar vision. A former contract communications adviser at the Department of Health and Human Services, Grossu had a vision of "people praying in the streets," beseeching God for election integrity, truth, and a restoration of American values. The daughter of Romanian immigrants, Grossu says part of her motivation for organizing the march was to avoid the communist oppression her family endured before emigrating to the United States.

In their press release for the December 12 event, Weaver and Grossu drew on classic Christian nationalist tropes to encourage "patriots and people of faith" to "march around the U.S. Capitol, Supreme Court, and Department of Justice seven times praying for the walls of corruption and election fraud to fall down, just as Joshua and the Israelites walked around the walls of corrupt Jericho." According to Weaver and Grossu, "America is a gift entrusted to us by our creator and a republic secured by our Founding Fathers and those who sacrificed to keep us free." In their vision, MAGA Nation plays the role of Israel in the reenactment of the Jericho story. Washington, DC, and the institutions it houses are cast as the corrupt city inhabited by infidels who must be removed.

Thousands of people gathered in DC for the main event. Just as the organizers hoped, they marched around the holy places of the American republic—the Supreme Court, the Capitol, and the Department of Justice. Eric Metaxas, author and radio host turned MAGA superstar, served as the emcee of the main rally at the National Mall. During the five hours or so of programming, one of the most popular (and infamous) speakers was General Michael Flynn, the man who was convicted of lying to the FBI and then pardoned by former president Trump. "Courts aren't going to decide who the next president is going to be," Flynn proclaimed ominously. "We the people decide."

At one point, Marine One flew over the rally (there's no verification that Trump was actually in the helicopter) and then came a series of presentations by religious leaders, who bathed the crowd in Christian nationalist rhetoric. Father Greg Gramovich, a specialist in exorcism, gave a prayer meant to exorcise the spirits of corruption from Washington, DC. "You realize we are in a spiritual battle. This cannot be solved by human needs," he told the crowd just before encouraging them to put on the full "armor of God" in order to prepare for the days ahead. Later, Archbishop Carlo Maria Viganò married Christian nationalism with themes from QAnon. "We are the silent army of the children of light," he said, on the large screen overlooking the rally. "The walls of the deep state, behind which evil is barricaded, will come crashing down."

Soon the provocateurs took the stage. Alex Jones, the disgraced host of Info Wars, gave one of his notorious screaming rants. He didn't so much speak as send bundles of non sequiturs to the audience in order to activate their anger and grievance. "God is on our side. . . . The state has no jurisdiction over any of us," he belted. When it came to President-Elect Joe Biden, Jones was clear that "we will never recognize him." He then gave a dire warning: "Joe Biden will be removed one way or another." In order to coat this rhetoric in religious authority, Jones finished with a call for the MAGA faithful to keep their attention on the Lord: "We need to keep our eyes on Christ and never back down and never surrender."

A few minutes later Ali Alexander, the organizer of "Stop the Steal"—the campaign that would help mobilize the lie that Trump won the election—sent a message to all Republicans in Congress who wouldn't help Pence overturn the election: "I don't have a speech as much as I have a warning to the establishment. We will shut this country down." Drawing on the Joshua-Jericho theme of the rally, Alexander prophesied that "We will occupy D.C.," because, "We can do all things through Christ who strengthens us," a direct citation of Philippians 4:13—a popular Bible passage among conservative Christians.

When the "prayer" rally ended, the Proud Boys and other groups spread throughout downtown DC, wreaking havoc and instigating violence. They vandalized numerous historic Black churches, tearing down Black Lives Matter flags and causing other damage. According to reports, four people were stabbed and thirty-three were arrested. In the spirit of the Israelites who violently seized Jericho after their prayer walk, MAGA Nation descended on DC the night of December 12. The violence of that night, of course, turned out to be only a preview of what was ahead.

After the success of the first Jericho March on December 12, a second round of marches was planned for January 5, 2021, to take place in DC and in the swing states where there was supposed election fraud. This was, of course, the day before the certification of the electoral votes—a formality in the presidential election process with no bearing on the election result or power to change its outcome. Before the event kicked off, the Jericho March organizers released a statement outlining what they hoped would happen on January 6: "Vice President Pence has the ability to elect the President himself and Jericho March calls on him to exercise his rightful power in the face of the blatant election fraud and corruption."

What is striking about this call—even if you were to support the theory behind it—is that it doesn't say that Vice President Pence has the ability to throw out fraudulent electors who misrepresent the will of the people in their states. It says he has the power "to elect the President himself"—as if the goal is not a democratic outcome but the installation of the man they want regardless of the process or the cost.

On Tuesday, January 5, thousands of "Joshuas" once again gathered to pray that God would "stop the steal" and restore Trump to the presidency. This time the prayer for the walls to come down was the direct precursor to the actual invasion of America's Jericho.

JANUARY 6, 2021

Leandra Blades is a blond woman in her forties with a high-pitched voice and a straightforward demeanor. She speaks plainly but assertively. Leandra attends Friends Church in Yorba Linda, the sister church of Rose Drive where I once served in ministry—and the church where Dr. Marshburn threw the American flag out of the sanctuary a century ago. A former youth soccer coach and classroom helper, Leandra was elected to the Placentia-Yorba Linda Unified School District's board in 2020. This is the school district I attended from kindergarten through high school. Some of my friends now teach in the district. Dozens of people I went to school with now have their kids enrolled in one of the district's elementary, middle, or high schools. It's an institution dear to my heart, and one that continues to play an integral part in my loved ones' lives.

Leandra flew to Washington, DC, on January 4, 2021, with two friends for what she described later as a "girls' trip." As a supporter of Donald Trump, she planned to visit DC at this moment so that she and her friends could attend the rally on January 6. Though she had visited a few summers prior, neither of her friends had ever been to DC. They landed on Monday and had a full day of sightseeing on Tuesday. She described the trip as akin to a teenage slumber party with friends but with wine. Leandra was surprised to meet so many other Orange Countians in their hotel and marveled at making so many new acquaintances on such a short vacation.

Southern Californians aren't used to any weather below fifty degrees, so the cold Washington morning was probably a shock to their systems. Though there was no snow or sleet on Wednesday, January 6, the air was frigid. It was also extremely windy. The three women woke in their comfy hotel room in the "District," as locals refer to DC. Unaccustomed to dealing with cold temperatures, they bundled up and left their hotel to fulfill a dream of joining MAGA Nation for the Save America rally.

As the rally waned, the thousands of people gathered for the event began marching toward the Capitol at Trump's behest. Leandra and her friends were caught up in the crowd and marched with them to the Capitol. Soon they sensed tear gas in the air and commotion ringing through the throngs of people. No matter what she would later claim, Leandra was no longer on a "girls' trip." She was part of the crowd marching on her own country's Capitol to stop the certification of the 2020 presidential election.

January 6, 2021, is a day of infamy, a day that marks a Before and an After in American history, similar to the bombing of Pearl Harbor or 9/11. The difference with J6 is that the attack was by a mob of Americans incited by the sitting president rather than a foreign enemy.

After months of listening to Trump and his political cronies repeat the falsehood that the election was stolen, tens of thousands of Trump supporters like Leandra and her friends gathered in DC to express their outrage while Congress and the vice president certified the election results. By this time, Trump's dozens of legal attempts to have votes thrown out in Pennsylvania, Arizona, and other states had failed in the courts. His illegal pressuring of Georgia's attorney general and other state officials had also failed. Unable to overthrow the election by way of the courts or state legislators, he turned to the mob as one of the last weapons in his arsenal.

On the morning of January 6, Leandra and thousands of others gathered to hear Trump and other MAGA superstars speak at the Save America rally at the Ellipse, an open space near the National Mall. Before the former president took the stage, his spiritual adviser Paula White gave the opening prayer. "I declare that you would give us a holy boldness in this hour," she exclaimed. "Today let justice be done." Rudy Giuliani used his time on stage to foment violence. "Let's have a trial by combat," the disgraced former mayor of New York City said.

After MAGA celebrities such as Representative Mo Brooks and Donald Trump Jr. did their part to rile the crowd into a frenzy, former President Trump encouraged everyone in attendance to walk the short distance to the Capitol. "Anyone you want, but I think right here, we're going to walk down to the Capitol, and we're going to cheer on our brave senators and congressmen and women, and we're probably not going to be cheering so much for some of them," Trump said. "Because you'll never take back our country with weakness. You have to show strength and you have to be strong. We have come to demand that Congress do the right thing and only count the electors who have been lawfully slated, lawfully slated."

After arriving at the Capitol, the mob quickly turned violent. Waving MAGA flags and donning MAGA apparel, members of the mob began assaulting Capitol Police with pieces of broken barricades and other makeshift weapons. They pushed past the police line, broke windows in order to enter the Capitol, and once inside began searching for the politicians they considered to be enemies of the republic—Vice President Mike Pence, Speaker of the House Nancy Pelosi, Representative Alexandria Ocasio-Cortez, and others. Millions of Americans turned on their televisions to see Trump flags waving from the Capitol and MAGA-ites storming the building's every nook and cranny. Meanwhile members of Congress donned gas masks, huddled down between seats while Capitol Police barricaded the doors and literally prayed for safety before running for cover. Vice President Pence, the man on whom Trump and MAGA Nation was counting to overturn the election, was moved quickly to a secure—and secret—location. Congressional staffers, some in their mid-twenties, hid under desks in locked offices, contemplating whether or not to text their parents goodbye for the last time.

The country watched in horror as the rioters breached every part of the Capitol—defecating in the halls, stealing documents, putting their feet up on the desk of the Speaker of the House, and shouting in victory after having stopped, albeit briefly, the certification of the election. Outside, in one of the most chilling scenes, insurrectionists erected gallows in order to hang Mike Pence for not overturning the election for Trump. In another, a man marches with the Confederate flag on his shoulder—a symbol of the White supremacy that was at the heart of the attempted coup.

Capitol Police officer Brian Sicknick died in his office after responding to the riot. Later, four additional Capitol Police officers would die by suicide. The Capitol Police Union reports that 140 officers were injured as a result of the mob violence. Capitol Police officer Harry Dunn, an African American, testified before Congress that while he had never been called the n-word while in uniform, that changed on January 6. He heard similar stories from his Black colleagues. "One officer told me he had never in his entire 40 years life been called a n—— to his face and that streak ended on January 6. Yet another Black officer later told me he had been confronted by insurrectionists in the Capitol who told him, 'Put your gun down, and we'll show you what kind of n—— you really are.'" Officer Dunn's testimony confirms that the mob who attacked the Capitol was not only Christian nationalist but also overtly White supremacist.

It was nearly midnight when Andy Kim, a Democratic representative from New Jersey, made it back to the Capitol rotunda on

January 6. When the siege happened, he was in a separate building, so he didn't see the wreckage until the waning moments of the day. "I was just overwhelmed with emotion," Kim said. "It's a room that I love so much—it's the heart of the Capitol, literally the heart of this country. It pained me so much to see it in this kind of condition."

For the next couple of hours Kim worked on his hands and knees to clean up the debris left by the rioters. There is now a famous picture of Representative Kim on all fours, scooping up a pile of trash in the Capitol rotunda. He worked in stunned silence, overcome by the damage to the building—and to American democracy—done in only a few hours. Outside the streets were largely quiet. DC was a city under curfew after Trump's White Christian nationalist mob laid siege to the Capitol. An eerie quiet, similar to Kim's mood, had overtaken the District. The city and the nation were in shock. Inside the building, Kim, the son of Korean immigrants and only the second Korean American to serve in Congress, was cleaning up their mess before joining his congressional colleagues to certify the 2020 presidential election.

When I turn my attention from Representative Andy Kim back to Leandra Blades, the story of January 6 hits home. Leandra looks like my mom—and countless other Orange County moms I knew growing up. She reminds me of my mom when she was that age in other ways too: someone who may appear unassuming by appearance but who is formidable and forthright when it comes to her beliefs—and certainly when it comes to standing up for her family. Leandra is a former police officer who decided to run for school board as a way to serve her community. Her kids attend the public schools in the district my brothers and I attended. On Sundays, she sits in the pews at Yorba Linda Friends Church. In many ways, her story maps onto mine. When I reflect on whether I would have been at the rally on January 6, I think of Leandra: an active and dedicated member of the suburban community in which I grew up—someone who saw, and still sees, nothing wrong with supporting the president she voted for by attending a rally where he called on his supporters to overthrow the American government and the outcome of a free and fair election. When asked about her presence there, Leandra claimed that it was an unfortunate coincidence that she and her friends chose this rally, on this day, at this moment in history, that just so happened to boil over into an attempted coup d'etat. In her telling, attending a rally framed as an attempt to stop the certification of a presidential election was just part of a normal tourist visit.

It's not the maliciousness or cunning of Leandra Blades that plagues me. It's the banality of her actions and rationale. It's the ordinariness of her thought patterns. She is not exceptional. She is not a super villain who wakes up every morning with the hopes of tearing apart the country piece by piece. She's a suburban parent in her forties who did what she thought was right seemingly without considering how it might hurt others or how it might contribute to the destruction of our republic. In terms of the region where I grew up, she's pretty average. And that scares the hell out of me.

#CAPITOLSIEGERELIGION

As soon as video and images of the insurrection became available, scholars of religion began archiving the religious artifacts present at the riot. Writer and Smithsonian curator Peter Manseau started #capitolsiegereligion in order to archive them under one hashtag.

Examining these artifacts, you can't help but notice the pervasiveness of Christian imagery, symbols, rituals at the insurrection. The video and photographs show that Trump flags of various kinds waving throughout the mob, but mixed into the crowd are various religious banners. One of the most popular was "Jesus Is My Savior, Trump Is My President." Other images show people waving "Jesus Saves" and "God, Guts, Guns" flags throughout the crowd. In one landscape photo showing a facade of the Capitol overrun by rioters, the Christian flag flies amid a sea of Confederate flags, Gadsen flags (a rattlesnake and the inscription "Don't Tread on Me" on a yellow background), and Trump flags.

At least one rioter carried the Deus Vult flag—a red medieval cross on a white background. As the scholar of religion Matthew Gabriele observes it, "The red cross on a white field was supposedly the uniform of the medieval Christian crusaders, exemplified perhaps best in the military religious order of the Knights Templar—a group founded in the early 12th century as a kind of permanent warrior class to defend the frontiers of Christendom against its perceived enemies." At the insurrection, it underscored the way in which the White Christians in attendance saw themselves as warriors, protecting the nation.

Flags weren't the only religious artifacts manifest at the insurrection. Some of the most violent perpetrators wore vest patches with a portion of Psalm 144 that read "Blessed be God, My Rock Who Trains My Hands for Battle, My Fingers for War." One man wore a biker-style leather jacket that read "God, Guns, and Trump." Some rioters went the extra backbreaking mile to cart around statues of Mary and Jesus as they paraded in and around the Capitol. At least one person improvised by attaching a large crucifix to a Trump flag. Others carried paintings. There was one of a White Nordic-looking Christ with the inscription "Jesus I Trust in You." One rioter put all their cards on the table by carrying around a large poster of a European-looking Jesus wearing a MAGA hat.

And those gallows? Close-up images show the inscriptions that rioters left on the frame: "God Bless America" and "In God We Trust." Next to these inscriptions someone else wrote "Amen," agreeing with the sentiments written on an instrument meant to assassinate the vice president of the United States.

"By building the gallows, they signaled that they were done with democracy," writes the scholar of evangelicalism Anthea Butler. "Murder was the only way they could put Trump back into office. Rather than prayer, rather than engaging in a democratic process in the next election, murder was the choice they made."

In contrast to the murderous spirit in the air, the insurrection was marked by impromptu praise and prayer sessions. It wasn't that rioters chose one or the other. Rather, the insurrectionists used prayer and other rituals to justify murderous intention. Every time the mob crossed a new boundary—past another police barricade or through another doorway or up a flight of steps—certain rioters stopped to pray and thank God. One video clip shows a dozen or so people gathered on the Capitol lawn, near the police barrier, singing along with Kari Jobe's "Revelation Song," a popular praise and worship song in White evangelical congregations. In the frame, a woman wears a Trump flag as a cape while she sings, her hands raised over her head. Once rioters advanced past security and to the boundary of the building, they stopped to pray again. Couy Griffin, a county commissioner from Otero County, New Mexico, and founder of "Cowboys for Trump," led a throng of rioters in prayer, claiming the sacred space of American democracy in the name of patriots and their God. After he breached Capitol security barriers, Griffin used his bullhorn to pray and proclaim January 6 "a great day for America."

In the Senate Chamber, the infamous QAnon Shaman, Jacob Angeli—shirtless, wearing horns on his head, adorned with blue face paint, and carrying an American flag on a spear—led the rioters in prayer: "Let's all say a prayer in this sacred space," he said, as he gathered them on and around the Senate dais. "Thank you, Heavenly Father, for this opportunity to stand up for our God-given inalienable rights," he prayed. "To all the tyrants, the communists, the globalists: this is our nation, not theirs. We will not allow the American way to go down. Thank you for filling this chamber with patriots that love you." After praying, Angeli left a note for then vice president Pence that read, "It's only a matter of time, justice is coming."

One of the most visible religious symbols throughout the riot was the shofar, an ancient instrument made from the horn of an animal such as a ram and used in Jewish religious rituals. In recent decades Pentecostal Christians like the event organizer Robert Weaver, as well as My Pillow CEO Mike Lindell and Trump's spiritual adviser Paula White have adopted the shofar in worship, appropriating it from Jewish rituals as a weapon of spiritual warfare meant to ward off God's enemies. The scholar of religion Leah Payne notes the significance of the numerous shofars on display at the January 6 insurrection: "Shofarists draped in American flags and dancing to the Contemporary Christian culture war anthem 'God's Not Dead' on January 6th, 2021, confounded many outside observers," writes Payne. "But those familiar with the Pentecostal and charismatic communities who tie the United States to Israel to the apocalypse recognized the ritual's logic: blowing the shofar is an ancient Jewish act of war on behalf of Donald J. Trump."

Such ritual acts are no accident. Even amid the chaos of the riot, many in the crowd felt the need to stop to pray as they crossed into the inner depths of the congressional chamber. They recognized their entering the Capitol as a crossing-over—a breach of protocol, an occupation. The rituals of chanting, singing, and praying enabled them to collectively and psychologically transform the Capitol space into their own. As the theorist of religion Thomas Tweed maintains, religion "maps social space. It draws boundaries around us and them; it constructs collective identity and, concomitantly, imagines degrees of social distance."

Thus, when the QAnon Shaman thanked God for filling the Senate chamber with patriots who defend the American way and listed the globalists, communists, and tyrants as enemies of God, he drew boundaries around who is a true citizen and who is not. He provided a story that placed the rioters in the role of God-ordained citizens, turning them all into something like "Joshuas" defending the country from invaders and enemies. The Senate chamber became theirs to inhabit because they were on the side of the Almighty. Scholar Russell McCutcheon describes this kind of prayer as the act of granting an extraordinary reason for an otherwise ordinary thing.

In his writing on the January 6 insurrection, Peter Manseau argues that the rioters had a "permission structure" that provided the psychological mechanism needed to justify killing police officers and erecting gallows for the vice president. "Even for those without strong Christian convictions, the pervasive religious imagery provided both a permission structure and a psychological safety net that allowed self-declared patriots to rampage through a space they supposedly held sacred," Manseau writes. "If any had second thoughts as they charged up the Capitol steps, they perhaps needed only to see a Bible thrust in the air above the crowd to be put at ease. How could a righteous mob be wrong?"

The Christian flags, symbols, rituals, and Bible verses gave the rioters' actions a sense of divine permission, reassuring them that the desacralization of the Capitol was actually a sanctification of the American way. Through rituals of their White Christian nationalist faith, many insurrectionists rendered the profane act of desecrating the Capitol into a sacred act of reclamation on behalf of real Americans.

"WE ARE JOSHUAS"

The story of Joshua leading the Israelites in their siege of Jericho is a story of conquest and desolation. It's also a story about eradicating the other: the foreign interloper who has taken your place, the people group who has no right to your land.

It's so familiar to me—and I suspect many of the people who took part in the Jericho Marches and the insurrection itself—that it's easy to unconsciously glaze over its brutality and xenophobia. In the text, Joshua leads a group of people into a territory already occupied by the Canaanites. He and his followers believe that God has granted them rights to the territory. In a vision, Joshua is told to march around the corrupt city of Jericho in order that its walls might come tumbling down.

This is where most Christians either stop reading the text or start spiritualizing it. They see a bold act of faith. They are inspired by the willingness to abandon ordinary logic in order to witness extraordinary events. Some pastors and Bible teachers weasel out of confronting this passage by claiming that God wanted to root out corruption and idolatry rather than violence and the destruction of human life.

Yet when the Israelites overtook through Jericho, they destroyed everything. Men. Women. Children. Animals. Every living thing was annihilated. They were willing to ravage the city and ferociously exterminate all its Canaanite inhabitants in order to fulfill the mission and promise that had been granted to them by the Most High. There is no mercy or grace in Joshua 6, no patience or kindness or forgiveness. The central lesson from the text is that if God commands you to take what he has given to you and to no one else, then the proper response is to eradicate anyone and anything that stands in your way. Once the gates fall, your mission is to ransack the city—not only to make it yours, but to make sure no one dares challenge your proper place as the God-given rulers of the territory: "They devoted the city to the Lord and destroyed with the sword every living thing in it—men and women, young and old, cattle, sheep and donkeys" (Joshua 6:21). Some Christians have reclaimed the story for liberatory purposes, using it as inspiration to overcome enslavement or oppression. Some have attributed the annihilation of the Canaanites to the Israelites' xenophobia rather than to God's command. Despite these readings, when Joshua 6 is employed by a dominant group trying to justify its violent rampage against others, it is hard to escape its viciousness.

Any honest accounting of the January 6 insurrection—one that takes seriously the religious symbols and language of the rioters—must reckon with the very real sense in which many of the rioters, perhaps including Leandra Blades, were reenacting key parts of the Jericho narrative. By locating themselves in the position of Joshua and the Israelites, the MAGA faithful rewrote the story. In this version, Jericho, the occupied city, is transformed into the United States of America. Instead of attacking a city filled with foreign gods, the assailants are entering the corrupted sacred spaces of the American republic in order to root out the idols that stand in the way of another Trump presidency.

Even those who didn't see themselves as modern-day Joshuas used religious rituals and symbols at the insurrection to draw boundaries and create divisions between "us" and "them." The stories, prayers, chants, and Bible verses enabled them to play the part of righteous crusaders retaking a country that has been occupied by their enemies: "communists," "socialists," "globalists," "antifa," "Black Lives Matter," "baby killers," "feminists," "tyrants," and the politicians who support them. In this narrative, they were not laying waste to a city, as barbarians at the gate; they were reconquering what has been promised to them. Their violent actions were not random acts of brutality; they were holy acts of war against God's and America's (and by default, Trump's) enemies.

The bloodthirsty aura that pervaded January 6 is reminiscent of Joshua 6. When I reflect on that day, I ask the same questions that the irksome kid in Sunday school used to bring up when we finished a lesson on the walls of Jericho falling down. If the patriots trying to save the country didn't want to do anything except root out corruption, why did they act so violently? If the storming of the Capitol wasn't about punishing enemies but ensuring God's will would be done in the election, why did they erect gallows for Mike Pence and attempt to hunt down Nancy Pelosi, Alexandria Ocasio-Cortez, and Mitt Romney? If they wanted to push back the spiritual powers, why did they think they had to desecrate the holy sanctuary of American democracy?

Because the goal was domination, not simply rooting out corruption. One doesn't erect gallows and express the desire to kill the Speaker of the House for anything less than vengeance. In Joshua 6 and on January 6, the walls falling down is only the cover of the story. The spiritual lesson is a way to glaze over the real meaning of the narrative: When God gives you a mission, you have the right—no, the directive—to vanquish your enemies.

The video footage from January 6 is breathtaking in its scope and horror. This was not a group of patriots patiently trying to make their way into the Capitol. This was not a sit-in or a silent, peaceful act of resistance or a nonviolent expression of the freedom of assembly and freedom of speech. It was a mob released from inhibition and fear, ready to overtake anyone or anything that stood in the way of them taking back their country.

In essence, the January 6 insurrection was a religious ritual carried out by the Americans who believe they have a God-given right to rule the country. For them, a siege of the most important space in United States government was a crusade against the enemies of the United States. The framework that guided them was Christian nationalism. And the story of Jericho provides a window into the spiritual mechanics of the most traitorous attack on the country in modern history.

"We are Joshuas. And we need the sound of praise to bring down the walls of the Swamp," said Julia Bithorn, from Knoxville, Tennessee, at the first Jericho March on December 12, 2020. As she spoke, Julia and her sister were marching around the Supreme Court with thousands of other rallygoers, surrounded by raised Christian and Trump flags and the echoes of shofars. "This is not gloom and doom. This is the glory of God being revealed," she explained. "We've come here to bind the enemy in the name of Jesus."

Chapter 10

MAGA MYTHS

"WE ALL LIVE ACCORDING to myths. It's just a matter of which ones." I say something like this every semester in my introduction to religion courses. Some of my students are nonreligious science majors, and when I say this, they look at me like I'm insane. In their minds, they are rational people who live according to data and evidence and history.

"If you don't want to live by myths, I have a solution," I goad them. They look at me expectantly. "Thanksgiving is next week. We have three days off. Many of you are going home to see family for the first time since the summer. But we all know that the Thanksgiving holiday is based on a set of events that included the murder and betrayal of Native American peoples *and* that the history is hardly what we make it out to be. The holiday is built off a fragment of historical truth—a myth, we could call it—and one that is in many ways tragic."

At this point the room is a mix of disappointment and realization. Many of them understand that they are implicated. "So, if y'all want to stand up and quit living by this myth, let's stage a sit-in," I continue. "All of us in this room could demand that our school no longer recognize the holiday. Everyone get their phones out right now. Call your moms. Tell them you aren't coming home."

Nervous laughter fills the room. They can't tell if I'm serious.

"Come on, y'all! Let's do this."

No one bites. They want the time off. The myth allows them to see their loved ones at a hard point in the semester. The food they'll eat at Thanksgiving is comforting. Many of them have traditions of cooking with their grandma or playing football with friends before Thanksgiving dinner. Even if they know the myth isn't historically accurate, it's too much to give it all up.

As opposed to conspiracy theories, myths are often based in history, rooted in fact, but marked by elaboration and imagination that turns them into something else. A myth, above all, is a story that organizes our lives. "We all tell stories about who we are, where we came from, and how we should live," I tell the class. "Humans live through narratives that are often made up of facts—and more."

Myths inform the present by teaching lessons that help individuals and communities form their identities, cultivate virtues, and give an account of who they are that stretches from the generations before them to the ones they anticipate will follow. In essence, myths are a narrative version of some past set of events—like the Israelites marching around the city of Jericho—that motivates the present and helps cast a vision for the future. From Adam and Eve, to the tale of the first American Thanksgiving, to Paul Revere riding through the night to warn that "the British are coming!," myths are powerful because they open space for us to participate in something bigger than ourselves and to locate our feelings and passions in a collective memory. Myths give us room to perform who we are—or who we want to be—and in turn to create the world as we think it should be. In this sense, myths are a bridge between the world as we encounter it and the world we think should exist.

And for all these reasons, myths can be wondrous and life-affirming. Myths can give our identities texture and richness. In the evolutionary perspective, myths enabled humans to work together to accomplish tasks that transcended the individual—to work together to accomplish tasks greater than ourselves. When Martin Luther King Jr. said that "the arc of the universe bends toward justice," he espoused a myth that inspires Americans of different backgrounds to play a part in that story—to be characters in the narrative of universal justice. The story provides not only an ideal to work toward but a community—what King called the "beloved community"—in which to participate.

But myths can also be dangerous. The world humans often want to create is brutal and vicious, and the stories we live by sometimes make us the worst version of ourselves. The martyrs, relics, and stories that have grown out of the January 6 insurrection are more powerful than many outsiders to White Christian nationalism realize, and they are shaping a dangerous future.

THE POST-J6 WORLD WE COULD HAVE HAD

Let's imagine a world in which the January 6 insurrection had been taken seriously. What if a consensus about the event had developed among a wide swath of leaders? What if our leaders had dealt with January 6 as a coup attempt by an aggrieved former president unwilling to cede power? If they had done that, we would have seen the second impeachment lead to conviction. Trump and his cronies could have been prosecuted for conspiracy or treason, and up to a dozen members of Congress could have been expelled and possibly prosecuted. All members of both the Senate and the House would have condemned the lie that Trump actually won the election, and we would have seen Republican leaders—from Congress to state legislatures to city councils and school boards across the country—disavow Trump and his movement.

Imagine if we had heard that White Catholic priests and evangelical ministers—including Franklin Graham, Robert Jeffress, and Paula White—had joined the multifaith coalition of religious leaders, such as Bishop William Barber, Imam Omar Suleiman, and Rabbi Danya Ruttenberg, who condemned both the insurrection and the Big Lie. What if we had witnessed them asking their followers to accept the election results as lawful and legitimate, to pray for the new president, and to ask God to heal the United States as it recovers from the treachery of the Capitol riot and other violence?

Finally, we the people could have denounced it wholeheartedly. What if Americans of all backgrounds had held gatherings to mourn the deaths of the police officers? What if there had been nonviolent rallies calling on citizens to show their support of American democracy and the peaceful transfer of power? We could have had a moment of national unity—something so rare in the Trump era and over the last two decades. Like millions of Americans of all backgrounds did in the aftermath of 9/11, we could have chosen to come together as a national body, in the wake of January 6, in the face of a threat to our way of life.

But that is not what happened.

The Big Lie has grown more expansive and powerful since January 6, 2021, because local and national politicians, religious leaders, and media figures have used it to foment the resentment and rage of MAGA Nation. They realized early on that the mob wasn't ready to let go of their grievance and hatred, and so they kept giving those emotions space to grow by telling the story of the stolen election and the country taken from "real Americans." All but a few of the Republican members of Congress who initially condemned Trump and the insurrection have changed course. They are back to supporting the former president and hoping for his support in return; some are offering revisionist histories of J6, calling it a "normal tourist visit" or blaming the violence on antifa and other groups. Fox News host Tucker Carlson produced a documentary on January 6 that frames the coup attempt as a false flag operation—an act made to look like it was planned by one's opponents in order to place blame on them. Some megachurch pastors and spiritual leaders continue to fuel the fires of the Big Lie in sermons and at rallies. For many Americans, even those who didn't riot on J6 and who think that such violence is wrong, the myth of the stolen election has become the bridge to building back their nation.

As a result, we now face a stark question: What if January 6 was not the end of an era but the beginning of one? What if it was not the last gasp of a movement devoted to a leader on his way out but the start of a more extreme iteration of MAGA terrorism? What if January 6 is not history we are now viewing safely via the rearview mirror but the basis for a new civil war?

Trump may have lost the presidency, and the January 6 insurrection may not have prevented the certification of the 2020 election. But these setbacks, like the Goldwater defeat in 1964, do not spell the end of White Christian nationalism. They do not represent the finale of MAGA Nation. Instead, these temporary defeats may be exactly what the movement needs to overcome America as we know it.

TRUMPISM IS A LOST CAUSE

Americans went to the polls on November 3, 2020. But due to close races in Pennsylvania, Arizona, Georgia, and Wisconsin, Joe Biden wasn't declared president until November 7. By then, Trump's Big Lie was already gaining steam. He tweeted that Democrats had stolen votes "where it matters," and by contrast to theirs, all the votes for him were "legal." He called the election a fraud and urged supporters not to accept the results.

Even in those early postelection days, it wasn't hard to see how the myth of a stolen election would gain traction among his base. As political theorist Hannah Arendt says in *The Origins of Totalitarianism*, "In an ever-changing, incomprehensible world the masses had reached the point where they would, at the same time, believe everything and nothing, think that everything was possible and that nothing was true. . . . Mass propaganda discovered that its audience was ready at all times to believe the worst, no matter how absurd, and did not particularly object to being deceived because it held every statement to be a lie anyhow."

According to analysis from the *Washington Post*, Trump told approximately thirty thousand lies or falsehoods during his presidency. He claimed COVID was under control, that Representative Ilhan Omar supports Al-Qaeda, that millions of people voted illegally in California for the 2016 election, that windmills cause cancer, and that the crowds at his inauguration were the largest in history. He even claimed that his tweet of "covfefe" had a secret meaning rather than just admitting it was a typo. His loyal base never wavered as over and over again, he shaped reality to his own liking. Instead, they found in the web of untruths a world they wanted to exist—and thus ones they pursued.

What we have witnessed since the 2020 election, and certainly since January 6, 2021, is *mythmaking in real time*. National myths often develop slowly, over several generations, so that by the time they wield power over any of us as individuals, we are fuzzy on the details of the origin story. But in the space of a few short months, we watched the formation of a story in which MAGA Nation is playing the role of aggrieved citizens who had their country stolen from them.

The Big Lie is one narrative piece of a larger myth, and the United States has suffered the consequences of this larger myth before. After the Civil War, the Confederate myth of the Lost Cause—which has startling resonances with Trump's Big Lie—took root in the South and then spread throughout the country, with disastrous results.

The period known as Reconstruction (1865–1877) saw the passage of the Thirteenth, Fourteenth, and Fifteenth Amendments, which abolished slavery and granted equal citizenship to Black Americans. In the years after the war, the nation witnessed Black Americans' integration into southern political life. Local chapters of the Union League and other organizations mobilized Black voters and fostered Black candidates for local and state elections. In 1868, South

Carolina had a Black-majority state legislature, and in 1870, Hiram Revels of Mississippi became the first Black American to serve in the United States Senate. For a short while, it seemed that liberty and justice for all was an attainable legal goal.

In the late 1860s and early 1870s, however, White southerners developed the notion of the Confederacy as the Lost Cause to combat the "radical" changes taking root in Dixie. According to proponents of the Lost Cause, the South was the victim of an invasion by "Yankee vandals," as Caroline Janney, a University of Virginia historian, phrases it. In response, they framed themselves as occupying the moral high ground in the conflict—a class of honorable and loyal families who defended their soil and way of life in the face of undue northern aggression. To make their case, they argued that slavery was not the real issue of the war but rather a pretext for a political and economic power grab by the North.

Like the myth of the stolen election, these claims are historically untenable. But the historical realities were less important to the power of the myth among its adherents than the stories, rituals, and symbols that developed in conjunction with the Lost Cause. As Charles Reagan Wilson, a southern historian, has shown, Lost Cause mythology was enacted through the rituals of Confederate civil religion: the funerals of Confederate soldiers, the celebration of Confederate Memorial Day, the pilgrimages made to the hundreds of Confederate monuments that had been erected by the dawn of World War I. The rituals and symbols instilled in the younger generation a sense of the nobility of the Confederacy and the moral vacancy of its enemies. Together, they supported a myth that was deeply religious in nature and that, for many southerners, supplanted the historical record. The men who died in battle became its martyrs. The generals became its patron saints.

The civil components of the Lost Cause were combined with Christian mythology. The South played the part of Christ in the Christian drama—crucified, yet unrisen. The heroes of the Confederacy—most notably Robert E. Lee and Stonewall Jackson—were saints in this Lost Cause theology. Scholar of southern religion Paul Harvey put it this way: "Key to this mythology was the exalting of southern war heroes as Christian evangelical gentlemen. Evangelists of the New South era immortalized the Christian heroism of the Confederate leaders and soldiers and dovetailed them into revivals of the era." Regardless of denominational affiliation, the Lost Cause offered a story and a set of high holy days every White southerner could celebrate.

The Lost Cause exerted immense influence over American law, foreign policy, and culture for a century after its inception. In *How the South Won the Civil War*, historian Heather Cox Richardson argues persuasively that even though the Union defeated the Confederacy on the battlefield, the South actually won the war. By using the Lost Cause myth, southern Whites were able to cultivate the reemergence of the Ku Klux Klan and create the context for Jim Crow laws. The myth then spread west to provide fuel for the Chinese Exclusion Act and acts of violence against Native Americans—all on the basis of resentment, ritual, and symbol rather than facts or historical truth. The Lost Cause didn't whimper and die in the face of historical criticism. It persisted, and it grew. Generation after generation of White people used it to justify a world of prejudice and injustice—an America where White Christians remained at the top of America's political and cultural hierarchies, from sea to shining sea.

The Lost Cause is an example of how myth works. Even if myths draw on a measure of reality, they aren't primarily about historical accuracy. Myths are preoccupied with the past and based on a desire to mobilize a vision for the present and create a prospect for the future. A myth shapes reality through ritual, which dramatizes its story and brings its adherents into collective participation.

When Trump supporters took hold of the Capitol, temporarily halting the counting of the electoral college votes, they brought the fiction down on the levers of government through temporary mob rule. But the enactment of the myth of the Big Lie did not stop when dusk fell on January 6. In fact, January 6, and the way it is being remembered, has given the myth of the stolen election the martyrs, the sacred objects, and the rituals that any good myth needs to survive. January 6 made space for MAGA Nation to create a new American reality.

MAGA MARTYRS

Ashli Babbitt was killed during the siege on the Capitol. A US military veteran, Babbitt had for months said on her social media feeds that the 2020 election was stolen from Trump. She arrived at the Capitol on January 5 to participate in the Stop the Steal rally the next day. On January 6, Babbitt was the first to climb through a broken window leading into the Speakers' Lobby, near to where members of Congress were hiding, and was shot by a Capitol Police officer. If one considers the January 6 riot as an attempted coup inspired by the former president, it's natural to view Babbitt as someone who lost her life in the midst of a traitorous attack on American democracy. When John Hinckley Jr. tried to assassinate Ronald Reagan, no one, including Reagan's political opponents, tried to make him out to be a misunderstood hero or a sympathetic figure. He was seen as a threat to national security.

Yet in MAGA circles, Babbitt has become a martyr in the quest to retake the stolen country. "Who was the person who shot an innocent, wonderful, incredible woman?" Trump asked Fox pundit Maria Bartiromo. "I will tell you, they know who shot Ashley [sic] Babbitt. They're protecting that person. I've heard also that it was the head of security for a certain high official—a Democrat."

This is mythmaking in real time. Trump turns Babbitt into an innocent female victim, despite the fact that she was attempting to enter the chambers where the Speaker and other members of Congress were sheltering from a violent mob. Next, the story becomes that the person who shot her is MAGA Nation's enemy—a security officer for a Democrat. Trump offers no evidence, but it doesn't matter. Everyone listening got the idea in just a short paragraph: Ashli Babbitt was an innocent woman who died at the hand of a nefarious political opponent who stands against Trump and the real Americans trying to reinstate him to the presidency.

"We all saw the hand, we saw the gun," Trump said. "You know, if that were on the other side, the person that did the shooting would be strung up and hung. OK? Now they don't want to give the name. . . . It's a terrible thing, right? Shot. Boom. And it's a terrible thing."

Fox News host Tucker Carlson expanded on Trump's martyr myth. "Who *did* shoot Ashli Babbitt and why don't we know?" Carlson asked on his show, which averages four million viewers. "Are anonymous federal agents now allowed to kill unarmed women who protest the regime? That's OK now? No, it's not OK." Again, Carlson's crafted narrative provides the foundation for turning Babbitt into a martyr for the MAGA cause. The words "unarmed" and "regime" frame Babbitt as a righteous protester standing up to an unjust government rather than a violent perpetrator taking part in the worst attack on the American Capitol since it almost burned down during the War of 1812.

Trump and Carlson weren't the only ones memorializing Babbitt. "Trying to find the name of a woman that was gunned down by Capitol Police today," wrote Larry Brock, who identifies as a 3 Percenter and an Oathkeeper, which are both violent far-right militia groups, on Facebook on the night of January 6: "She was unarmed and is the first Patriot Martyr in the Second American Revolution."

Since then, the image of the "first Patriot Martyr" has been used as a totem for MAGA Nation's remembrance of January 6 as well as by right-wing groups propagating antigovernment and White supremacist messages. Her face appears on the flag used as the symbol for the proposed "Million Martyr March" on January 20, 2021, a rally at the Capitol meant to remember and celebrate those jailed and "persecuted" as a result of the insurrection. US representative Paul

Gosar from Arizona tweeted a picture of Babbitt in May 2021 with the words: "They took her life. They could not take her pride." The Anti-Defamation League reports that "posts across platforms have specifically noted Babbitt's race, one such post referring to her as 'a brave white woman' and the white supremacist National Partisan Movement Telegram channel posted a memorial image with the text 'Rest in White Power.'"

Babbitt is not MAGA Nation's only January 6 martyr. Since the insurrection, more than seven hundred alleged rioters have been arrested. Some were still imprisoned as of 2022 on felony charges of conspiracy. In the eyes of many Trump supporters, the jailed insurrectionists have become political prisoners.

"Our hearts and minds are with the people being persecuted so unfairly," former president Trump said in a statement in September 2021. According to Trump, they are being unfairly treated for their participation in a "protest concerning the Rigged Presidential Election." In the summer of 2021, Representatives Paul Gosar, Marjorie Taylor Greene, Louie Gohmert, and Matt Gaetz made headlines when they tried to visit the jailed rioters to check up on the conditions of their confinement and ensure their safety. "We have concerns about reports of the conditions of the prison where these detainees are being held and whether, in fact, there have been instances of abuse inflicted by other prisoners or guards," Gaetz, Greene, Gosar, and Gohmert said in a joint statement. Madison Cawthorn, the twenty-five-year-old freshman congressperson from North Carolina, said he would like to "try and bust them out" of prison. On November 5, 2021, QAnon supporter and Georgia representative Marjorie Taylor Greene visited the rioters in jail—the "Patriot Wing," as she called it. According to Greene, the prisoners are receiving "virtually no medical care, very poor food quality, and being put through re-education which most of them are rejecting." In perhaps the most startling declaration, the Republican Party labeled the actions of rioters on January 6 as "legitimate political discourse."

There have been rallies around the country, including in New York and Washington DC, for the jailed rioters. Organizers compared their conditions to those of prisoners at Guantanamo Bay. In a letter from prison, one insurrectionist explained that he and his fellow insurrectionists "are just regular freedom-loving Americans, with a tendency towards humorous shenanigans."

Making martyrs out of the jailed rioters is strategic. Martyrs are the exemplars of myth. They are the figures who embody the virtues that the community must emulate in order to create their ideal world. As the scholar of right-wing movements Daniel Koehler says, dying for the cause is "usually connected to a heroic fight to the death against ideological enemies, who in the end are responsible for the martyr's death or ideological steadfastness." Ashli Babbitt is now valorized as the first "Patriot Martyr" of the MAGA Lost Cause. She exemplifies the sacrifice necessary to take back the country. The jailed rioters are its political heroes, celebrated for their suffering at the hands of a fraudulent government.

MAGA RELICS

On October 13, 2021, supporters of Virginia gubernatorial candidate Glenn Youngkin held a rally in Richmond, Virginia. While Youngkin didn't attend, a number of MAGA heavyweights led the rally. Former president Trump addressed the crowd via a recorded message, and his former adviser Steve Bannon was the headline speaker.

But their presence isn't what makes the rally worth remembering. When the rally got underway, an American flag that, the crowd was told, a "patriot" had carried at the January 6 insurrection was brought to the front and raised on stage. Rallygoers then participated in the pledge of allegiance to what, in essence, became the January 6 American flag.

It was an impromptu ritual, created from the fabric of the traditional American pledge of allegiance, but imbued with new and startling meaning. As the rally attenders pledged allegiance to the American flag, they also pledged allegiance to the nation that Trump, Trump's team, and the rioters tried to create during the failed coup.

The American flag to which they pledged allegiance that day became more than an item of ceremony; it became a sacred object. As the scholar of religion Mircea Eliade explains, sacred objects exceed their bounds. They are more than just fabric, wood, or stone. "The sacred tree, the sacred stone are not adored as stone or tree; they are worshipped precisely because they are hierophanies, because they show something that is no longer stone or tree but the sacred." A hierophany is an event that unveils the sacred. It reveals objects, lands, people, and words to be set apart and special. For those pledging allegiance to the January 6 flag, the American flag—already a sacred object—became more than an object of American patriotism. January 6 turned it into a symbol of a sacred battle and the holy mission of MAGA Nation. The flag expanded into an object that manifests the story that Trump's followers are living out—one in which an election is stolen and a group of Americans attempts to overthrow a fraudulent government. In the wake of temporary defeat, the flag reminds them, God's patriots continue the war by remembering the lives lost in battle and the righteous cause for which they fight.

ONLY THE BEGINNING

In the days following the attack, prominent Republicans denounced the riot and Trump's actions. Minority leader Kevin McCarthy said, "The president bears responsibility for Wednesday's attack on Congress by mob rioters. He should have immediately denounced the mob when he saw what was unfolding. These facts require immediate action by President Trump." Senator Lindsey Graham of South Carolina, a staunch Trump ally throughout the former president's term, said he had never been so humiliated for the country. Their rhetoric shifted, however, once it became clear that Trump and his mob would continue to determine the fate of the GOP on local, state, and national levels.

Republicans refused to support a bipartisan investigative commission focused on January 6. According to Senator Ron Johnson of Wisconsin, the rioters are "people that love this country, that truly respect law enforcement." Representative Jody Hice of Georgia went a step further by claiming, "It was Trump supporters who lost their lives that day, not Trump supporters who were taking the lives of others." Not to be outdone by her Peach State colleague, Representative Marjorie Taylor Greene said in a speech on the House floor that "the people who breached the Capitol on Jan. 6 are being abused." A third congressperson from Georgia, Andrew Clyde, described the riot as a "normal tourist visit."

Public opinion about January 6 shifted dramatically in the year after it happened. Whereas 80 percent of polled Republicans condemned the insurrection in January 2021, by the summer of 2021, more than 50 percent of them were labeling it an act of patriotism and "defending freedom." By September 2021, 78 percent of Republicans believed that the election had been stolen. In a Pew Research poll from the same month, researchers found that "only about [a] quarter of Republicans (27%) view the prosecution of the rioters as very important; six months ago, half said this was very important."

The danger here is clear: When leaders mythologize January 6, they not only tell inaccurate accounts of what happened that day, accounts that belie the overwhelming photographic and video evidence of the violent mob attacking Capitol Police. They also erode trust in democratic institutions and insinuate that the ensuing presidential administration, and perhaps other elected officials, have been elected fraudulently. They are also fomenting public opinion against those attempting to prosecute the perpetrators of the failed coup.

The myth, in other words, creates sympathy for the insurrectionists, and it legitimates the MAGA movement's violence. History shows us that this can have tragic consequences.

STABBING DEMOCRACY IN THE BACK

In 1918, German politicians and generals began discussing surren-der in World War I. They were militarily outmatched and wanted to avoid the invasion of German towns and villages by the Allied forces. For many Germans, however, surrender seemed ridiculous. When they looked around, Germany seemed as powerful as ever. War had not reached their homeland. They couldn't see the destruction or defeat happening on the battle fronts. For a century their country had proved to be the dominant military and political force in Europe. Why would their leaders decide now to humiliate the nation? Some found the facts simply too much to bear.

In response, they turned to a series of insidious myths, first to one offered by the head of the German army, General Erich Luden-dorff, who blamed politicians, Marxists, and others for sabotaging the German military effort. The lie quickly circulated among both civilians and military. The *Dolchstoßlegenden*, or "stab-in-the-back" myths, offered an explanation of the present situation by claiming that traitorous politicians, Jews, and foreigners had stabbed Germany in the back by intentionally leading it to military failure. The defeat, in other words, was a false flag operation meant to destroy Germany from within.

When Germany signed the Treaty of Versailles in 1919, thereby agreeing to harsh economic, political, and military terms of surrender, the stab-in-the-back myths offered convenient explanations as to how the greatest force in Europe could be defeated—and be willing to agree to such humiliating terms. The only way, the myth instructed, was by sabotage and fraud. "It was especially incomprehensible that Germany, in just a couple of years, had gone from one of the world's most respected nations to its biggest loser," notes German journalist Jochen Bittner.

The myth was weaponized against German Jews, who became, in the minds of many Germans, the group to blame for Germany's traitorous surrender and acceptance of the Treaty of Versailles. By the early 1920s, the historian Klaus Schwabe observes, "the image of a Dolchstoß (stab in the back) became common currency in the public discourse. By implication, it indicted democracy as inadequate in dealing with military problems."

In the wake of World War I, Germany's first democracy, the Weimar Republic, was formed in 1919. But it was fragile and marked by internal turmoil across the vanquished nation. Different political factions and parties developed platforms and movements that they believed would return Germany to glory. One of them was the German National Socialist Party, also known as the Nazi Party. Founded in 1919 just after the war, the Nazis originally appealed to working-class Germans who had seen their economic status and national pride stripped from them. In 1921, the party was handed over in the form of a one-person dictatorship to the charismatic, cunning, and narcissistic young leader Adolf Hitler.

Hitler shaped the Nazis into a hypernationalist, anti-immigrant, and anti-Semitic party. He used the stab-in-the-back-myths to justify his hatred of Jews and his call to replace the Weimar Republic with a government—and a leader—that could avenge Germany's economic, military, and political humiliation. "The literal term 'stab-in-the-back' ('*Dolchstoss*') does not appear in his autobiography *Mein Kampf*, but he referred to it in many of his speeches and publications, at times, even verbally," notes Klaus Schwabe. "Needless to add that other Nazi publications abounded with references to the *Dolchstoß*."

In 1923 Hitler led thousands of his followers on a march in Munich in an attempt to overthrow the German government in the state of Bavaria—and eventually the entire Weimar Republic. The "Beer Hall Putsch," as it came to be known, since the insurrectionists set out from a beer hall, famously failed. Sixteen Nazis and four police officers were killed in the attempted coup. Hitler was sentenced to five years in prison, though he only served nine months. By German law, he and some of his coconspirators should have been expelled from the country because they were Austrian rather than German citizens. Hitler renounced his Austrian citizenship in 1925 and later became a German national. Despite their antagonism to the Weimar Republic—they used the term "Jew Government" to describe it—the judge presiding in the case gave Hitler and his cohorts the minimum sentence and allowed them to remain in the country.

While in jail, Hitler turned into a celebrated political prisoner who received visitors and gained the admiration of even more of the German Right who resented the new postwar reality. Richard Steigmann-Gall, a historian of Nazi Germany, explained it to me this way in a 2020 interview: "He's found guilty. His term is five years, reduced to less than one for good behavior. And he takes this opportunity in jail to write *Mein Kampf*. And what you see from the photography we have of the period is that he is treated quite well in his prison. He gets visitors, and you know, there's not what you would think of as the fate of somebody who in a US prison system would be found guilty of treason."

So despite having been convicted of treason in the courts, Hitler won a key battle in the court of public opinion. The failed coup of 1923 only fueled the stab-in-the-back myth Hitler propagated, and it expanded the Nazi reach to further corners of German politics and society.

In addition to the stab-in-the-back myths, Hitler claimed that democracy was not the best form of government for the German people but rather one forced on them by their enemies after the war. As the 1920s wore on, his politics of resentment took hold in a German populace looking for a figure to lead them back to glory. The stab-in-the-back myths became the "heart of Nazi propaganda," and thus the basis for violence against anyone who opposed them. Hitler used the myth to cultivate resentment and rage. He railed against democracy in the name of national pride and the greatness of Germany. In other words, he used myth to call his followers to make Germany great again.

When the Great Depression took hold of Germany in 1928, Hitler had already won the war of truth and reality in the public square.

Historical accuracy meant nothing in the face of a national citizenry looking for a story in which to place their rage, grievance, and desire for vengeance. Hitler gave them that story. And so Hitler rose to power. He was installed as chancellor in 1933, a decade after his failed coup attempt. Germany's experiment in democracy failed in the face of an authoritarian leader whose myth telling and charisma had already persuaded the German people to accept anti-Semitic, nationalist, xenophobic Nazi ideology. The traditional German conservatives of the day thought they could mold him for their own purposes. They allowed Hitler and his fringe political coalition to take the seat of power with the naive intent of "riding him like a horse." Instead, ten years after his failed coup, Hitler and the Nazis had conquered Germany's fledgling democracy. The rest is tragic history.

AMERICA'S MYTHICAL FUTURE

Myths are like ivy. They grow in all directions, and after a short time it's not only hard to tell where they came from but almost impossible to root them out. When you cut back one branch or prune away a whole section, the ivy often grows back and expands further. Myths root themselves in the public imagination when they become accepted knowledge that most people refuse to investigate. When a story rises to the level of "Everybody knows that," then it is a myth that exists in public consciousness. It is a shared reality. A foundation of the world in which people live and navigate.

January 6, 2021, could have been the end of MAGA Nation's role in the story of American politics. If politicians, media voices, religious leaders, and celebrities had formed a united front that painted the insurrection as a disqualifying event that barred Trump and anyone who advocated for the attempted coup from serving in political office, our political future might look differently. As it stands, however, it seems that J6 will become the foundational event in a long, perhaps slow-moving attempt to thwart American democracy. Like the 1923 Beer Hall Putsch in Germany, the 2021 Capitol insurrection may have been a "failure" only for a time, and in name only. When authorities stop a coup attempt, and when that insurrection births martyr stories and rituals and symbols among its adherents, any effort to trim back the myths that led to the coup simply end up stimulating their growth.

Some historians are raising parallels between the Capitol riot and the Beer Hall Putsch. "What if the events of Jan. 6, like the Beer Hall Putsch, only mark the beginning of the rise of the far-right?" asks the historian of World War I Robert Gerwarth. "After all, militant right-wing nationalism as a political force in American life will not disappear. The question is how the Republicans will deal with Trump's legacy and with his most fanatical supporters."

We already know how Republicans are dealing with Trump's legacy. He remains the leader of the party. The Big Lie is the foundation of the MAGA movement. And January 6 is viewed as the first battle in the war for the country. The question is not if there will be another attack on our democracy. The question is when.

Chapter 11

RIGHT FLIGHT

IT FEELS ALARMIST TO forecast January 6, 2021, as the beginning of a new American conflict. Whenever I say it out loud, it seems hyperbolic, as if I have turned into one of the talking heads on television or radio trying to drum up hysteria for the sake of attention, clicks, or views.

But in a postinsurrection context, where the Big Lie has come to define the Republican Party and a majority of the party's constituents believe the election was stolen from Trump, staid academic reserve just won't cut it for the task ahead of us. This book is about history: the history of White Christian nationalism and my own history in the movement. The Trump years taught us that any prognostication is unstable. Yet the times demand that we follow the evidence and do our best to anticipate what might come next.

While it is impossible to know the future in detail, one thing seems certain: even after Trump is out of the public eye, the MAGA movement he energized on the foundation of White Christian nationalism will remain. Once you open Pandora's box, there is no way to put everything back nice and tidy like you found it. The animus Trump unleashed is not dependent on Trump himself. As a result, there are already indications of the types of conflict that will characterize our future once he's gone: the intimidation of election workers, the threats against school board members, the attempt to kidnap the governor of Michigan, and the refusal to abide by COVID-19 regulations. They are the little fires all around us that portend bigger blazes—or one big wildfire—in the years ahead.

Yet there's another trend to consider beyond the localized conflicts popping up from Virginia to California to Michigan: The movement for geographical consolidation and de facto secession—what one might call the Make America Great Again Migration. I'm not talking about states officially leaving the Union but of members of MAGA Nation banding together in semiautonomous regions where they take over local government, cultivate Christian nationalist churches, and do everything possible to create a theocratic society where White Christians have all the power. Such a migration is already happening from places like California, coastal Washington, and parts of the East Coast to what is now known as the "American Redoubt"—the region comprising Idaho, Montana, Wyoming, eastern Washington, and eastern Oregon. *Redoubt* means stronghold or fortification. Etymologically, it is similar to *refuge*. The American Redoubt is, in essence, a safe space to which some White Christians are fleeing in order to take refuge from the rest of the country.

And so, when I think of the future of MAGA Nation, I have to return home to Orange County, where I, and this book, began. It's in Orange County, or at least in the ways that my former church friends and classmates *are leaving it* in order to migrate to the American Redoubt, that I see the future of White Christian nationalism and MAGA Nation after Trump.

TEARING DOWN THE ORANGE CURTAIN

When I was growing up, Yorba Linda Bowl was our neighborhood bowling alley. It was nothing fancy. No neon lights or lasers. No high-tech sound system. Just a musty bowling alley with an equally greasy diner, situated in a strip mall next to a bike shop and a gas station. The sign outside was an analog relic, a holdover from the 1970s, and the shoes for rent were apparently from the same era.

A few years ago, Yorba Linda Bowl went under. It was replaced by Tokyo Central, a modern Japanese market with a sushi counter, ramen bar, and all the Japanese sweets my brothers and I grew up eating at our grandmother's house. Every time I walk the aisles of Tokyo Central, picking out rice crackers and bottles of green tea from the market's huge selection, I am taken aback. When I was growing up in North Orange County, it would have been almost unthinkable that there would someday be enough East Asian folks to support a sprawling market. Dad used to trek an hour away to Japantown in LA on Saturdays to fetch various foods, treats, and Japanese items we just couldn't get closer to home. Sushi bars, noodle counters, and boba shops are now everywhere in my hometown, alongside taquerias and taco trucks. It's not that they've replaced the diners or pizza parlors. It's just that they exist side by side in a way I could never have imagined as teenager.

Orange County's change is a testament to the changing demographics of the country as a whole. Following nationwide trends, the county is more diverse than it's ever been. Communities of color have lived, struggled, and resisted for decades in Orange County. Santa Ana is a majority Mexican city. Westminster and Garden Grove are home to one of the largest Vietnamese populations outside of Vietnam. Yet, on the whole, Orange County has been a White enclave since the Sunbelt migration in the mid-twentieth century. That is changing.

According to the 2020 census, the White population decreased by almost a quarter in the last ten years, while the Asian American and mixed-race populations have grown by a third. There are also more Latinx and Black people than a decade ago. Orange County is also less conservative than at any point in my lifetime. The region that championed Goldwater, raised Nixon, and paved the way for Reagan voted 53.5 percent Democrat in the 2020 election. When Hillary Clinton won Orange County by 5 percent in 2016, it was the first Democratic presidential victory in the county since the Great Depression. Perhaps most shockingly, in 2018 three congressional seats flipped from red to blue. The Blue Wave broke through the conservative stronghold over Orange County in a torrent of cultural, demographic, and political change. Once the epicenter of the extremist takeover of the GOP and the conspiratorial cosmos of the John Birch Society, Orange County is now a purplish, increasingly diverse, and democratically represented region.

The transformation didn't take place through converted hearts and minds, however. Though the Trump years made some Orange Countians rethink their political commitments, the county's shift is not the result of all those old Christian nationalist Goldwater and Reagan supporters becoming born again. The story of Orange County's makeover is a story of White exodus. The county that once defined White flight is now undergoing its own "right flight."

THE ORANGE EXODUS AND THE REDOUBT MIGRATION

As we saw in the first few chapters, in the mid-twentieth century migrants came to Orange County from the South and Midwest in massive numbers. The defense industry boomed after World War II, providing well-paying jobs in a place with great weather, beautiful beaches, and affordable housing. It is easy to see why people like my grandfather picked up their lives and families to head west.

By the 1990s, however, Orange County had become expensive and crowded. The defense-industry jobs dripped away. Many people became tired of commuting two hours one way to jobs in Los Angeles, only to be left unable to buy a home or live beyond paycheck to paycheck. So they began to leave—heading to Portland, Austin, Nashville, and Colorado Springs. This is the story I've always heard when I go home: a story about friends and neighbors leaving paradise because they were priced out and tired of the rat race.

But when I started paying attention to *where* my former church friends and high school classmates had been moving over the last two decades, an interesting pattern emerged: Idaho was the most prominent destination. By my last count, more than fifty people from my home community have moved to Idaho, more than any other state with perhaps the exception of Tennessee, where Nashville is a major draw.

This migration is apparently not limited to my circles. Boise has seen an 9.3 percent increase in population since 2010. It has gone from "flyover country" to the hottest metro area west of the Mississippi. It was the fastest-growing US city in 2018, and the population growth isn't expected to slow down during the 2020s. Boise is expected to surpass one million residents by 2040. The expansion continued during the global pandemic, when nearly 200 percent more people moved into the state than left it. Most of the people moving to Idaho are from Washington and California. In 2018 alone, eighty thousand Californians moved to the Gem State.

Longtime residents of Boise worry that the influx of newcomers from these blue states will change the political makeup of the city and the state as a whole. However, Boise State political scientist Jeffrey Lyons found in a study that the Californians moving to Idaho are by percentages more conservative than the state itself: "If anything, Californians coming to Idaho are more conservative than native Idahoans." Instead of turning Idaho blue, the new migrants are reinforcing Idaho's staunch conservativism, "and those hailing from California are no exception."

White Christians from places like Orange County are moving to Idaho because they see it as a haven for conservative politics and "religious freedom." Kory and Bonnie Martinelli own a real estate company called Live Better in North Idaho. They left California for Coeur d'Alene, which is in the northern strip of the state known as

North Idaho—and what some consider the capital of the American Redoubt—in 2009. Kory Martinelli now advocates for North Idaho as the "best place" to live in the United States. In California, he says, liberal politics were a menace to "our spiritual rights, our family values, our economic stability and our constitutional rights, especially the right to bear arms." Part of the reason the Martinellis chose Idaho is that it a highly conservative place with over 20 percent more conservatives than liberals. The Martinellis' lived experience backs up what the numbers says—the growth in population is moving Idaho to the right, rather than to the left, politically. "North Idaho is a direct contradiction to the theory that population growth turns communities liberal," Martinelli said. "North Idaho is a conservative culture and it's only growing more conservative with population growth."

There's another important factor at play in the exodus from California: Idaho is 93 percent White. When my White Christian friends and classmates leave California, they not only separate themselves from a democratically controlled state legislature but also the communities of color that have a meaningful place in the state's politics and culture. They may say that moving is not about race and certainly not about racism. They are adamant that all people, of any background, are welcome to join. But when 93 out of 100 people in their new state are White, they are extending the invitation from a place where their sense of being the dominant group is in no way threatened—where White people are the unquestioned majority to whom all others must adapt and conform.

There are no cities in Idaho that show up as blue circles in an otherwise red state, as with Tennessee or Texas or Pennsylvania. There are no deeply rooted immigrant communities that have made inroads in statewide politics, as there are in Arizona, Louisiana, or Minnesota. Parts of Idaho are what Orange County used to be: an unzoned land with a stunning White majority, a homogenous political culture, and by contrast to Los Angeles or San Francisco or Seattle, very little religious pluralism. It is the perfect setting for a self-segregated

White Christian society without the bother of religious, racial, or ethnic minorities.

When I bring up these factors to friends and family, they often scoff. Stop trying to turn this into a big issue, they say. What's the big deal if people want to move somewhere more affordable in order to be around like-minded folks who share their religion and values? This isn't some American crisis. They aren't moving there to be part of some extremist thing or to join a White supremacist church. It's just nice to be able to buy a piece of land, have a bigger house, own guns without pesky regulations, and be in a place where the school district and local government and small-town culture all align with your idea of America.

Then I remind them of who else is moving to Idaho—and why.

AMERICAN THEOCRACY

Californians and others have been moving to the American Redoubt region for decades in order to escape what they take to be the overthrow of American society by leftist politics, the breakup of the nuclear family, and the diminishment of religious freedom. When folks from my high school and former church move there now, they are joining a decades-long caravan of migrants who see the Gem State as the last frontier of freedom left in the United States.

In 2011, James Wesley Rawles, a former US military intelligence officer born and raised in Northern California, dubbed the region including Idaho, Montana, Wyoming, and parts of eastern Washington and eastern Oregon the American Redoubt. In a now infamous blog post, Rawles identified this region of the country as the last fortress for traditional Americans to protect themselves against what he predicts will be an economic and political crisis. "I believe that it is time for freedom-loving Christians to relocate to something analogous to "Galt's Gulch" on a grand scale," Rawles wrote.

Rawles was following the lead of Chuck Baldwin, a pastor who was once Jerry Falwell's Moral Majority lieutenant in Florida and who himself had called for a mass migration to the Redoubt region. "America is headed for an almost certain cataclysm," Baldwin wrote. "As Christians, we suspect that this cataclysm could include the judgment of God. As students of history, we believe that this cataclysm will most certainly include a fight between Big-Government globalists and freedom-loving, independent-minded patriots. I would even argue that this fight has already started." Baldwin moved his extended family to Montana and relaunched his ministry there in 2010.

For Rawles and Baldwin, the goal is to create a separate society of American Christians who will defend their families and communities when the next civil war dawns. "I am a separatist, but on religious lines, not racial ones," Rawles writes in the blog post that now serves as the foundation for the Redoubt Migration. "I'm inviting people with the same outlook to move to the Redoubt States, to effect a demographic solidification. We're already a majority here. I'd just like to see an even stronger majority."

For Rawles, separatism and demographic isolation are the antidotes to the tyranny of a federal government and American society overrun by unconstitutional taxation, regulations on gun ownership, and limits to religious liberty. And it's not an unprecedented move, Rawles says. "Closing ranks with people of the same faith has been done for centuries. It is often called cloistering. While imperfect, cloistering got some Catholics in Ireland through the Dark Ages with both their skins intact and some precious manuscripts intact. . . . Designating some States as a Redoubt is nothing more than a logical defensive reaction to an approaching threat."

According to Rawles, closing ranks and setting up a de facto separate society is a way to prepare for "the Second Civil War, here in America and caused by the gulf between the right and left—or between the godly and the godless—or between the libertarians and the statists—or between the individualists and the collectivists." For him, this means autonomy from the United States, a seceded state that is "a stronghold of conservative, traditional values while we see the rest of the United States sink into oblivion."

While it may be tempting to write off Rawles as an extremist on the fringe, his popularity speaks to the resonance his worldview has with millions of Americans—and the influence it is having on the Redoubt region. Rawles claims his website, survivalblog.com, has 320,000 unique visitors per week. He is a *New York Times*–bestselling author. He has five novels and two nonfiction books published by major houses—Simon and Schuster and Penguin Random House.

Others are helping to implement his vision for the creation of the American Redoubt. His son runs Survival Realty, which specializes in off-the-grid properties in the region. There are other "Redoubt Realtors" who specialize in helping "refugees" from California and other places find land. They offer relocation services and consulting for newcomers becoming accustomed to Redoubt life. Todd Savage operates American Redoubt Realty. Each year, he helps nearly three thousand Americans locate properties and make preparations to move to the Redoubt Region. He met Rawles in 2003 and soon moved his family from California to a homestead near Sandpoint, Idaho.

"We didn't quite 'fit in' with the changing landscape" in California, Savage told the *Sandpoint Reader*, a local newspaper. "We were libertarian Christians who home-schooled, refused to poison our children through vaccinations, owned evil black rifles and supported what would one day be known as the Blue Lives Matter movement." On his company website, Savage leaves no room for interpretation as to who is welcome in the Redoubt: "Snowflakes, Liberals, Socialists, Marxists, Communists, and other Tyrants that hate our Constitutional Republic, the Bill of Rights and want to defund law enforcement are not allowed to engage our services."

The American Redoubt movement isn't just spearheaded by writers and survivalists like Rawles and his allies in the real estate industry. Elected officials are also leading the charge. Matt Shea was a state representative for a district in eastern Washington that includes the outskirts of Spokane and borders North Idaho from 2008 to 2020. In 2016, he supported the armed takeover of federal public lands in Oregon. A 2019 report revealed how Shea took part in the effort, led by ranchers such as Cliven and Ammon Bundy, to forcibly occupy federal territories in an effort to reclaim them from the government. The most worrying aspect of the report was the revelation of Shea's desire for an alternative Christian government nearly identical to Rawles's vision for the American Redoubt. According to Ozzie Knezovich, the former sheriff of Spokane County, Washington, Shea and his companions "compiled manuals on everything from how to escape handcuffs to the operation of military weaponry and, according to the report to the legislators, laid the groundwork to form an alternative government that would be poised to take over after the expected fall of the United States government." Knezovich, who has known Shea for decades, is clear that Shea does not want to "preserve America," but instead, he and others "want to start their own country."

This ideal came into clearer focus when Shea's manifesto on biblical warfare was leaked in 2018. In the four-page document, Shea outlines his theory of just war. First, he lays out his vision for government: "Tyranny is never a divinely appointed means of government. A tyrant is someone who rules without God. Tyranny is not a lawful form of government. Godless civil rulers are no more than bands of robbers. When the rule of law dies as sin prevails throughout the land, tyranny is not far behind." The manifesto reads like a theocratic manual for the American Redoubt.

After casting his vision for theocracy, Shea sets the terms for negotiating with anyone who resists: "Make an offer of Peace before declaring war. Not a negotiation or compromise of righteousness. Must surrender on terms of justice and righteousness: 1. Stop all abortions; 2. No same-sex marriage; 3. No idolatry or occultism; 4. No communism; and 5. Must obey Biblical law. If they yield—must pay share of work or taxes. If they do not yield—kill all males."

In a meeting with supporters, Shea clarified that he doesn't see this as a future fight. It's one that has already arrived at America's doorstep: "But the bad guy is already here. How many of you have pulled your trigger on your AR-15 in the fight we are in yet? Not one. But there is a fight. Right now. The war is here. The bad guy is here."

Shea's political career ended when these documents came to light. Somehow, he had become too extreme for one of the most radically conservative parts of the country. But he found a safe landing spot: the church.

Shea is now the pastor of On Fire Christian Ministries and Kingdom Christian Academy in Spokane, Washington, where he regularly preaches the Gospel of the Redoubt. In early 2021, days before the election, he went to US representative Jim Risch's office in Coeur d'Alene. "We're fighting and we're going to continue to fight. We're heading into a war," Shea yelled. "This was not an election! This was an attack on our country! That's what this was." He then made his feelings about democracy loud and clear: "We do not live in a democracy! Democracies are what have led us to this point, where people think they can rob us, loot us, close our businesses down, eviscerate our elections, try to destroy our institutions and our livelihoods and our farms! I don't want to live in a democracy! I love the rule of law."

PASTORING THE MAGA MIGRATION

Shea is not the only influential religious leader doing his part to develop the Redoubt as a Christian haven. Doug Wilson has been building a Christian supremacist empire in Moscow, Idaho, since the late 1970s. Over the last half century, he has made it his goal to make the town of twenty-five thousand into a Christian town where the schools, city government, and businesses are controlled by evangelicals. Wilson is the controversial founder of Christ Church, a congregation that is more than a church. In Moscow, Christ Church has established a day school, a liberal arts college, and a media center from which Wilson spreads his message via radio, podcast, and his prolific writing. He has written over thirty books. His homeschooling network includes nearly two hundred schools across the country. Crawford Gribben, a scholar of religion who has written extensively about the church and Wilson, observes: "Followers believe that abortion rights and same-sex marriage, among other evidences of what they would see as moral decline, will eventually be repealed. Their goal is simple—the conversion of the people of Moscow to their way of thinking as the first step toward the conversion of the world."

Wilson has made waves in the past for his views on slavery. In *Southern Slavery as It Was*, coauthored with Steve Wilkins, Wilson argues that "slavery as it existed in the South . . . was a relationship based upon mutual affection and confidence. There has never been a multiracial society which has existed with such mutual intimacy and harmony in the history of the world." The authors go on to say that enslaved people enjoyed simple pleasures, "such as food, clothes, and good medical care."

Just about the time Wilson was setting the foundation for his ministry in Moscow, Richard Butler established a White supremacist church as part of the Christian Identity movement eighty-five miles north of Moscow in Coeur d'Alene. "In simplest terms," writes Bill Morlin at Boise State University's the *Blue Review*, "Christian Identity believers are convinced that the Bible tells them white people of Northern European ancestry are God's chosen—direct descendants of Adam and the 'true Jews.'" Butler left California in the 1970s in order establish his compound outside of Coeur d'Alene. Soon it became a kind of headquarters that attracted hundreds of White supremacists and also became a central node in the Christian Identity movement. The group flew the Nazi flag, called the property the "Aryan Nations," and eventually became the host site of the annual Aryan World Congress.

Butler, who was an early California migrant to North Idaho, was eventually shut down after becoming too brazen. When he and his community marched through Coeur d'Alene waving Nazi flags and other racist symbols, it set in motion events that resulted in the shuttering of the compound. Some Coeur d'Alene residents remain proud that the community didn't allow the hate group to continue to root and grow in its midst—that when they tried to become part of the public square in the town, they were run out.

However, White supremacy has not been rooted out from the area completely. In nearby Sandpoint, America's Promise Ministries carries on the Christian Identity cause in the region. It is, according to the Southern Poverty Law Center, a central node in the "informal local network of neo-Nazi and Ku Klux Klan groups" and White separatist groups. Before he was shut down, Richard Butler used to speak at the church regularly. In 2001, America's Promise Ministries leader Dave Barley said this in a Sunday sermon: "America's greatness . . . didn't come from the blacks. It didn't come from the Asians, and it certainly didn't come from the Jews. They [the Jews] wanted to become a part of our nation because of the light. Now, they want it because of greed."

In 2017, Boise State Public Radio did a series on the legacy of White supremacist Christianity in North Idaho. They interviewed shocked residents who couldn't believe that White supremacist pamphlets were still being left on cars and shop windows in the present day. The journalists interviewed Cynthia Delmonte, a Californian who relocated to Coeur d'Alene in 2012. She admits that there are still remnants of White supremacist Christianity, but for the most part, the region is just known as a place that is religiously and politically conservative. But near the end of the article, Delmonte comes, perhaps by accident, to an important conclusion: "Everyone's really nice up here, but I wonder how much of that is because I am a middle-aged, white woman?" Indeed, Shawn Keenan, a native of North Idaho whose family members were once held at gunpoint by White supremacists, holds a different perspective. "I've been calling this now the South of the North, because I've never seen so many Confederate flags ever here in my life."

THOSE PEOPLE ALL LOOK THE SAME

When I bring up these issues with my former church friends, they reiterate that for them moving to Idaho was an opportunity to live in a conservative state with affordable housing and beautiful terrain. They didn't move there, they explain, to associate with White supremacists or separatist Christian communities. If they are part of the Redoubt movement, they either don't know it, or they aren't admitting it outright.

But let's look at it from a different angle. What if there were a part of the country known as the epicenter of violent Muslim communities populated by people of Arab descent (which, to be clear, does not exist in the United States)? What if there were expansive networks of radical Muslim separatists who moved to New Mexico in order to prepare for the next civil war and what they saw as the impending doom of American society (which again, does not exist in the United States in any substantive form)? And what if throngs of nonradical Muslims of Arab descent were also moving to the same region—in many cases the very same cities—as these radical and violent communities but claiming that they simply wanted to find a more affordable and amenable place to raise their families and enjoy the outdoors? Would they be given the benefit of the doubt? Would this be viewed as a happy coincidence unworthy of analysis or concern?

This is what is happening in the case of the White Christian migration to Idaho and the American Redoubt. While run-of-the-mill White Christian families from Anaheim, Sacramento, or Seattle may say they have no intention of associating with extremists—and truly believe it—they appear to be completely fine moving to places where extremism is part of the culture and politics of everyday life. Once there, they or their children may be radicalized by dint of exposure and proximity to these radical ideas and figures at school board meetings, city council elections, and debates over state and national policies on guns, land, civil rights, and so on.

"A lot of good people are going to get sucked into that vortex," Sheriff Knezovich says. "And they are going to wake up and go, 'I didn't buy into that. I didn't buy into breaking away from the United States and forming my own country, because ultimately that's what the Redoubt stands for.'" For Knezovich, the promise of liberty through authoritarian religion and governance is an illusion. "They're using religion once again to suck people into come live wherever everybody believes the same way you believe.... You might think you are going into something where you will have freedom and liberty. No. You are going into tyranny. And the day you step out of line they will slap you back in line."

None of this is meant to indict all Idahoans or others in the Redoubt states. Many people in Idaho have fought hard to root out White supremacy, welcome diversity, and create safe places for all people to live. There are people of color in Idaho. There are LGBT communities in the Gem State. There are progressives and independents and hippies and all kinds of Americans. My point is not that Idaho is unilaterally populated by White Christian supremacists. My point is that many White Christians are fleeing to Idaho because they envision it as a welcoming place for radical conservative politics, extremist libertarianism, and Christian supremacy—and they are making inroads in local government, state government, and throughout the religious culture of the region.

What scares me about how migrants imagine the Redoubt as a haven for a segregated MAGA Nation free of liberal politics and the complications of religious and racial diversity? It's the foundations of their vision: self-separation, geographical removal, intentional homogeneity, outright Christian supremacy, and the belief that America is on the precipice of civil war in which some believe there will be a need to "kill all males" who do not yield to their demands. Unfortunately, the extremism that has long plagued the region serves as a mechanism for radicalization and the entrenchment of antidemocratic views.

JUDGMENT IS HERE

In the mid-twentieth century, the Sunbelt Migration transformed American politics, religion, and culture. White Christians' movement from one area of the country to a largely "unzoned" area laid the foundation for the New Religious Right and its takeover of the GOP. It seems that in the twenty-first century, the Redoubt Migration may have the potential for a similar effect. Only this time, the goal is not to take control of a political party. The goal is to prepare for the collapse of the United States and the chance to rebuild a theocratic state. Even after Trump is no longer part of American public life, the movement to make America great again will remain. And it may be more extreme than even he could have ever imagined.

"No one wants to believe that their beloved democracy is in decline, or headed toward war," writes scholar of international relations Barbara Walter in *How Civil Wars Start*. Yet "if you were an analyst in a foreign country looking at events in America— the same way you'd look at events in Ukraine or the Ivory Coast or Venezuela—you would go down a checklist, assessing each of the conditions that make civil war likely. And what you would find is that the United States, a democracy founded more than two centuries ago, has entered very dangerous territory."

My cohost Dan Miller and I say similar things on *Straight White American Jesus* regularly. In our view, if one looks at the state of American democracy from the outside, it's a country wherein one of the two major political parties is giving in to the impulses of authoritarianism, xenophobia, propaganda, and conspiracy in order to leverage power. If it means maintaining their cultural supremacy and minority rule, they are willing to place all their hopes in a wannabe autocrat like Trump.

Researchers around the world are coming to the same conclusion. "The United States, the bastion of global democracy, fell victim to authoritarian tendencies itself, and was knocked down a significant number of steps on the democratic scale," states the International IDEA's Global State of Democracy 2021 report. The authors of the report go on to lump the United States in with India and Brazil as undergoing "democratic backsliding," creating "a witches' brew for the global health of democracy."

At this point, the question for me is less about where we are and more about where we are headed. The history recounted in the foregoing chapters should make it evident that White Christian nationalists have been preparing for war since Barry Goldwater lost the 1964 election, if not before. Now is the time for those of us who value multiracial democracy, free and fair elections, and majority rule to admit that blithe prescriptions for dialogue and understanding won't cut it. One side has been readying for conflict for sixty years. It's time for the rest of us to admit that the normal ebbs and flows of American politics have been usurped by the forward march of MAGA Nation. What lies ahead is not a contest for electoral majorities or policy initiatives. It's a test of democracy's resilience in the face of an apocalyptic threat.

"I believe personally that America is already under the judgment of God," says Chuck Baldwin, the pioneer pastor of the Redoubt movement and a key figure in Falwell's Religious Right. "It's not that judgment is coming. Judgment is already here."

Epilogue

THOSE WITH EYES TO SEE

WOULD I HAVE BEEN THERE? That was the question I asked myself as I watched the insurrection on television that day. It's the inquiry that set in motion the writing of this book, the refrain that sometimes still haunts me when I watch the videos and images from January 6. I hear people praying in the familiar cadence and vocabulary we used in my evangelical circles. The way that some of the rioters raised their hands to the heavens as they sang and worshipped brings back visceral memories of doing the same motions in church and at summer camp. Several friends from my former church were, in fact, at the Jericho March on December 12. Others were present on January 6. Those with whom I used to pray and break bread and worship and serve *were* there.

Even if I hadn't actually been there, I think, would I have been at home, quietly or not so quietly cheering them on? Would I have felt something akin to relief, or joy, in watching the patriots fight to retake the country for God and his righteous servants? For every person in the Capitol that day, my guess is that there were a hundred or a thousand cheering them on. Had history unfolded differently, perhaps I wouldn't have been in DC but at home, praying alone, or in an impromptu group asking God to somehow reinstate Trump to office and protect the people fighting in his name.

Nearly twenty years after leaving the church, I realize that I cannot know what I would have done. The thought exercise that animated the writing of this book proves useful insofar as it offers lines of inquiry to pursue, but games of imagination can only take us so far. Ultimately, a more pressing and urgent question remains for all of us to consider: that is, *Why didn't we see this coming?*

I am not so much talking about the Trump presidency itself as the White Christian coalition that helped create the pathway for his ascendancy and then supported him every authoritarian and traitorous step of the way. I'm talking about the megachurch congregations, Jericho Marchers, Proud Boys, QAnons, Oath Keepers, Redoubt Migrants, and other MAGA-ites who used God's name to justify the worst domestic attack on the Capitol in the history of the United States.

As the history we have traced throughout this book testifies, the clues were there all along. In 1964, Goldwater won the hearts and minds of radical conservatives by proclaiming that extremism is a virtue. In the wake of his defeat, Paul Weyrich and Richard Viguerie launched the counterrevolution that reshaped American politics. "We are radicals, working to overturn the present power structure," they proclaimed. In order to propel their recapturing of America, they teamed up with conservative White evangelicals and Catholics who claimed victimhood every time they didn't get their way. The family became a versatile weapon deployed to counter advances in gender equality and civil rights for BIPOC Americans. James Dobson called children the "foot soldiers in the second American civil war."

The New Religious Right always envisioned the cross and the flag together. There was no separating national identity from the divine calling of the United States. This meant sacrificing the republic in order to save the America they wanted—a nation where White, straight Christians maintain power. If authoritarianism and conspiracy were necessary to retake America, then democracy be damned. What mattered was a pure nation constructed according to White Christian supremacy rather than multiracial democracy. In the case of Jimmy Carter versus Ronald Reagan, White Christians chose power over piety. Over the decades from the 1960s to the 2010s, power became the *marker* of piety—the sign of doing God's will the ability to conquer and eliminate political and cultural opponents.

Historian Kristin Kobes du Mez summarizes this brilliantly in *Jesus and John Wayne*. Though she names White evangelicals, I would expand it to include White Christian nationalists as a whole. "By the time Trump arrived proclaiming himself their savior, conservative White evangelicals had already traded a faith that privileges humility and elevates 'the least of these' for one that derides gentleness as the province of wusses," she writes. "Rather than turning the other cheek, they'd resolved to defend their faith and their nation, secure in the knowledge that the ends justifies the means."

If one accepts, as the data says we should, that Christian nationalism is the standard worldview for not only a large number of the January 6 rioters but White Americans as a whole, it becomes clear that what happened on January 6 was the inevitable outcome of an American cold civil war half a century in the making. When one puts together the history of political and culture wars, fought over the fault lines of race, gender, sexuality, family, immigration, and foreign policy, it becomes clear that the January 6 insurrection was simply the logical next step.

But the homegrown terrorist threat that culminated in the J6 insurrection went unheeded for decades. Why so many investigators, historians, and journalists missed it is a complex question. But it's clear that one reason so few observers saw January 6 coming is because, for centuries, the assumption has been that White American Christians—like my former classmates and church friends who have moved to the Redoubt region—are the default demographic of the nation. This is what the ex-evangelical author and scholar Chrissy Stroop calls Christian privilege: "Christian supremacy and privilege are every bit as real as white and male privilege, for example, and are part of the unjust social hierarchies that need to be dismantled in order for equity to be achieved in our society." Under the guise of (White) Christian privilege, people like Leandra Blades are often envisioned as the heart of Americana—the pesky but harmless moralists of a nation founded on religious principles. They're seen as more Ned Flanders—the irritatingly pious neighbor from *The Simpsons*—than Mr. Burns, the power-hungry corporate authoritarian who cares little for democracy, fairness, or inclusion, much less loving his neighbor.

Seeing this story in its full light doesn't leave me bereft of hope. There are many reasons to think that the United States might continue to reach its promise of equality, freedom, and the pursuit of happiness for all its people in the coming decades. After all, the night before J6, Stacey Abrams and a host of other organizers helped to pull off one of the most stunning electoral victories in modern American electoral politics, when Jon Ossoff and Raphael Warnock were elected to the Senate from Georgia. In 2020, Delaware's Sarah McBride became the first transgender candidate elected to a state senate in the country's history. In 2021, Michelle Wu became the first Asian American and first woman to become Boston's mayor by running on a thoroughly progressive platform. During the same election cycle, Elaine O'Neal became the first Black woman to win the mayor's office in Durham, North Carolina, a city with a history of voter suppression aimed at preventing African Americans from voting. These aren't isolated stories. All over the country Americans are fighting for labor protections, voting rights, immigration reform, new gun laws, and climate policies for a sustainable future. There are bright lights illuminating the arc that bends toward justice, from Georgia to Delaware to Oregon and everywhere in between.

But after January 6, 2021, we need to acknowledge this isn't the only path possible for our future. A new picture should come into focus for anyone paying attention. Many Christian nationalists are a clear and present danger to the United States of America. They are homegrown radicals who prioritize White Christian supremacy over multiracial democracy. They are not interested in pluralism. Their goal is not a model of governance based on dialogue and debate. The goal is to take back America by any means possible.

In a very real sense, January 6 was not the end of a movement—some last-gasp attempt of a weakened and aggrieved group supporting a politician who didn't want to admit he'd lost an election. No. If we are paying close attention to the extremist backstory of the people who stormed the Capitol that day, we will see that the insurrection was the logical next step for a certain diminishing White Christian population trying desperately to retake what they considered theirs. Acclimating or adjusting themselves to the inevitable waves of religious, racial, and other forms of diversity, for White Christian nationalists, is no option at all. This was not the last stand of a dying faction. It was the first violent battle in what they foresee as the coming civil war.

ACKNOWLEDGMENTS

THE BEST THING ABOUT cohosting *Straight White American Jesus* is getting to talk to smart people about the most fundamental questions of our time every week. This book would not be possible without the genius of my cohost, Dan Miller, or all the guests who answered my emails, came on the show, and taught me so much about so many things—Katherine Stewart, Phil Gorski, Sarah Posner, Anne Nelson, Randall Balmer, Chrissy Stroop, Blake Chastain, Ryan Stollar, and dozens and dozens more. Special thanks are due to Sara Moslener, Susannah Crockford, and Dan Miller for their edifying and encouraging feedback on various drafts. I am indebted to my editor, Valerie Weaver-Zercher, for not only making this text more readable and coherent but for offering intellectual, theological, and historical insights that expanded its horizons significantly. My agent, David Morris, always puts his authors' interests above all else, while pushing them to be their best. I could not write without the love and support of my partner, Kendra, who is my most honest reader, my best friend, and the one who first encouraged me to tell *this* story through the prism of *my* story. And most of all, Kaia, whose smile is the only theodicy I'll ever need.

NOTES

PREFACE TO THE PAPERBACK EDITION

white supremacist Theodore Beale: "Jack Posobiec," at the Southern Law Poverty Center. https://www.splcenter.org/fighting-hate/extremist-files/individual/jack-posobiec. Accessed April 2024.

conspiring to keep US borders open: Tess Owen, "Protest Convoy Headed to Southern Border Is Calling Itself an 'Army of God,'" at Vice. https://www.vice.com/en/article/5d9adk/trucker-convoy-eagle-pass-texas-border-dispute-christian-nationalism. Accessed April 2024. '

participating in the insurrection as "hostages": Anni Karni, "Goldman Files Censure Against Stefanik for Calling Jan. 6 Defendants 'Hostages'" at the New York Times, January 27, 2024. https://www.nytimes.com/2024/01/17/us/politics/goldman-censure-stefanik-jan-6-hostages.html. Accessed April 2024.

"political prisoners": Lisa Mascaro, "Marjorie Taylor Greene's jail visit pulls GOP closer to Jan. 6 rioters," at the Associated Press March 25, 2023. https://apnews.com/article/marjorie-taylor-greene-jan-6-capitol-attack-20f06d75072a563d56a86b0ecf2d89b8. Accessed April 2024.

with a "red Caesar" or "Christian prince": On the call for a Christian prince, see Stephen Wolfe, The Case for Christian Nationalism. Cannon Press, 2022. For a discussion of the "Red Caesar," see Kevin Slack, War on the American Republic: How Liberalism Became Despotism. Encounter Books, 2023.

PROLOGUE

Some scholars have: Kevin Kruse focuses on Graham, Nixon, and the ties between big business and Protestant America. See Kevin Kruse, *One Nation Under God: How Corporate America Invented Christian America* (New York: Basic Books, 2015). Anthea Butler centers the racist past of White evangelicalism in *White Evangelical Racism: The Politics of Morality in America* (Chapel Hill: University of North Carolina Press, 2021). Katherine Stewart's *The Power Worshippers: Inside the Dangerous Rise of Christian Nationalism* (New York: Bloomsbury, 2020) provides an inside look at Christian nationalism through the lens of a seasoned investigative journalist. Sarah Posner's *Unholy: Why White Evangelicals Worship at the Altar of Donald Trump* (New York: Penguin Random House, 2020) provides the most incisive view into the ways conservative Christians have revered authoritarian leaders and regimes for decades. In her groundbreaking work on evangelical masculinity, historian Kristin Kobes du Mez analyzes the toxic models of manhood operative in evangelical culture from the early twentieth century to the Trump presidency. See Kristin Kobes du Mez, *Jesus and John Wayne: How White Evangelicals Corrupted a Faith and Fractured a Nation* (New York: W. W. Norton, 2020).

As Nell Irvin Painter says: See Nell Irvin Painter, "Why White Should Be Capitalized Too," *Washington Post*, June 2, 2020, accessed April 2022, https://www.washingtonpost.com /opinions/2020/07/22/why-white-should-be-capitalized/.

CHAPTER 1

Recent data shows: Samuel Perry and Andrew Whitehead, *Taking America Back for God: Christian Nationalism in the United States* (Oxford: Oxford University Press, 2020), 30.

historical identity: Perry and Whitehead, *Taking America Back for God*, x.

As Perry and Whitehead argue: Perry and Whitehead, *Taking America Back for God*, 11.

Throwing God out: See Michael E. Naparstek, "Religion after 9-11: Falwell and Robertson Stumble," *Religion in the News* 4, no. 3 (Fall 2001), accessed December 2021, https:// www3.trincoll.edu/csrpl/RINVol4No3/Falwell.htm.

This is one wicked: See Matthew Yglesias, "Hagee on Katrina," *Atlantic*, March 5, 2008, accessed December 2021, https://www.theatlantic.com/politics/archive/2008/03/hagee -on-katrina/45516/.

It is as ethnic: Perry and Whitehead, *Taking America Back for God*, 10.

The hard truth: See "RNC 2020: Pence Warns Americans 'Won't Be Safe' if Biden Wins," BBC, August 27, 2020, accessed December 2021, https://www.bbc.com/news/election -us-2020-53928422.

a choice between: See Jim Tankersley, "Why Trump's Efforts to Paint Biden as a Socialist Are Not Working," *New York Times*, October 14, 2020, accessed December 2021, https:// www.nytimes.com/2020/10/14/business/socialist-biden-trump.html.

win for Marxism: See Cheryl K. Chumleky, "A Win for Joe Biden Is a Win for Marxism," *Washington Times*, October 12, 2020, accessed December 2021, https://www.washingtontimes .com/news/2020/oct/12/kentucky-pastor-win-joe-biden-win-marxism/.

Black Americans: Samuel Perry and Andrew Whitehead, "America in Black and White: Racial Identity, Religious-National Group Boundaries, and Explanations for Racial Inequality," *Sociology of Race and Ethnicity* 5, no. 1 (2019): 130–46.

connecting Christian and American identities: Perry and Whitehead, "America in Black and White."

I've been trying: See Curtis Bunn, "'My Ideals Are Driven by My Faith': Raphael Warnock on His Senate Runoff Race," NBC News, November 7, 2020, accessed December 2021, https:// www.nbcnews.com/news/nbcblk/my-ideals-are-driven-my-faith-raphael-warnock -his-senate-n1246879.

White evangelicals: Janelle Wong, *Immigrants, Evangelicals, and Politics in an Era of Demographic Change* (New York: Russell Sage Foundation, 2018), 23.

CHAPTER 2

a frontal assault: Focus on the Family Broadcast, January 16, 2020, accessed December 2021, https://www.focusonthefamily.com/episodes/broadcast/restoring-godly-values-to -america/.

Government represents power: Barry Goldwater, *The Conscience of a Conservative* (Shepherdsville, KY: Victor Books, 1960), 16–17.

I am not prepared: Goldwater, *Conscience of a Conservative*, 37.

Goldwater was signaling: David Farber, *The Rise and Fall of Modern American Conservativism* (Princeton, NJ: Princeton University Press, 2010).

Either the Communists: Goldwater, *Conscience of a Conservative.*

I would remind you: Barry Goldwater, "Address Accepting the Presidential Nomination at the Republican National Convention in San Francisco," July 16, 1964, accessed December 2021, https://www.presidency.ucsb.edu/documents/address-accepting-the-presidential -nomination-the-republican-national-convention-san.

CHAPTER 3

Some of them: For a deeply researched and compelling treatment of the Great Migration, see Isabel Wilkerson's *The Warmth of Other Suns: The Epic Story of America's Great Migration* (New York: Penguin Random House, 2010). For a brilliant analysis of the ways African Americans cultivated religious identities that subverted racial categories—and thus the mechanisms of racism in American society—see Judith Weisenfeld, *New World A-Coming: Black Religion and Racial Identity During the Great Migration* (New York: NYU Press, 2017).

the famous March on Washington: See this public opinion survey from 1964: Roper Center for Public Opinion Research, "Public Opinion on Civil Rights: Reflections on the Civil Rights Act of 1964," Cornell University, accessed December 2021, https://ropercenter .cornell.edu/public-opinion-civil-rights-reflections-civil-rights-act-1964.

It was the perfect petri dish: John Compton, *The End of Empathy: Why White Christians Stopped Loving Their Neighbors* (Oxford: Oxford University Press, 2020); Darren Dochuk, *From Bible Belt to Sun Belt: Plain-Folk Religion, Grassroots Politics, and the Rise of Evangelical Conservatism* (New York: W. W. Norton, 2010); Lisa McGirr, *Suburban Warriors: The Origins of the New American Right* (Princeton, NJ: Princeton University Press, 2001).

to defeat worldwide communism: Mark Mulder and Gerardo Martí, *The Glass Church: Robert H. Schuller, the Crystal Cathedral, and the Strain of Megachurch Ministry* (New Brunswick, NJ: Rutgers University Press 2020), 100.

Schuller found a recently migrated: Mulder and Martí, *Glass Church*, 3.

The profit motive: Robert Schuller, *God's Way to the Good Life* (Grand Rapids, MI: Eerdmans Publishing, 1971), 84.

Those who are blessed: On the prosperity gospel, see Kate Bowler's *Blessed: A History of the Prosperity Gospel* (Oxford: Oxford University Press, 2013).

Big business began: All interviews referenced throughout this work are public and available on the *Straight White American Jesus* podcast feed (https://cms.megaphone.fm/channel /PPY9950636314).

In 1954 he tried to purchase: McGirr, *Suburban Warriors,* 44.

The John Birch Society: Christopher Towler, "The John Birch Society Is Still Influencing American Politics, 60 Years after Its Founding," *The Conversation,* December 6, 2018, accessed December 2021, https://theconversation.com/the-john-birch-society-is-still-influencing-american-politics-60-years-after-its-founding-107925.

Goldwater's volunteers: McGirr, *Suburban Warriors,* 4.

Anyone who joins us: Goldwater, "Address Accepting the Presidential Nomination."

prism for understanding: McGirr, *Suburban Warriors,* 132 and 273.

Goldwater's defeat: See Anne Nelson, *Shadow Network: Media, Money, and the Secret Hub of the Radical Right* (New York: Bloomsbury Publishing, 2019), 10.

The next major area: Daniel Schlozman, *When Movements Anchor Parties: Electoral Alignments in American History* (Princeton, NJ: Princeton University Press, 2016), 85.

CHAPTER 4

The abortion myth: Randall Balmer, *Bad Faith: Race and the Rise of the Religious Right* (Grand Rapids, MI: Eerdmans, 2021).

One report from the early 1980s: Schlozman, *When Movements Anchor Parties,* 91.

This was the model: Sophie Bjork-James, *The Divine Institution: White Evangelicals' Politics of the Family* (New Brunswick, NJ: Rutgers University Press, 2021).

historian Elizabeth Jemison points out: Elizabeth L. Jemison, "Proslavery Theology after the Emancipation," *Tennessee Historical Quarterly* 72, no. 4 (Winter 2013): 255–68.

Doing away with slavery: Luke Harlow, "The Long Life of Proslavery Religion," in *The World the Civil War Made,* ed. Gregory P. Downs and Kate Masur (Chapel Hill: University of North Carolina Press, 2015).

the position of Southern Methodism: Jemison, "Proslavery Theology after the Emancipation," 266.

After the war: Alison Collis-Greene, "Reckoning with Southern Baptist Histories," *Southern Cultures* 25, no. 3, *https://www.southerncultures.org/article/reckoning-with-southern-baptist-histories/.*

Klan members displayed: "Seven Symbols of the Klan," *Imperial Night-Hawk,* December 26, 1923, 8.

The cross served: Kelly J. Baker, "The Artifacts of White Supremacy," *Religion and Culture Forum,* June 14, 2017, accessed August 2021, https://voices.uchicago.edu/religionculture/2017/06/14/813/.

There is an inherent right: Schlozman, *When Movements Anchor Parties,* 98.

CHAPTER 5

Who dared: H. Larry Ingle, *Nixon's First Cover Up: The Religious Life of a Quaker President* (Columbia: University of Missouri, 2015), 25.

The latter marked: J. Brooks Flippen, "Carter, Catholics, and the Politics of the Family," *American Catholic Historical Society* 123, no. 3 (Fall 2012): 35.

The education system: Flippen, "Carter, Catholics, and the Politics of the Family," 43.

worried Catholics: Flippen, "Carter, Catholics, and the Politics of the Family," 29.

In some lessons: See Rebecca Klein, "These Textbooks in Thousands of K-12 Schools Echo Trump's Talking Points," HuffPost, January 15, 2021, https://www.huffpost.com /entry/christian-textbooks-trump-capitol-riot_n_6000bce3c5b62c0057bb711f.

She claimed: See Leigh Ann Wheeler, "Could the ERA Pass in the #Metoo Era?" *The Conversation*, March 8, 2017, accessed January 2022, https://theconversation.com/could-the -era-pass-in-the-metoo-era-87901.

The Moral Majority: Seth Dowland, "'Family Values' and the Formation of a Christian Right Agenda," *Church History* 78, no. 3 (September 2009): 606.

As Christians: Jerry Falwell, "The Man I Want for President!" *Faith Aflame*, 1976.

A gospel choir: Jeremy Hatfield, "For God and Country: The Religious Right, the Reagan Administration, and the Cold War" (PhD diss., Ohio University, 2013), 120–21.

We have to make a choice: Bruce Buursma, "Moral Majority: Crusade Has Just Begun," *Chicago Tribune*, November 6, 1980.

You and I are told: Ronald Reagan, "A Time for Choosing," October 27, 1964, accessed August 2021, https://www.reaganlibrary.gov/reagans/ronald-reagan/time-choosing-speech-october -27-1964.

CHAPTER 6

He then paints: Charles Murray, "The Coming White Underclass," The American Enterprise Institute, October 29, 1993, https://www.aei.org/articles/the-coming-white -underclass/. Murray is not a fringe figure. His 1994 book, *The Bell Curve: Intelligence and Class Structure in American Life*, made the *New York Times* best-sellers list, despite many viewing its core argument as resting on misguided—and racist—assumptions.

So I think the time: Dan Quayle, "Standing Firm," May 19, 1992, accessed December 2021, http://www.vicepresidentdanquayle.com/speeches_StandingFirm_CCC_3.html.

By the turn of the millennium: Encyclopedia Britannica, "Focus on the Family," last updated January 24, 2022, https://www.britannica.com/topic/Focus-on-the-Family.

Focus on the Family: Susan Ridgely, "Conservative Christianity and the Creation of Alternative News: An Analysis of Focus on the Family's Multimedia Empire," *Religion and American Culture* 30, no. 1 (Winter 2020): 1–25, https://www.cambridge.org/core /journals/religion-and-american-culture/article/conservative-christianity-and-the -creation-of-alternative-news-an-analysis-of-focus-on-the-familys-multimedia -empire/104B94DD4CACF996F9DCB2BF3A8DE25C.

For Dobson: Sara Moslener, *Virgin Nation: Sexual Purity and American Adolescence* (Oxford, UK: Oxford University Press, 2015).

Men and women: Moslener, *Virgin Nation*, 96.

You also have to remember: Vyckie Garrison, "My Life as a Daughter of Christian Patriarchy," Rewire News, September 12, 2011, accessed January 2022, https://rewirenewsgroup .com/article/2011/09/12/lifedaughter-christian-patriarchy/.

As the scholar and author: Audrey Clare Farley, "The Eugenics Roots of Evangelical Family Values," *Religion & Politics*, May 12, 2021. *https://religionandpolitics.org/2021/05/12/the-eugenics-roots-of-evangelical-family-values/.*

Like many evangelical leaders: Itabari Njeri, "Faith, Hope, and Racial Disparity: As Multiracial Marriages Increase, Churches Face a Call for Greater Sensitivity, Support," *Los Angeles Times*, August 20, 1989, https://www.latimes.com/archives/la-xpm-1989-08-20-vw-1058-story.html.

The family is for him: Bjork-James, *Divine Institution.*

the biblical foundation of marriage: James Dobson, "Why Marriage Matters Now More Than Ever," CBN News, October 11, 2020, accessed August 2021, https://www1.cbn.com/cbnnews/us/2020/october/dr-james-dobson-why-marriage-and-family-matters-now-more-than-ever.

Our culture: James Dobson, March 2015 newsletter, accessed August 2021, https://www.drjamesdobson.org/newsletters/dr-james-dobsons-march-2015-newsletter.

Children are the prize winners: Cited in Moslener, *Virgin Nation*, 102.

American Christian nationalism: Daniel Miller, introduction to *Queer Democracy: Desire, Dysphoria, and the Body Politic* (New York: Routledge, 2021).

White Christian nationalist imagination: Miller, introduction to *Queer Democracy.*

Christian nationalism therefore represents: Miller, *Queer Democracy*, chap. 5.

The historical privileging: Miller, *Queer Democracy*, chap. 5.

the civil war of values: See Dobson's lecture, "A Civil War of Values," given at Prestonwoods Baptist Church, accessed December 2021, https://www.dobsonlibrary.com/resource/audio/7d5962a1-f4e6-49f4-995e-9b0f8f2b640c.

I am endorsing Donald J. Trump: See Sarah Eekhoff Zylstra, "Dobson Endorses Trump, While Evangelical Leaders Advise Voting for Lesser Evil," *Christianity Today*, July 21, 2016, accessed December 2021, https://www.christianitytoday.com/news/2016/july/dobson-endorses-trump-nae-leaders-vote-for-lesser-evil.html.

CHAPTER 7

I believe it should be: Billy Graham, *Storm Warning* (Nashville, TN: Thomas Nelson, 1993).

There are great experiments: Cited in Posner, *Unholy*, 210.

American national interest: Edward Lozansky and Paul Weyrich, "A Brave New Russia," *Washington Times*, October 26, 2001, accessed December 2021, https://www.washingtontimes.com/news/2001/oct/26/20011026-030444-2642r/.

illiberal autocrats: Sarah Posner, "The End of the City on a Hill: A Burgeoning Alliance with Europe's Far Right Is Radically Altering the Christian Right's View of American Democracy," *Type Investigations*, March 11, 2019, accessed December 2021. https://www.typeinvestigations.org/investigation/2019/03/11/european-american-christian-conservative-alliance/.

the World Congress of Families: Posner documents these developments in detail in *Unholy.*

Deviations from natural sexual behavior: Allan Carlson and Paul Mero, *The Natural Family: A Manifesto* (Dallas: Spence Publishing Co., 2007).

Tell the LGBT tolerance tyrants: Fr. Josiah Trenholm speech at the World Congress of Families gathering in Tbilisi, Georgia, May 2016. *See "World Congress of Families Gathering in Tbilisi Showcases Anti-LGBT Rhetoric and Conspiracy Theories," Southern Poverty Law Center,* accessed December 2021, https://www.splcenter.org/hatewatch/ 2016/06/01/world-congress-families-gathering-tbilisi-showcases-anti-lgbt-rhetoric-and-conspiracy.

experiments with a godless cosmos: Bernadette Szabo, "Hungary's Orban Calls for Central Europe to Unite around Christian Roots," NBC News, August 20, 2020, accessed December 2021, https://www.nbcnews.com/feature/nbc-out/hungary-s-orban-calls-central -europe-unite-around-christian-roots-n1237460.

Make Families Great Again: Shaun Walker, "Orbán Deploys Christianity with a Twist to Tighten Grip in Hungary," *The Guardian,* July 14, 2019, accessed December 2021, https:// www.theguardian.com/world/2019/jul/14/viktor-orban-budapest-hungary-christianity -with-a-twist.

We know there are: Alexei Anishchuk and Steve Gutterman, "Putin Says Russia's Power Is Moral as Well as Military," *Reuters,* December 12, 2013, accessed December 2021, https://www.reuters.com/article/us-russia-putin-idUSBRE9BB0TM20131212.

What a great idea: See Brian Tashman, "World Congress of Families Praises Russian Laws 'Preventing' Gays from 'Corrupting Children,'" Right Wing Watch, June 3, 2013, accessed December 2021, https://www.rightwingwatch.org/post/world-congress-of -families-praises-russian-laws-preventing-gays-from-corrupting-children/.

exactly the right thing to do: John Bolton, *The Room Where It Happened: A White House Memoir* (New York: Simon and Schuster, 2021).

in the 2020 election: See Justin Nortey, "Most White Americans Who Regularly Attend Worship Services Voted for Trump in 2020," Pew Research Center, August 30, 2021, accessed December 2021, https://www.pewresearch.org/fact-tank/2021/08/30/most-white -americans-who-regularly-attend-worship-services-voted-for-trump-in-2020.

hypermasculine aggression: Leslie Dorrough Smith, *Compromising Positions: Sex Scandals, Politics, and American Christianity* (Oxford: Oxford University Press, 2020), 47.

claim to authority: Dorrough Smith, *Compromising Positions.*

Christian idolization of Trump: Kristin Kobes du Mez, *Jesus and John Wayne: How White Evangelicals Corrupted a Faith and Fractured a Nation* (New York: W. W. Norton, 2020).

The American people: See Miranda Devine, "Donald Trump's Lesson for Mitt Romney," Fox News, October 7, 2019, accessed December 2021, https://www.foxnews.com/opinion /miranda-devine-donald-trumps-lesson-for-mitt-romney.

CHAPTER 8

what makes a theory: Susannah Crockford, *Ripples of the Universe: Spirituality in Sedona, Arizona* (Chicago: University of Chicago Press, 2021), 177.

When it comes to the true believers: Religious fundamentalisms vary across time and space but can be understood to demand participants in the community forfeit meaningful external social ties, including but not limited to family, friends, and other forms of community. They often reduce the world to a cosmic binary, pitting their community against the evils of the world beyond it. Their morals are thus formed in an either/or framework where one is either with or against, us or them, good or bad, in or out.

Understanding is granted: Crockford, *Ripples of the Universe*, 155.

The overall effect: Crockford, *Ripples of the Universe*, 164.

private networks of belonging: Giovanna Parmigiani, "Magic and Politics: Conspirituality and COVID-19," *Journal of the American Academy of Religion* 89, no. 2 (June 2021), https://academic.oup.com/jaar/article/89/2/506/6299191?login=true.

Trump retweeted: See Alex Kaplan, "Trump Has Repeatedly Amplified QAnon Twitter Accounts. The FBI Has Linked the Conspiracy Theory to Domestic Terror," Media Matters, August 1, 2019, accessed December 2021, https://www.mediamatters.org/twitter/fbi-calls-qanon -domestic-terror-threat-trump-has-amplified-qanon-supporters-twitter-more-20.

Among the 25 percent: Paul Djupe and Jacob Dennen, "Christian Nationalists and QAnon Followers Tend to Be Anti-Semitic," *Washington Post*, January 26, 2021, accessed December 2021. https://www.washingtonpost.com/politics/2021/01/26/christian-nationalists -qanon-followers-tend-be-anti-semitic-that-was-visible-capitol-attack/.

to restore: See The John Birch Society, "An Introduction to The John Birch Society," YouTube, March 15, 2016, https://www.youtube.com/watch?v=vCL1_h_D654&t=1020s.

Illuminati's efforts: See Dan Kelly, "Birchismo," *The Baffler*, no. 13 (December 1999), https:// thebaffler.com/salvos/birchismo.

communist subversion: Towler, "John Birch Society."

They believe in the Constitution: See Erick Trickey, "Long Before QAnon, Ronald Reagan and the GOP Purged John Birch Extremists from the Party," *Washington Post*, January 15, 2021, accessed December 2021, https://www.washingtonpost.com/history/2021/01/15 /john-birch-society-qanon-reagan-republicans-goldwater/.

Reagan once told: Rick Perlstein and Edward H. Miller, "The John Birch Society Never Left," *New Republic*, March 8, 2021, accessed December 2021, https://newrepublic.com /article/161603/john-birch-society-qanon-trump.

While America's military strength is important: The transcript can be found at Voices of Democracy, "Ronald Reagan, 'Evil Empire Speech' (March 8, 1983)," accessed December 2021, https://voicesofdemocracy.umd.edu/reagan-evil-empire-speech-text.

Nightly news programs: Megan Goodwin, *Abusing Religion: Literary Persecution, Sex Scandals, and American Minority Religions* (New Brunswick, NJ: Rutgers University Press, 2019), 32.

moderately severe character defect: See Jim Rutenberg, "The Man Behind the Whispers about Obama," *New York Times*, October 12, 2008, https://www.nytimes.com/2008/10/13/us/ politics/13martin.html.

Martin also claimed: See Matthew Mosk, "An Attack That Came Out of the Ether," *Washington Post*, June 28, 2008, https://www.washingtonpost.com/wp-dyn/content /article/2008/06/27/AR2008062703781.html?hpid=topnews&sid=ST200806 2703939&pos=.

Don't know who the original: See Matthew Mosk, "Scholar Traces Online Obama Smears," *Seattle Times*, June 29, 2008, https://www.seattletimes.com/nation-world/scholar -traces-online-obama-smears/.

One soldier even challenged: See Brian Montopoli, "Who Are the Birthers?" CBS News, June 23, 2009, https://www.cbsnews.com/news/who-are-the-birthers/.

He was born a Muslim: Graham made these remarks on CNN in an interview with John King. See Andy Barr, "Rev. Graham: Obama 'Born a Muslim,'" Politico, August 20, 2010, https://www.politico.com/story/2010/08/rev-graham-obama-born-a-muslim-041292.

One out of five: See Stephanie Condon, "Poll: 'Birther' Myth Persists among Tea Partiers, All Americans," CBS News, April 14, 2010, https://www.cbsnews.com/news/poll-birther-myth-persists-among-tea-partiers-all-americans/.

emotionally satisfying: See Michael Scherer, "Birtherism Is Dead, But the Birther Industry Continues," *Time*, April 27, 2011. https://swampland.time.com/2011/04/27/birtherism-is-dead-but-the-birther-industry-continues/.

statement of values: See Adam Serwer, "Birtherism of a Nation," *Atlantic*, May 13, 2020, https://www.theatlantic.com/ideas/archive/2020/05/birtherism-and-trump/610978/.

Supposedly dozens of children: "The Saga of 'Pizzagate': The Fake Story That Shows How Conspiracy Theories Spread," BBC, December 2, 2016, https://www.bbc.com/news/blogs-trending-38156985.

By December 2020: See the poll at "More Than 1 in 3 Americans Believe a 'Deep State' Is Working to Undermine Trump," Ipsos, December 30, 2020, https://www.ipsos.com/en-us/news-polls/npr-misinformation-123020.

CHAPTER 9

The conquest was more: Andy Patton, "Why Did God Command the Invasion of Canaan in the Book of Joshua?" *BibleProject*, accessed December 2021, https://bibleproject.com/blog/why-did-god-command-the-invasion-of-canaan-in-the-book-of-joshua/.

patriots and people of faith: Jericho March press release, December 7, 2020, https://jerichomarch.org/2020/12/jericho-march-and-stop-the-steal-announce-the-december-12-let-the-church-roar-national-prayer-rally-speakers-and-march-details/.

America is a gift: Peter Montgomery, "Right-Wing Religious and Political Activists Trying to Overturn Biden Victory Will Converge on Washington Dec. 12," Right Wing Watch, December 8, 2020. https://www.rightwingwatch.org/post/right-wing-religious-and-political-activists-trying-to-overturn-biden-victory-will-converge-on-washington-dec-12/.

Vice President Pence: The Jericho March website has been largely scrapped. But the document is preserved in part here: "Who We Are," Hamilton Strategies, accessed December 2021, https://hamiltonstrategies.com/who-we-are.

Leandra flew to Washington: See her interview on *The Andy Falco Show*, accessed December 2021, https://www.facebook.com/ZeroToHeroSchool/videos/493185694996560.

One officer told me: Nick Niedzwiadek, "Capitol Police Officer Says Jan. 6 Rioters Used N-Word against Him and Others," Politico, July 27, 2021, accessed December 2021, https://www.politico.com/news/2021/07/27/captiol-police-racial-slurs-500846.

Inside the building: Claire Wang, "Behind the Viral Photo of Rep. Andy Kim Cleaning Up at Midnight after Riots," *NBC News*, January 8, 2021, accessed December 2021, https://www.nbcnews.com/news/asian-america/behind-viral-photo-rep-andy-kim-cleaning-midnight-after-riots-n1253519.

The red cross on a white field: Matthew Gabriele, "The Deus Volt Cross," in Uncivil Religion: January 6, 2021, part 1, Christian Nationalism on January 6 (4/6), accessed January 2021, https://uncivilreligion.org/home/the-deus-vult-cross. Uncivil Religion is a digital exhibit by the Smithsonian Museum of American History, in partnership with the University of Alabama.

By building the gallows: Anthea Butler, "Hanging Democracy on the Gallows," in Uncivil Religion: January 6, 2021, part 3, Religion behind the Events (3/6), accessed January 2021, https://uncivilreligion.org/home/index.

After he breached: United States Department of Justice, Affidavit for Couy Griffin, accessed March 2022, https://www.justice.gov/opa/page/file/1355981.

But those familiar: Leah Payne, "The Trump Shall Sound: Politics, Pentecostals, and the Shofar at the Capitol Riots," *Political Theology*, September 2, 2021, https://politicaltheology.com/the-trump-shall-sound-politics-pentecostals-and-the-shofar-at-the-capitol-riots/?fbclid=IwAR042YQf3w9UgLldj8j0KU_OKcx-jeOwFSDzzW4Lw2XDt0LrcRM5s2Ue7Vk.

maps social space: Thomas A. Tweed, *Crossing and Dwelling* (Cambridge, MA: Harvard University Press, 2008), 110.

The Senate chamber: Russell McCutcheon, "The Sacred IS the Profane, Part 2," *Political Theology*, May 1, 2013, accessed December 2021, https://politicaltheology.com/the-sacred-is-the-profane-part-2-russell-mccutcheon/.

Even for those without: Peter Manseau, "Some Capitol Rioters Believed They Answered God's Call, Not Just Trump's," *Washington Post*, February 11, 2021, accessed January 2021, https://www.washingtonpost.com/outlook/2021/02/11/christian-religion-insurrection-capitol-trump/.

This is not gloom and doom: Andrea Morris, "'Let the Church ROAR!': National Prayer Rally Comes to DC for Jericho March to 'Stop the Steal' at CBN," December 12, 2020, accessed December 2020. https://www1.cbn.com/cbnnews/us/2020/december/let-the-church-roar-national-prayer-rally-comes-to-dc-for-jericho-march-to-stop-the-steal.

CHAPTER 10

In an ever-changing: Hannah Arendt, *The Origins of Totalitarianism* (San Diego: Harcourt, 1973), 367.

According to one analysis: See the report by the *Washington Post* here, accessed March 2022, https://www.washingtonpost.com/graphics/politics/trump-claims-database/.

Lost Cause mythology: C. R. Wilson, *Baptized in Blood: The Religion of the Lost Cause, 1865–1920*, 2nd ed. (Athens: University of Georgia Press, 2009).

Key to this mythology: Paul Harvey, *Moses, Jesus, and the Trickster in the Evangelical South* (Athens: University of Georgia Press, 2012), 109.

I will tell you: Max Burn, "Trump Makes Ashli Babbitt, Killed in the Capitol Riot, into a Martyr. Why That's So Dangerous," NBC News, July 12, 2021, accessed December 2021, https://www.nbcnews.com/think/opinion/trump-makes-ashli-babbitt-killed-capitol-riot-martyr-why-s-ncna1273750.

We all saw the hand: Jonathan Chait, "The Chilling Message of Trump's Embrace of Ashli Babbitt Martyrdom," *New York Magazine*, July 7, 2021, https://nymag.com/intelligencer/2021/07/trump-who-shot-ashli-babbitt-january-6-insurrection-riot.html.

Who did shoot Ashli Babbitt: Sinéad Baker, "Tucker Carlson Said Putin Was Asking 'Fair Questions' about Ashli Babbitt's Killing at the Capitol Riot," *Business Insider*, July 16, 2021, accessed December 2021, www.businessinsider.com/tucker-carlson-says-putin-fair-question-ashli-babbitt-killing-2021-6.

She was unarmed: Jordan Fischer, Eric Flack, and Stephanie Wilson, "'Who Shot Ashli Babbitt?' Inside the Effort to Make a January 6 Martyr," WUSA, July 21, 2021, accessed 2021, https://www.wusa9.com/article/news/national/capitol-riots/who-shot-ashli-babbitt-inside-the-effort-to-make-a-january-6-martyr-right-wing-paul-gosar-donald-trump-white-supremacist-anti-semitic-qanon/65-6641f710-99d0-42ba-b657-4c568e132ef1.

first Patriot Martyr: "Furious Extremists Call for More Violence Around Inauguration Day," ADL, January 13, 2021, accessed December 2021, https://www.adl.org/blog/furious-extremists-call-for-more-violence-around-inauguration-day.

Anti-Defamation League reports: "Far-Right Extremists Memorialize 'Martyr' Ashli Babbitt," ADL, January 15, 2021, accessed December 2021, https://www.adl.org/blog/far-right-extremists-memorialize-martyr-ashli-babbitt.

We have concerns: Will Sommer, "Republicans Recast Jan. 6 Riot Defendants as 'Political Prisoners,'" *Daily Beast*, July 27, 2021, accessed December 2021, https://www.thedailybeast.com/republicans-recast-jan-6-riot-defendants-as-political-prisoners.

Madison Cawthorn: Bryan Metzger, "Rep. Madison Cawthorn Calls Jan. 6 Rioters 'Political Prisoners,' Suggests He Wants to 'Try and Bust Them Out' of Jail," *Business Insider*, August 30, 2021, accessed December 2021, https://www.businessinsider.com/rep-cawthorn-bust-jan-6th-rioters-out-jail-political-prisoners-2021-8.

prisoners are receiving: Alia Shoaib, "Marjorie Taylor Greene Visited Accused Jan. 6 Rioters in Jail and Told Steve Bannon the Prisoners Cry While Singing the National Anthem Every Night," *Business Insider*, November 6, 2021, accessed December 2021, https://www.businessinsider.com/marjorie-taylor-greene-visited-jan-6-rioters-jailed-patriot-wing-2021-11.

legitimate political discourse: Jonathan Weisman and Reid J. Epstein, "G.O.P. Declares Jan. 6 Attack 'Legitimate Political Discourse,'" *New York Times*, February 5, 2022, accessed February 2022, https://www.nytimes.com/2022/02/04/us/politics/republicans-jan-6-cheney-censure.html.

one insurrectionist explained: Sommer, "Republicans Recast Jan. 6 Defendants."

dying for the cause: Daniel Koehler, "Dying for the Cause? The Logic and Function of Ideologically Motivated Suicide, Martyrdom, and Self-Sacrifice within the Contemporary Extreme Right," *Behavioral Sciences of Terrorism and Political Aggression*, September 17, 2020, accessed December 2021, https://www.tandfonline.com/doi/abs/10.1080/19434472.2020.1822426?journalCode=rirt20.

Rallygoers then participated: Zachary Petrizzo, "MAGA Faithful Pledge Allegiance to Supposed Jan. 6 Flag; Glenn Youngkin Forced to Back Away," *Salon*, October 14, 2021, accessed December 2021, https://www.salon.com/2021/10/14/maga-faithful-pledge-allegiance-to-supposed-jan-6-flag-glenn-youngkin-forced-to-back-away/.

The sacred tree: Mircea Eliade, *The Sacred and the Profane: The Nature of Religion*, trans. Willard R. Trask (New York: Harcourt Brace Jovanovich, 1987), 12 (emphasis in original).

Senator Lindsey Graham: Josh Dawsey, "Lindsey Graham Said 'Count Me Out' after the Capitol Riot. But He's All In with Trump Again," *Washington Post*, February 20, 2021, accessed December 2021, https://www.washingtonpost.com/politics/lindsey-graham-donald-trump/2021/02/20/178afc0a-72ca-11eb-a4eb-44012a612cf9_story.html.

A third congressperson: For Clyde's comments, see C-SPAN, "Normal Tourist Visit," YouTube, May 13, 2021, accessed December 2021, https://www.youtube.com/watch?v=WLI0OH1ZWWc.

Public opinion: David Leonhardt and Ian Prasad Philbrick, "Valorizing January 6," *New York Times*, September 17, 2021, accessed December 2021, https://www.nytimes.com/2021/09/17/briefing/january-6-capitol-riot-rally.html.

researchers found: "Declining Share of Republicans Say It Is Important to Prosecute Jan. 6 Rioters," Pew Research Center report, September 28, 2021, accessed December 2021, https://www.pewresearch.org/politics/2021/09/28/declining-share-of-republicans-say-it-is-important-to-prosecute-jan-6-rioters/.

It was especially incomprehensible: Jochen Bittner, "1918 Germany Has a Warning for America," *New York Times*, November 30, 2020, accessed December 2021, https://www.nytimes.com/2020/11/30/opinion/trump-conspiracy-germany-1918.html.

the image of a Dolchstoß: Klaus Schwabe, "World War I and the Rise of Hitler," *Diplomatic History* 38, no. 4 (September 2014): 866.

Needless to add: Schwabe, "World War I and the Rise of Hitler," 876.

He railed against: Bittner, "1918 Germany Has a Warning for America."

What if the events of Jan. 6: Robert Gerwarth, "Weimar's Lessons for Biden's America," *Foreign Policy*, February 6, 2021, accessed December 2021, https://foreignpolicy.com/2021/02/06/weimars-lessons-for-bidens-america/.

CHAPTER 11

According to the 2020 census: See Brandon Pho and Hosam Elattar, "New Census Data Shows More Populous Diverse Orange County," *Orange County Register*, August 21, 2021, accessed December 2021, https://voiceofoc.org/2021/08/new-census-data-shows-more-populous-diverse-oc-how-will-this-affect-the-countys-services/.

The expansion continued: Katie Warren, "I talked to 3 millennials who gave up big-city lives in California and moved to Boise. Here's how they feel about adjusting to small-town life in Idaho," *Business Insider*, August 25, 2020, accessed December 2021, https://www.businessinsider.com/why-millennials-are-moving-from-california-to-boise-idaho-2019-12.

eighty thousand Californians: Jeffrey Lyons, "Don't California My Idaho?" *Blue Review*, October 30, 2017, accessed December 2021, https://www.boisestate.edu/bluereview/dont-california-idaho/.

If anything: Lyons, "Don't California My Idaho?"

Martinellis' lived experience: See Martinelli Realty Team's YouTube video, "North Idaho: The Best Place to Live in America," December 24, 2017, accessed December 2021, https://www.youtube.com/watch?v=aTgnZIbRBjc.

direct contradiction: "North Idaho."

I believe: James Wesley Rawles, "The American Redoubt—Move to the Mountain States," Survivalblog.com, updated March 24, 2021, accessed December 2021, https://survivalblog .com/redoubt/.

As Christians: Chuck Baldwin, "Why We Are Moving to Montana," News with Views, September 15, 2010, accessed December 2021, https://newswithviews.com/baldwin /baldwin615.htm.

I'm inviting people: Rawles, "The American Redoubt."

the Second Civil War: Southern Poverty Law Center, "Far-Right Survivalist and Icon of 'Patriot' Movement Predicts Religious Civil War," January 3, 2019, accessed March 2022, https://www.splcenter.org/hatewatch/2019/01/03/far-right-survivalist-and-icon-patriot -movement-predicts-religious-civil-war.

a stronghold of conservative: In a 2013 episode of the *God and Guns* podcast, Rawles makes clear his apocalyptic worldview in which the United States is destined to disintegrate into chaos

We were libertarian Christians: Justin Franz, "For Sale: God, Guns and Separatism in the American Redoubt," *Montana Free Press*, November 24, 2021, accessed December 2021, https://montanafreepress.org/2021/11/24/selling-the-american-redoubt-in-montana/.

Snowflakes, Liberals, Socialists, Marxists: Franz, "For Sale."

compiled manuals: Mike Baker, "G.O.P. Lawmaker Had Visions of a Christian Alternative Government," *New York Times*, December 23, 2019, accessed December 2021, https:// www.nytimes.com/2019/12/23/us/matt-shea-washington-extremism.html.

Make an offer of Peace: Shea's manifesto is titled "Biblical Basis for War." It was leaked October 2018 and referenced in this article at the Spokesman Review: "Rep. Matt Shea takes credit, criticism for document titled 'Biblical Basis for War,'" October 31, 2018. The manifesto can be accessed on December 2021, https://media.spokesman.com/documents /2018/10/Biblical_Basis_for_War.pdf.

But the bad guy: Baker, "G.O.P. Lawmaker Alternative Government."

We're fighting: Daniel Walters, "At 'Stop the Steal' Protests, Former Rep. Matt Shea Blames Capitol Mob on 'Antifa,' Says We're 'Heading into a War,'" *Inlander*, January 6, 2021, accessed January 2022, https://www.inlander.com/spokane/at-stop-the-steal-protests -former-rep-matt-shea-blames-capitol-mob-on-antifa-says-were-heading-into-a-war /Content?oid=20918768.

Followers believe: Crawford Gribben, "In Moscow, Idaho Conservative 'Christian Reconstructionists' Are Thriving Amid Evangelical Turmoil," *The Conversation*, August 9, 2021, accessed December 2021, https://theconversation.com/in-moscow-idaho-conservative -christian-reconstructionists-are-thriving-amid-evangelical-turmoil-162652.

America's greatness: Southern Poverty Law Center, "America's Promise Ministries," accessed December 2021, https://www.splcenter.org/fighting-hate/extremist-files/group/americas -promise-ministries.

Everyone's really nice: Tim Wilson, "Legacy of Hate: The Specter of North Idaho's Past Still Haunts Region," Boise State Public Radio, October 2, 2017, accessed December 2021, https://www.boisestatepublicradio.org/law-justice/2017-10-02/legacy-of-hate-the -specter-of-north-idahos-past-still-haunts-region.

I've been calling this: Kirk Siegler, "Are Paramilitary Extremists Being Normalized? Look to Idaho for Answers," NPR, October 17, 2020, accessed December 2021, https://www

.npr.org/2020/10/17/924461164/are-paramilitary-extremists-being-normalized-look-to-idaho-for-answers.

A lot of good people: Inside the American Redoubt, film by *The Times* and the *Sunday Times* (London: United Kingdom, 2021), YouTube, November 1, 2021, 38:21, accessed January 2022, https://www.youtube.com/watch?v=Qy6RQJQ6J5w.

No one wants to believe: Barbara F. Walter, *How Civil Wars Start: And How to Stop Them* (New York: Penguin Random House, 2022).

Researchers around the world: Institute for Democracy and Election Assistance, "Global State of Democracy Report 2021," accessed January 2022, https://www.idea.int/gsod/global-report#chapter-2-democracy-health-check:-an-overview-of-global-tre.

I believe personally: Chuck Baldwin, "The American Redoubt," speech at Lordship Church, YouTube, October 8, 2015, accessed December 2021, https://www.youtube.com/watch?v=9zUgnbX8Tb4.

EPILOGUE

By the time Trump: Kobes du Mez, *Jesus and John Wayne*, 3.

Christian supremacy: Chrissy Stroop, "One Year After 1/6, Media Still Refuse to Recognize Authoritarian Christianity," *Religion Dispatches*, January 4, 2022, accessed January 2022, https://religiondispatches.org/one-year-after-1-6-media-still-refuse-to-recognize-authoritarian-christianity/.